Following in Ted's Footsteps

Piero Vitelli

Copyright

For Maria, Red and Railay

Foreword

We arrived at Stone House at the end of July 2011 in need of a fresh start, having been forced by circumstance from our life in London the previous year. In this sturdy, squat and somewhat tattered country cottage, set in three and a half acres on the border between Worcestershire and Herefordshire, we had chosen to embrace a lifestyle which we hoped might encourage the deep wounds of a life-changing workplace accident to heal as best they can. We also wanted to leave the past behind us and to tread a little lighter on the ground underfoot.

Within days of moving in it became abundantly clear that we had leapt in much haste and with little forethought, and I took the opportunity to chronicle the transition as best I could. Originally written as a blog between July 2011 and May 2015 under pseudonyms borrowed from BBC Television's *The Good Life*, these one hundred and forty seven letters chart the progress that we made during our first four years here, and are collected in this book for posterity and personal vanity.

October 2015

Letters

Photos

Piero Vitelli

The Good Life (July 29th 2011)

This is my first letter as Tom and, as you would expect, Barbara is here too. The purpose of this book is to chart our new life course and document the impact of a serious workplace foot injury. To date this has included the loss of a significant amount of personal freedom for Barbara and the current tally of two major surgical procedures, with the promise of more to come. It has meant spending month after month in a cast, endless sessions of physiotherapy, and a good deal of counselling not to mention miles and miles of *Kinesio* tape.

In order to do this, we have had to shine a light on the corporate irresponsibility, negligence and callousness which was the cause of it, and which has so far required three years of legal battles to resolve, despite an almost instant admission of liability. It has left us with a foul taste in our mouths, and a distrust of some who practise within the legal system.

As you might imagine, all of this has caused enormous stress and upset, and so it has been the reason for our rout from London, sojourn in Gloucestershire and eventual arrival here at Stone House: three and a half acres in the beautiful rolling hills on the border between Herefordshire and Worcestershire. This is where we now plan to make our home, to raise a family, to live a quieter life, to watch the seasons change with laughter, with mistakes and to lick our wounds with all the grace we can muster.

It goes without saying, right from the start, that we have absolutely no idea of what we have let ourselves in for. Three-and-a-half acres? What on earth were we thinking of? We moved in less than a week ago, and already there are nasty thorny things growing in places that used to be innocent and pure. Our arsenal of tools with which to combat, coerce and control nature is woefully inadequate; it is the same arsenal that was just about a match for the suburban garden in Hanwell that we ran from a year ago, and the only addition has been a tractor. Much to my annoyance, Barbara calls it a ride-on mower; but the manual says it's a tractor, and that's good enough for me. And anyway, lawnmowers do not have five speed gearboxes.

So who is Ted and why are we following in his footsteps? Well, Ted and his wife Jan lived here before us, and they had spent over forty years growing vegetables, rearing livestock and making cider. Sadly Jan died a few years ago, and so Ted decided to sell Stone House and move in with his sister in Malvern. In all our meetings over the months, Ted has been a true gentleman; kind, humorous, polite, helpful, honest and an absolute pleasure to deal with, and when we shook hands and exchanged keys I imagined how terrible a wrench it was for him to leave his home for the last time. Since first viewing the house in January, we had fallen in love with the feel of the house, the land and the area, and I think part of that came from Ted's spirit, sense of peace and generosity.

The plot comprises of a three bedroom house built of Malvern Stone, four wooden sheds of varying sizes, a large garage that contains a separate workshop, a large animal shelter, a well, a greenhouse, a cider barn, a chicken house, an apple orchard and a two-acre field. It's a five-minute walk to the nearest house, which happens to be a pub, and which we visited for the first time yesterday. For the purposes of this book, we shall call the landlady, our next-door neighbour, Margo.

Before we moved in, I had mentioned to Barbara that I thought we should rename this house, and she didn't disagree. There are many other houses in this area called Stone House, and I thought it would be nice to change the name to something more unique that reflected our ideals and personalities. Now, having been here for a week, I have a feeling that we are custodians rather than owners, just as Ted and Jan were before us. The name will most likely stay, and one day in the years ahead, another family will take over from us in, I hope, a similar manner.

Until then, this is going to be our very long project; one about which I feel sure we will doubt ourselves more than a few times along the way, one for which we do not yet have a clear vision, and one that will challenge and test us. We have no idea what is going to happen, but when we know, we'll let you know. Along the way though, you might like to laugh with us, not to mention at us.

Reduce, Reuse, Recycle (7th August)

I remember seeing those three words for the first time on Network Southeast trains a number of years ago. From time to time, my work would require me to use the over-priced, over-filled and under-cleaned trains that ferried passengers around various destinations in and around Greater London. It was as if the passengers took this advice to heart with newspapers, half-eaten food and other detritus being strewn across the carriages in an effort to be kinder to the environment in some strange way. It's a mantra that Barbara likes to repeat quite often as we get to grips with the big changes in our life here, although hopefully it will manifest itself in a different way than on the 7.22 from Hanwell to Paddington.

Stone House is a maze of boundaries; the vegetable garden is separated from the front of the house by a long row of Leylandii, the driveway from the orchard by a wooden fence, side gates on two sides of the house separate one piece of path from another piece of grass, a featheredge fence bisects the land next to the Cider Barn for no obvious reason, and all of this is divided from the field by a long hedgerow interspersed with three gates. We can only imagine that Ted liked to keep the land in smaller, more manageable areas, and it's something we plan on reversing over time so that we can enjoy as many of the wonderful views as we can. Oddly, the one place without a fence is the public boundary with the road; a line marked by a straggling collection of waist-high shrubs.

At the back of the house, there is direct access from the road to a flat area of scrubland for large deliveries like firewood, and the fence there is both rotten and less than serviceable. We use the area for drying laundry and, a bit farther up, as a sheltered spot to enjoy sundowners on a warm evening. The fence, standing three foot high and made of more gap than fence, makes a pitiable attempt at shielding you from passing cars, and so Barbara suggested a cunning plan the other day during our evening walk. "Why not take down the pointless featheredge fence by the Cider Barn, and use part of it to build some kind of replacement fence at the back of the house?" It was an excellent idea and, having spent yesterday indoors, we decided that today was the day for this project; a dull overcast day with temperature in the high teens and, importantly, no rain in the forecast. Though my strengths may be many, planning ahead and an eye for detail elude me, and so after my morning coffee I went to the workshop to equip myself with each and every tool that I felt I would need to accomplish a task such as this. After considering all the options for at least a minute, I selected a crowbar and a mallet. Feeling pleased with my tools of choice, I set to work and I have to say that removing the featheredge fence went very smoothly. By noon the fence was gone, I had less than ten cuts to my hands and there had been only two revisions to my original plan; which were to use a larger crowbar and a car jack to lever the gate panels from their hinges, resulting in only very minor additional bruising. The result was to open up and reveal the area we plan to use for chickens.

Now I had all the materials needed for plugging the hole in the road boundary behind the house. I removed the existing fence section, which took little more than leaning on it, and I found that there were fence post spikes already in the ground at more or less the right intervals. Now it was a simple matter of robbing from Peter to pay Paul, but they clearly felt it only right that I should receive three more cuts and a large blister in exchange for their contribution to our welfare. Happy with their price and in less than an hour, I had three fence posts secured in a vaguely upright fashion. To these, two of the better-looking featheredge fence panels were then attached, with only a bit of minor improvising being required to make the structure sturdy.

We have worked hard today, both of us rolling up our sleeves and getting stuck in. Having satisfied caveman and nesting instincts, as well as honing our Southend Smiles, we are now the proud creators of a free-range chicken area and an effective, if crude, boundary fence. If my hands hadn't been so sore, Barbara and I would have given each other a "high five". We have reduced the number of view-hampering boundaries, reused some panels and posts and, mindful of the recent 18% increase in energy prices, recycled what remained of the old fence into what we hope will be enough firewood to last three or four days this coming winter.

Henry F. Phillips (14th August)

There is a part of me that enjoys amateur DIY; I love the sense of achievement I get from solving the problem whether it's flat-pack furniture, basic plumbing or wiring. It's a part of me that Barbara understands only too well and several years ago, knowing that I conform to the norm that advertising agencies try to appeal to, she gave me the best present ever; a cordless screwdriver. There is no end of things I can do with it, and it's ideal for living out that daytime fantasy of being Mr Perfect; it makes a great noise, is highly effective and I find it indispensable for almost every job I undertake. Better than all of that, I imagine it looks really good as I raise it above my head in slow motion whilst mopping my brow with my shoulder. It is to me what the advertisers say Yorkie Bars are to lorry drivers.

Although it's quite a way off yet, there will come a time when our projects around the house and land involve constructing things like chicken runs outside and wardrobes inside, but at present most of our time is spent removing things like lights, fences and sheds. This focus has meant that I have become hugely frustrated with the very things that my precious screwdriver was invented for. Or, to be more precise, one particular type of screwdriver. We dismantled one of the sheds a few days ago, and this involved removing the hundreds of screws that fastened the roof to the walls, the walls to the floor and the wall sections to each other. It took much longer than it needed to for one reason only; it had been built using slot-head screws.

Using a slot-head screwdriver, be it manual or powered, will invariably be the source of much annoyance and, if you are an amateur like me, a little bloodshed. You need to use your fingers to centre it on the screw first, and also to keep it centred as you start turning it. If you are using a manual screwdriver, it will slip off repeatedly. With a cordless screwdriver, the head will first shave a layer or two of skin, then pirouette off the screw like Torvill & Dean and finally bury itself in either the surrounding surface or, more commonly, your fingers. Although persistent, I do like keeping my hands intact, and so in the end I had to get the crowbar out again before the shed finally admitted defeat. The total cost was one large and shiny bruise.

I imagine that something like this must have happened to a certain Mr Henry F. Phillips, and he probably swore a great deal too. Unlike me though, he focussed his frustration more effectively, resulting in the invention of the Phillips-head screw. His brilliant creation meant that angle, balance or lack of patience would no longer affect the ability to insert or remove screws. He managed this by exploiting the fact that we live in three dimensions and not two. Phillips-head screws turn amateurs into professionals; they allow anyone to use a screwdriver with expert precision and no blood-loss. They have rendered the slot-head screw a pointless dinosaur whose sole attraction can only be aesthetic. I can't imagine they would be welcome anywhere except in that house from the film "Sleeping with the Enemy" where the hand towels and soup tins had to line up. As for Stone House, they are completely banned, and one day soon Henry F. Phillips will allow this particular daytime fantasy of mine to return. In fact, I may suggest that we name a sheep in his honour.

Fruit-picking Politics (21st August)

About ten years ago the western world was recoiling from the terror of 9-11, the media had a new diet of shock & awe, smart bombs and sexed-up dossiers, and the heavyweight political players on the world stage engaged in a great deal of sabre-rattling and posturing. Everyone had an opinion but nobody really knew what was going on. In fact, so little was known that a sort of collective bewilderment at the emerging new world order became the norm. Just in case there was anyone who really did think they knew what was going on, US Secretary of Defence Donald Rumsfeld comforted us all with this gem:

"There are known knowns. These are things we know that we know. There are known unknowns. That is to say, there are things that we know we don't know. But there are also unknown unknowns. There are things we don't know we don't know."

It's lovely, don't you think? Mr Rumsfeld taking the time to slowly walk us through this simple life lesson as though it were a colourful wall chart from the Early Learning Centre. This quote has come to mind over recent weeks as the reality of our move here has begun to sink in. Well, the bits we know about anyway. What, for example, are the blue known unknowns growing in the tree behind the house, and what do we do with them?

Do we make jam? Clothing dye? Perhaps we could idly throw them against a fence-post on a Sunday evening? Barbara has tried to find out what they are, and articles found through Google warned her that most berries are poisonous. As far as we can tell by looking at pictures, they are Shropshire Damson Prunes. You'd think that this would be enough information for us to harvest the three trees we have laden with these beauties and rustle up a tart or twenty, wouldn't you? But we are discovering that as townies we are also big cowards, and despite all the evidence available on the web, Barbara and I have several times found ourselves standing under these trees, one fruit apiece and three paces apart, nervously smiling at each other and saying "no no, after you, please - I insist."

You might conclude from this that chivalry is dead around here, but I argue that the available evidence is not conclusive, and we could unwittingly be playing host to a bumper crop of the notorious Worcestershire *blue-orb-of-instant-death*. OK, I made that one up, but I liken my cautious nature to that of Dr Hans Blix* when he repeatedly asked an impatient coalition of trigger-happy politicians for more time to be certain about the existence of WMD in Iraq. And, to feebly cover my cowardice with yet more chaff, I might add that it was he who said, "You don't know what you don't know." Indeed I don't, but at this rate, the one thing I do know is that I've probably just found names for two more animals; Rumsfeld and Blix, and as the dodo is extinct, a pair of ducks will have to do.

Luckily we have plenty of things we do know about; plums, apples, pears, strawberries, raspberries, rhubarb and potatoes were all growing here when we arrived. To these we will add more vegetables and perhaps plant a few more fruit trees, but these are all known knowns. Equally there is much we have to learn and be surprised by, and as these unknowns ambush us, I hope we will confront them rather than cower behind syntax. Perhaps unsurprisingly, the one thing Mr Rumsfeld never talked about was the unknown knowns; the things that you know you are going to have to do, but either have no idea how to set about it, or haven't quite the stomach. For the politicians of today it's balancing an urgent need to reduce deficits against economies that are crying out for fiscal stimuli, and for us it's plucking up the courage to try one of these juicy blue berries.

Laugh if you like, but if we survive you're getting jam for Christmas. And that's a known known.

Dr Hans Martin Blix was, at the time this letter was written, chairman of the Weapons of Mass Destruction Commission which searched for and ultimately failed to find any in Iraq during 2002/3.

Mowing in Hyperspace (29th August)

During my early teen years, summer days were often spent with friends huddled in the back of the Toy Cave on Chiswick High Road. We emptied our pocket money into Asteroids and Space Invaders video games, and although the colourful Space Invaders looked more exciting, I felt that the monochrome Asteroids was top trumps for a number of reasons. Firstly, almost no skill was required as it was possible to spin the space ship endlessly with one finger while firing wildly at everything with another and secondly, you could improvise a crude cruise control by firing your rockets once and then leaving your craft to lazily cross the screen ad infinitum while you blasted away in all directions. Lastly, as the game progressed, the number of asteroids increased and it got hotter in the intergalactic kitchen, there was a hyperspace button. All you had to do was hit it at the last moment and you magically vanished from the path of imminent destruction. Dominating the universe had never been so relaxing or easy; even Darth Vader couldn't do that! Mind you, he probably wouldn't have wanted to as you almost always reappeared somewhere you hadn't been looking, just in time to be pulverised by something you hadn't been expecting. Little did I realise it then, but under the guise of entertainment Atari was really trying to teach me that the best-laid plans often go awry.

When we lived in London, mowing the lawn was a simple job, the sort of thing you do before lunch on a Sunday when you have a spare half hour. Out with the Flymo, on with the grass box and away you go pushing it first one way, and then the other. All you had to do was keep the lever pressed and walk, and before you knew it you had earned enough points for a beer in the sun. Minimum effort, maximum reward. The other Sunday the grass was looking a bit long, and so I set aside a sunny morning for my first attempt at some large-scale garden maintenance. There are some parts of the garden where the old Flymo is still perfect for the job; the small areas of grass outside the kitchen and dining room, for example. I am glad that it's equal to the task, and I hope we get a good few more years out of it yet. The big field and part of the orchard field will be used for livestock at some point, but for the moment are left to produce hay for a local farmer. All I need to do is keep a mown path around the outside of them for access and for our evening walks. As you might imagine, a one metre wide path cut around three acres of land is a big ask of a Flymo in its twilight years, so for this the tractor is perfect.

My new pride and joy is a robust classic at over twenty years old, lovingly maintained by Ted since new, and part of the bargain we struck with him for Stone House. It's economical, quiet, reliable and, with no suspension to speak of, it's also rather good at revealing to you exactly how much of your body has slipped from your direct control into the clutches of gravity. Before using it for the first time, I read the manual and found out that it is really very straightforward to operate. I simply adjust all the settings like gear, cutting height and throttle, point it in the right direction, start the engine and off I go. I don't need to do anything except steer, and with a turning circle that would make a London Cabbie turn green with envy, it couldn't be easier.

Well, not exactly, and if you have ever driven a tractor right alongside a hawthorn hedgerow in anything less than full body armour, you'll know just what I mean. Thorny branches approached me at lightning speed, and I suddenly discovered what it's like to be a steak on a chopping board waiting to be sliced and diced. Then I remembered how I used to play Asteroids; I should take evasive action! Well, I tried shifting my carcass over and away from the hedge and found that as soon as I lift my bum from the seat, a safety device cuts the engine. It transpired that if I want to avoid being shredded to a pulp, I need to adopt a sort of side-saddle crouch while I mow; my left knee jammed under the steering wheel and my head and torso leaning out over the cut grass vent. Three and a half sides of the big field are hedgerow, and by the time I got to the blissful relief that is the post and rail fence dividing the big field from the orchard, I was ready for a long session with a chiropractor.

Thankfully from then on it was quite straightforward and as I completed my first lap, I even managed to pluck a juicy snack as I passed under the sagging branches of the plum tree. On my second round, I tossed one to Barbara who was taking her life in her hands by pruning some of the hedgerow, and we enjoyed our elevenses on the go. With three circuits of the big field complete, all that lay between the chequered flag and me was the orchard, and so I lifted the cutter up under the tractor, selected fifth gear and roared off like Mario Andretti.

The orchard is fifteen apple trees laid out in three equal rows spaced about thirty feet apart, and mowing it seems to be a question of performing a slow motion slalom between the trees to get the best result. I thought that the worst was over, having bested the hedgerow through ingenuity and posture, but now I was to discover that tree branches, although less sharp, are most definitely more dense. Realising that a number of different factors were at play here, I took the time to devise a mowing process in an uncharacteristic display of concentration and planning. I would start by aiming the tractor directly at the first tree, keep one eye on the left cutting edge and another on the tree. At precisely the right moment, without slowing down, I would execute a right-left-right flick of the steering wheel (inspired by over twenty years of watching Formula One cars going through Eau Rouge at the Belgian Grand Prix), and the mower would veer around the tree trunk just inches away in a perfect arc, before continuing towards the next tree and so on. Voila: one beautifully mown orchard, and it's cold beer o'clock. Despite this scientific approach I fell spectacularly at the first hurdle as although my plan seemed logical, it was essentially flawed by the fact that along with my two eyes, I have just enough mental power to keep up with the information they give me, and none left over for anything else. In the end, it was uncannily similar to when I used to play Asteroids; I was moving slowly and mowing indiscriminately. As imminent death loomed, I used the hyperspace button to evade the approaching tree trunk and as soon as had I managed it, my forehead smacked straight into the unseen low hanging branch just on the other side. Game over. Insert coin please.

Plum Job (4th September)

Having previously offered ourselves up for ridicule with the Worcestershire *blue-orb-of-instant-death* episode, Barbara and I felt that it was time to make more of an effort, to face up to reality and to make positive strides towards getting a grip on ourselves in the face of being too squeamish to taste a small, innocent fruit. On that particular matter, I have to tell you that we did finally try one of the damsons the other week, and found them particularly tart. As we have been wisely advised not to waste our time or even our gin on them, I wonder if they can be used to add flavour to something? As with everything around here, time and Google will tell. In the meantime we decided to err on the side of caution, or at least on the side of fruit that we recognise, and so it is with great pride, jubilation and fanfare that I write to share with you the great news that I have now made my first pot of jam using a large bowl of ripe plums from our tree.

Clearly plum season is late August around here; in the last month they have turned from small hard fruit to large, soft and meaty mouthfuls with a sweet delicious flavour. On our evening walks of late, it is hard to resist plucking one for a snack and our five-minute wander to the bench is completed with plum in one hand and the produce of a South African grape in the other. It seems that the ripe window for plums is something in the region of a week to ten days; those that we have picked and frozen will be used and those that we have not managed to collect are already splitting open, the exposed insides attracting wasps from far and wide to gorge themselves.

We did manage to collect an amount that had only just split; that were wonderfully edible but perhaps aesthetically challenged, and it was these that I used for my inaugural jam making session. It's amazing what you can find on the Internet; many recipes giving page after page of information with precise amounts and step-by-step instructions. Personally I like the other kind that optimistically say no more than "take plums, chop up, boil, add sugar, job done". And so I did just that, and in the fridge now sit two pots of jam; one plum and one plum and cinnamon.

By complete chance we got the proportion of fruit, sugar and cinnamon just right to produce a not-too-sweet and rather Christmassy jam that tastes absolutely lovely. One day Barbara plans on selling jars of jam, fruit, vegetables and all manner of produce at local farmers markets, and I am looking forward to this. However, we now know that when it comes to jam and baking in particular, we will need to remember adopt a more precise approach, possibly involving measurements, so that it can be repeated.

Already I can tell that jam making is a labour intensive, energy consuming and rather boring procedure. For me, the litmus tests of a fun job are; does it require the use of a petrol-powered tool? And, can mistakes be easily bodged into something else? Sadly, jam making fails both these tests and therefore, as someone who prefers butter and little else on my toast of a morning, I regret to conclude that jam making is not a plum job.

Directions with Wolves (12th September)

Stone House sits in the rolling hills between Malvern and Bromyard, and a delightfully rural and peaceful setting it is too. Technically we are just outside the parish of Stanford Bishop; the marker being on our southern boundary. The loose collection of about ten households boasts a village hall, a church, a fervent football fan and a pub. We have yet to see a sign of life at the hall, the church cannot be accessed directly from the road, the fan is a fanatically loyal and flag-flying devotee of Wolverhampton Wanderers, and The Herefordshire House pub is the focus of the community in more ways, it turns out, than one.

Finding out anything about Stanford Bishop or its history has been quite a difficult task. Our constant companion Google has little to say on the matter, and the locals that we have met have nothing to add. It sits right on the border between Herefordshire and Worcestershire, and that seems to have given it a bit of an identity crisis. The two counties were once one; the marriage lasting from 1974 until 1998. Divorces can often be rather messy arrangements, and here the decree absolute gave custody of the council tax revenue to Hereford while Worcester got the postcode. To squabble over ten households spread over a few square miles of land might seem churlish, but sometimes the simplest things turn out to be more complicated than you expect. Like giving directions, for example.

To call a property Stone House in this part of the world is a bit like living in Dublin and naming your son Patrick; there are at least three others in the surrounding villages that we have seen. Add to that the fact that almost every road that leads to, from or around Malvern is called 'Malvern Road' and you begin to get the picture. If that weren't enough, once you tell whoever is asking that you are in Herefordshire and then give them a Worcestershire postcode, you have to wait patiently while they process this information, and prepare an explanation for whichever way around they ask the next question. Local tradesmen will usually ask for specific directions in terms of not only where we are, but also the easiest way to get here from wherever they are coming. Given that they are asking for directions like "left at the knackered parrot, straight on past the piggery and don't whatever you do take the right fork before the legless hop-picker", this means that Barbara and I have sometimes felt rather inadequate in this regard; we don't really know the roads yet, and it seems that the local names mean we live in a generic anywheresville as opposed to a specific nowheresville.

However, none of this actually matters as Margo and Jerry chose for the colour of their pub a rather distinct shade of Day-Glo pink. As you approach from the south, it appears as a bright beacon about a mile ahead over the rolling hills and if you approach from the north it acts as a very efficient and sudden traffic warning system for an unsighted sharp bend that has apparently caught quite a few drivers out over the years. We now know to ask anyone wanting directions firstly if they know the Pink Pub. Almost everyone around here has, its local fame (not to mention visibility) having carried far beyond the parish boundaries. If they have, our directions are simple; "Well, head for it and if you pass the Wolves flag before it, we're just after the pub. If not, we're just before it. You can't miss either."

If they don't know either the flag or the pub, then it's anyone's guess which Stone House our more traditional directions will eventually lead them to.

The Katia Harvest (18th September)

With autumn approaching, the fruit is ripening and we have vaguely planned our first harvest. All of it will need to be collected and either stored, used, sold or given away. Thankfully the different varieties have already had a chat amongst themselves and agreed to ripen at different times, so as not to cause a bottleneck in our amateur harvesting process. We have planned for damson first, then plums followed by pears and finally apples. Most important, simply due to quantity, will be the apple orchard. They are 'Vilberie' bittersweet cider apples, and one bite will assure you that they are definitely not for eating. Ted told us that they were originally planted by the Magners Cider Company, and provide a crop in early November just before the frosts come. Even though we have a Cider Barn built for the purpose, we are wine drinkers and therefore are not of a mind to mass-produce cider. There are quite a few independent producers around these parts, and so our plan is to collect the harvest and exchange it for jobs on the land that are beyond our knowledge, strength or machinery. Well, as I have mentioned in previous letters, other things tend to happen while we are busy making plans.

As an insomniac, I often listen to the Shipping Forecast late at night, and have for years enjoyed the phrase "losing its identity" when used to describe a weather system that is on the wane. The system that was previously Hurricane Katia was forecast to be just such a leftover when it approached the UK in early September, but can I assure you that when I met her, she seemed absolutely certain of her identity. On our exposed hilltop, she arrived quite suddenly from the west and relentlessly attacked for eight hours as she passed. The house shook, the wind shrieked and the rain was at times horizontal. She scoured every inch of land; anything not tied down was relocated to the eastern boundary or beyond in record time, and she almost succeeded in toppling our enormous willow tree which at times looked a tall ship flying far too much canvas in a storm. Not content with this, Katia also lent us a helping hand by harvesting all our fruit for us, whether it was ripe or not.

We mentioned this to Margo over a Saturday pint, and she warned us that the slight chill in the air is a sign that wildlife will start to seek warm places to escape the coming winter. Thanks to Katia's efficiency, all the rotting food on the ground was acting as an open invitation for our outbuildings to be the wildlife winter sun destination of choice. With our current work and travel schedules, it would be a race against time to collect and dispose of it.

The thousands of apples that littered the orchard were far too small and hard to be of use to anyone, and so our original plan of bartering (or at the very least leaving buckets of them at the roadside with a sign saying "help yourself") had been dashed. Instead it was a day of raking, piling, collecting and tipping. For the sake of accuracy, I should also mention that swearing, hitting heads on low-hanging branches, sore backs, cuts and blisters were also involved. Ted had warned us on arrival that this year's crop was not going to be plentiful, and judging by the number of full barrow loads that we tipped, this may be nature's way of easing us in gently, as a bumper harvest might well have overwhelmed us.

As we adapt to our life here, some things are already starting to change. One of the first things I have noticed is that our idle Internet browsing habits have suffered from substantial 'mission-creep'. There was a time when Sunday evenings involved web-inspired conversations and daydreams about tropical travel, classic cars and hi-tech gadgetry, but now we find ourselves scouring eBay and Freecycle for second hand farm equipment, storage jars and freezers. We have plans to change boundaries, move the driveway entrance, build a wall along the road, create several large vegetable plots and replace the apple trees with more useful produce; which means I am now searching for a small tractor with an assortment of attachments that will allow us to dig, plough, rotavate and grade the earth.

Katia may have taken only a few hours to alter the landscape around here, but I hope that our impact will be both gentler and longer lasting.

Margaritaville (2nd October)

Not too long ago the temperatures here were barely making it into the teens at the height of the day, there was a distinct chill in the air at night and we were preparing to light the fire for the first time. Summer was over, the barbecue had been wheeled into the back of the garage, and our busy schedule of outdoor work was suspended. An autumn of indoor maintenance, repairs and odd jobs beckoned, and after some two months of living here, we felt settled and looked forward to shortening days, the changing colours and a brisker breeze. Then, on Tuesday, the weather forecast promised a whole week of hot sun and no clouds.

If you have ever seen what happens to people at an airport when they suddenly realise that the flight they have been patiently waiting for is due to depart from a different terminal in ten minutes, then that will give you some idea of the impact this forecast had on us.

Even allowing for the Met Office's standard margin of error, which usually involves hot and dry rain, wet and snowy sunshine and Michael Fish telling us not to worry about an approaching hurricane, this week's forecast sent waves of excitement through us. Barbara sent urgent text messages from her desk at work; "Oh my God, look at the forecast! Get my swimsuit out of storage, dig a swimming pool, find the barbecue and go buy meat and lots of beer!" The telecommunications network that connected us sizzled with as much heat as the forecast told us to expect.

Barbara and I both feel we were born to live the lives of sun-worshipping backpackers, which means winter will always be a season that lasts a little too long for us. We often discuss whether or not we should move somewhere tropical and make our living by serving cold beer and renting windsurfers to tourists covered in oil. For now though, this forecast gave us the chance for another week's outdoor living; something we prize so highly.

During the days this week, while Barbara worked at her desk in Worcester, I raced through my office chores early in the morning here in order to spend as much time as I could outside. Having wired the garden and outdoor area between the house and garage for sound, Jimmy Buffett sang while I worked. There were sewers to be cleaned, sheds to be dismantled, chicken houses to be built, cut branches to be burned and tractors to be repaired. By the time she came home, there were walks to be taken, views to be enjoyed and barbecues to be had. Once or twice I got my timing wrong, and we cleaned sewers together, but when we finished we still had time to watch the most beautiful sunset.

This week has been six glorious days of shimmering heat straight from the Caribbean; sharing cold drinks and making dreamy plans while fixing this, replacing that and taking an open-topped drive there. Insomnia has been less frustrating than usual with the distractions of warm star-filled nights, owls hooting in the small hours and the occasional meteor streaking across the sky. For the first time in a long time, the five-day weather forecast was absolutely correct, although now it says that cooler temperatures will return soon as they must.

But this evening the sun continues to shine, the temperatures remain high and there is still time for one more Cheeseburger in Paradise. It's always five o'clock somewhere.

Norwegian Wood (9th October)

After last week's brief Indian summer, autumnal weather has returned and with it the need to start lighting fires in our wood burning stove, which I have discovered is a rather nice example. I usually cringe when I hear the word 'designer' being used to signify a product of a particular quality; it strikes me as a bit silly to infer exclusivity of some sort by referring to a part of the production process that is common to all manufactured goods. I mean, somebody must have designed the sunglasses that I bought for two euros on holiday, and if I take the vast majority of companies producing designer goods as a measure, I'm not exactly sure that I recognise the ability to write their name on what they make as a notable skill. Getting someone to pay over the odds for something and carry free advertising is indeed a skill, but I think that's using the word 'design' in a slightly different context. Even so I imagine most companies would prefer to build their brand in the way that Kleenex and Hoover have managed; by turning their company name into generic noun. But then, they didn't actually do that; those of use who liked and used their product did. Notwithstanding the above, as the owner of a relatively new and rather sleek LED television, I willingly admit to enjoying design based on aesthetics alone.

However, when I come across a design that is the by-product of functionality, then I believe it's in a different league altogether.

Stone House was formerly two cottages that were built sometime around 1840 from stone excavated from the long-since closed Malvern quarries. In common with all such exposed and rural properties, the living rooms were designed around fireplaces, and here in particular I find evidence of Ted's influence on the conversion being led by function over form; not for him the impressive show-home. Putting to one side the range cooker, virtually all houses such as these will have either an open fire or a wood burning stove; if you will, the PC and Mac of the rural heating world. The former produces quick heat via an open flame and the latter radiates heat via a cast iron outer casing. They both have their pros and cons; few would argue against the romance of an open fire, but the Achilles' heels of safety and a significant amount of heat escaping up the chimney limit their appeal. Stoves offer night-time safety and heat that lingers long after the flames have gone, but are slower to heat up and often take up floor space. As with most things in life, striking the right balance is important, but compromise is never easy.

When we first viewed the house in January, during the coldest winter in over 30 years, I had never heard of a Jøtul convection and radiation wood burning stove. More importantly I hadn't been in the same room as one and experienced it in action. Made by a Norwegian company for the last century and a half, these stoves are a beautiful blend of the best of both worlds; not by being a compromise, but by changing the rules and being clever.

A Jøtul Stove is just a normal wood-burning stove, except that some models like ours can be built inside the chimney. Or rather, the chimney can be rebuilt around it in a particular way to take advantage of some of the laws of physics depending on how you want to use it. If, as Lennon & McCartney suggest in their song from which this letter takes its title; she asked you to stay and she told you to sit anywhere, you might sit on the floor staring hopefully into the flames whilst you drank her wine and bided your time. With it's doors wide open, you would be both be bathed in delicious heat radiating from the flames while your hearts melted. If it were a normal open fireplace, she would need to wait for the fire to die down a bit before safely inviting you to her bed. Here, she can simply close the doors and off you go. The fire will continue safely behind the vented doors, radiating heat until it eventually dies out. The best of both worlds all rolled into one fireplace.

But it doesn't stop there. Continuing with my Beatles' theme; if you awoke alone because she had flown and you wanted a fire to warm the room unattended whilst you were busy rueing your misfortune, you could light a fire and close the doors, because here is the really clever bit. The stove appears to be set in the chimney, but it's actually set in a large cavity behind what looks like the chimney.

There is a substantial amount of space above, behind, below and to either side of it, and a number of vents positioned above and below it are part of the magic. As the fire warms the cast iron stove, the air in the cavity warms with it, and the magic of convection begins. Slowly at first, the warm air from around the stove begins to rise and starts escaping from the top three vents, leaving behind a vacuum that sucks in the colder air at floor level, and so the cycle has begun. The fire burns happily inside the stove and before long the vents are feeding the room with a plentiful supply of warm air whilst constantly removing all the cold air. If you fill the stove last thing at night and close the doors, you'll find it still producing warm air at breakfast.

It doesn't surprise me in the slightest to discover that Jøtul ranks in the world's top international design award winners alongside the likes of Porsche and Prada. Slower and less pretty it may be; but isn't it good, Norwegian Wood?

Walking the Plank (16th October)

One of our current projects is the construction of an enclosure that will allow chickens to be safe at night, have a secure pen to roam in for those days when we are both away and a free range area for when someone is at home to watch over them and keep an eye out for Mr Fox. We have chosen to use the area between the garage and the Cider Barn, and have taken our time to design, plan and execute this build. It's an area of scrubland on which Ted used to keep a large container surrounded by a high fence, and over the last two months the fence has been gradually removed and reused, and the area cleared of rubble.

The first thing we discovered was how expensive everything to do with animal shelters is. If you want to buy a purpose built chicken run made with wood and fox-proof mesh, it's going to set you back hundreds of pounds and that's before you've considered the chicken house itself. Luckily we discovered that one of the sheds would be ideal for this purpose, as it was a large wire cage with exterior wooden cladding. The outer shell was removed and stored, and the wire cage was dragged to the side of the garage where it now stands ready for its new life as a chicken run, complete with breeze block base to discourage foxes from digging underneath its walls.

On consulting the Haynes Chicken Manual, we learned how we might build a suitably sized chicken house, but when we costed all the materials, it came to almost the same amount as a flat-pack one which would doubtless be built to a better standard, so that's what we bought instead. Now we had a house and a run, but the land it was on was not very suitable for chickens. Both Haynes and common sense tell us they like vegetation as well as soil to scratch around in, and the entire area was hard packed earth. Our rotavator would not be strong enough to plough this piece of land, and therefore a creative solution was needed.

There are all manner of attachments that you can get for garden tractors; I imagined that a plough and a scarifier would have been ideal for this purpose, but I felt sure that we could find a way to achieve the same end without having to spend more money. With the help of a bottle of Merlot, we conceived a rather ingenious tractor-drawn scarifier using a plank, some large nails, leftover wire-mesh, washing line and, er, Barbara standing on it.

I hasten to add that not only did she volunteer to act as ballast, but I also suggested that we swap places as I can provide significantly more of it. This piece of engineering brilliance allowed us to convert a large piece of scrubland into loose and fertile land which we then sowed with grass. As the autumn continues, we look forward to the first hint of green that will give our chickens a safe and free ranging home. Their house had arrived a few weeks ago, was constructed during the glorious hot week at the beginning of the month, and now stands ready to receive them within the next few weeks. All that remains for us to do is to erect two retaining fences that will prevent them from wandering onto the road on one side or into the field on the other.

If everything goes to plan and the grass takes hold, Barbara and I will be joined by a few clucking feathered friends sometime in early November. Anyone for a Pirate's Egg 'n' Bacon breakfast?

True Colours (23rd October)

Being cautious people, Barbara and I thought it would be money well spent to have a full structural survey carried out on Stone House before we bought it. Ian, a surveyor that we had used before, went over every inch of the house and gave us a full report detailing that the structure was sound but that we would need to update various things like wiring, plastering and central heating in the future. We were happy in the knowledge that for at least the first few years we would be fine.

About three weeks after moving in, we discovered that the shower was not draining as quickly as usual and I thought that it would be a simple matter of clearing hair or some such blockage from the drain. It wasn't, and being relatively new to private drainage systems, I once again turned to Google for help. It suggested that I explore the main sewer via the inspection hatches just outside the house and discover whether the blockage was in the house or in the sewer. Using a crowbar (the tool of a million purposes) I opened both of them and was confronted with two inspection chambers filled to the brim with raw sewage and paper. There was nothing else to do except call out an emergency drainage company to unblock it, and make sure from then on that nothing other than human waste and paper was put into it. A sobering lesson for the townies from Hanwell.

The man cleared the sewer easily and advised me to lift the inspection hatch once a month and send some water down the pipe to the septic tank just to make sure that all was kept in good working order. To satisfy my curiosity, I lifted the hatches a mere two weeks later and found the same blockage had occurred again. This time, rather than spend the money on a call out charge, I went to Travis Perkins and invested in thirty metres of flexi-pipe with plumbing attachments, and unblocked it myself. It's not the nicest job I can think of, but neither is it the worst; which turns out to be rather a good thing.

I phoned Ted and outlined the problem to him, mentioned that it seemed to be recurring and asked him how he maintained the system so as to avoid it blocking. "Oh", he said, "Well, I don't know. I've never had a problem with it, you see". Without noticing the word 'mug' tattooed on my forehead, I took him at his word and wondered where I might next look for a long-term solution. The sewer pipe is made of pitch-fibre which degrades over time, meaning that pipes made from this material are susceptible to collapse. In fact, it is an inevitable, although gradual process. Our survey had shown that this problem would be occurring in the future, but no structural survey includes a camera inspection of a sewer pipe.

Another chap, this time from Dyno Rod complete with flashy equipment and bright pink van, came last week and showed me the entire length of the pipe from the inside on his CCTV. Together we counted no less than seven areas of collapse or intrusion, any one of which would be enough to cause reoccurring blockages with only very light use. I asked him if these distortions could be recent, to which he replied, "Anything is possible, but I doubt it". Unfortunately it is now clear that we need to install a new sewer pipe; something which we had neither anticipated nor budgeted several thousand pounds for.

This afternoon, I stopped by our other neighbour, Andrew, in order to deliver one of Barbara's fruit pies and collect some wood he had kindly offered us. Amongst our chitchat of weather and local news, he mentioned that he had seen me waving a large length of flexi-pipe about during one of my regular unblocking episodes, and asked if we had drainage problems. I gave him a précis of what I have written here, and he asked me if Ted had told me there was a problem before we bought the house. When I mentioned that Ted hadn't mentioned anything before and had specifically said since that he hadn't had a problem, Andrew said "Well, he's a lying bastard and I'd tell him so to his face." He then outlined how

Ted had spent the last five years regularly unblocking the sewer in more or less exactly the same way as me.

In time our sewer will be replaced and all that will remain broken is our opinion of Ted, a man who seemed so genuine and honest when we first met him. From now on, all the footsteps we take will be our very own. Anyone for a game of Pooh sticks?

Tool Academy (6th November)

Flicking through the channels on television the other day, I came across a program called 'Tool Academy'. Being often of an immature and child-like disposition, I giggled at the title and elbowed Barbara in the ribs. As she rolled her eyes, I conjured up all manner of ideas for what the program might be about, and then assumed that it was about a group of reality-celebrity-engineers being tasked to invent the next wheel with their tool of choice, whilst the public influenced the progress of mankind with their libido. It seems I was wrong, and the program is not about engineering. It actually is about who, from a collection of applicants who defy understanding by appearing on this show, is the biggest tool of the lot. Sadly I didn't have the stamina for more then five minutes of it, but it did start me thinking about, well, tools.

Much laughter has been had at my expense around the issue of my tractor mower. For one thing, is it really a tractor? For another, does the fact that it increases my testosterone levels mean that I should be a contestant on the program? If I won, would I suddenly take up steroids injections, wolf-whistling and an annual membership to the Circus Tavern in Dartford? Joking aside, I am here to tell you that a lawn tractor is actually quite a tame measure when compared to what I now consider the ultimate rural testosterone yardstick: the chainsaw.

For what it does, a chainsaw is quite small, makes an annoying wasp-like noise and looks far less impressive than a tractor; so right from the start it appears a poor rival as, when it comes to tools of this kind, size does matter. As a toddler, it was completely natural for me to impersonate a car whilst my parents encouraged me to eat rather than wear my food, but I imagine it would have been somehow odd for me to crawl around the house spontaneously making chainsaw noises; one was a known quantity and the other was alien. For me, this partly explains why I thought a tractor was the ultimate tool. Having been around and influenced by cars since I can remember, driving is no mystery to me and therefore tractor driving is well within my comfort zone. It works exactly as I had expected, and therefore I believe I can excel.

Conversely, what experience had I of a chainsaw before I moved here? None whatsoever. From time to time I saw men in hardhats and goggles wielding them in the leafy trees of West London, but I never had a go with one, I had no idea of how they worked and as far as I know there is no Gilles Villeneuve of the chainsaw world that could have thrilled me in quite the same way. They are saws; you chop stuff up with them – that was it. Barbara's father and his wife recently came to stay, and as a housewarming present, they gave us a rather smart chainsaw. I was delighted to let him show me the ropes, and within fifteen minutes of taking it out of the box he was merrily decimating whatever was within reach. Being new to it, I opted to wait and read the manual at a later date, which I did. The manual, I discovered, was like most manuals in that it tells you what to do but not how to do it - or what to be wary of.

One of my on-going jobs around here is the removal of about thirty Leylandii trees which form just one of many pointless boundaries on the land; a row between the house and the garage. Notorious for causing disputes between neighbours, they grow rapidly and are an infernal weed. Left to their own devices they can become a mass of tangled branches that are a nightmare to deal with, and that is easiest done with a chainsaw. Each tree takes about an hour to cut, separate from its neighbour and then drag to the animal shelter where they will dry over the winter before we turn them into firewood and kindling. This is the job for which I am now so grateful to have a chainsaw.

I quickly discovered that it was a tool that I was going to have to master or use only once. Yes, it is a saw, and it works just like any other saw. Well, not quite. It is a chain too, and this is where looking at the mechanics of a bicycle are useful. Whilst it certainly will cut, the distance between you and whatever you are cutting will also evaporate rapidly if you are not careful. I know this because on a number of occasions the chainsaw has been ripped from my hands, and on one particularly memorable occasion I ended up wearing the Leylandii that I was trying to cut down.

It is also designed for cutting trees as opposed to roofs, metal or cement, and having accidentally used it inappropriately on a number of occasions, I have blunted the teeth to the point where I already need to buy a replacement chain. Compounding this error, I have also failed to realise that it needs oil to lubricate the chain, as well as the oil to lubricate the engine. The prospect of a winter's chain sawing ahead of me is quite a daunting thought, and I already yearn for the spring when the Formula One season will begin at roughly the same time that my tractor comes out of hibernation.

Therefore, when comparing farm machinery, it seems I have learned that the smallest tool is potentially the most dangerous tool, especially when operated by the simplest tool.

Dramatis Personae (14th November)

I remember very few facts about the television sitcom from which I have borrowed our names; I was young when it was first shown and paid little attention to it. The original treatment for the pilot must have read something like "Suburban childless couple living next door to quarrelsome couple quit their rat-race existence in favour of a more self-sufficient lifestyle". I have no doubt that it was more comprehensive than that, but even if my version is only an approximation, it encapsulates the flavour of what we are trying to achieve here at Stone House. My only concrete memory of the show is from an episode where the constantly henpecked Jerry finally gets the better of Margo. "Aha!", he cries triumphantly at the end, "You see? I'm not as stupid as I look!" Margo's instant response was delivered in her typically cool and calm fashion; "Oh you couldn't be, Jerry, you simply couldn't be."

We are becoming increasingly less like John Esmonde and Bob Larbey's characters, as I found out on Sunday 18th September. Barbara had gone first to find eggs from the local farmer, and then on to the supermarket in Ledbury to use up her loyalty points on buying mundane essentials like shampoo and bin liners. At the same time I was finishing my preparations for a week's work in Scotland before starting on a car washing and garage-tidying marathon for the afternoon. Barbara came back and invited me for a lunchtime walk around the field. As we sat enjoying the autumnal sunshine on the bench, she gave me a box and said, "It's a few days late, but this is for your birthday". Earlier this summer, we had agreed to forget about our birthdays this year for financial and practical reasons, and so faced with a box from an expensive design company in my hand, I felt a pang of guilt for ignoring her birthday, not to mention feeling mildly irritated that she had gone against our decision in remembering mine. Almost reluctantly I opened it.

Barbara often prefers to make rather than buy gifts as her many friends with bags, aprons and favours will know, but placing a pregnancy test stick in a presentation box on a bed of ribbon with the instruction card was taking things to a new level. 'Two stripes: pregnant. One stripe: not pregnant', it read. This is the sort of binary output that I normally find easy to understand, but as I studied the two plainly visible stripes, I couldn't quite grasp what they were telling me. In fact I don't think I was sure what it meant until I looked up and saw tears in her eyes.

It would not be an exaggeration to say that Barbara has been suffering a cruel and unnecessary fate at the hands of a former employer over these last three years or so, and it is increasingly clear that she will live with a degree of pain and immobility for the rest of her life. Even so, she carries herself with humour, great dignity and endless grace. She also has an ever-developing spine of steel wrought in part from the idiotic shenanigans of people who would instantly know better if they lost their grip on the cloak of corporate invisibility to which they cling. Despite this, we are very lucky. We want for nothing, we have most of our health, we work very hard, and it is not often that we get news as good as this.

As with most things in our life together, we have tended to come to them late and after much consideration. Getting this far has not been easy, and over the last few years we had formed a vague idea that we might move to somewhere in the Pacific Ocean and live out our days under a hot sun on a sandy beach next to a blue ocean with a cold beer in our hands. This alternative plan may yet happen as it is still early days and reaching the end of the first trimester has not been as easy as it might, but for now we continue our first tentative steps towards parenthood full of wonder and awe for all that we have yet to experience, to get wrong and to discover.

We have just returned from a twelve-week scan where baby has been seen wriggling and hogging the duvet. The jury is still undecided about which parent baby might take after, but as Barbara continues to be the light that guides our family with her pregnancy, ever-strengthening spirit and beauty both inside and out, I shall simply borrow and distort a phrase from The Good Life; 'She couldn't not, she simply couldn't not.'

Room for a Baby (27th November)

Since September, we have been reassessing many of our plans due to the arrival next May of Barbara's bump, who for some reason is currently referred to as 'Bagel'. I am becoming slightly worried that this moniker will stick beyond next May, but more of that another time. The two most pressing issues that concern us are our drainage system and our bedrooms. Having prepared to unleash the Rottweiler that is our solicitor onto the as yet unsuspecting Ted, we have largely cleared our desks of the drainage issue in order to take care of the problem of living spaces.

Stone House is a three-bedroom cottage, where Barbara and I have one bedroom, guests another and my office is currently the third. We want to make some changes before May, and so we are planning a slow game of dominoes-like upheaval that will hopefully settle after six months. Bagel will eventually turn my office into a nursery, which will move into the wood store, which then relocates to the animal shelter, which needs to be cleared and prepared

The animal shelter is a large green ugly structure that sits just inside the big field opposite the Cider Barn. One day we would dearly love to move it to a corner of the field where it would appear less dominant, but it is a solid structure that will be hard to move and for the time being is ideal for storing wood, rubble, supplies, miscellaneous items and eventually will provide shelter for livestock. Fire logs are delivered by the tonne on the back of a tip-truck and having spent the last year ferrying and stacking hundreds of logs at the expense of my back, I took one look at the front wall of the animal shelter and decided that if the section on the right hand side were to come down, then the trucks could simply reverse in, tip their load in the right spot and it would be beer o'clock that much earlier.

This morning dawned a bright and sunny day, and I felt that there was no time like the present for the wall to come down. With a coffee inside me and seriously bad 'just-out-of-bed' look on my head, I wandered off to the field pausing only to collect the tools of choice for the day; newly repaired chainsaw, sledgehammer, wrecking bar, methylated spirits and matches. Destruction is just another kind of construction, right? Armed with this lethal arsenal, I decided that the metal cladding would be reused as a roof for the chicken pen, and so I removed it with uncharacteristic care and stored it in the Cider Barn. The wood that was behind it was a mixture of reasonable and rotting support beams, so I used the 'boot test' to decide which planks should stay and which should go. The boot test is as crude as it is effective, and is based on absolutely no science whatsoever. I have decided that any piece of wood that cannot withstand one swing from my steel capped boot is of little structural use to me and, as treated wood, cannot be used in our fireplace. Therefore anything that withstands my boot is stacked inside the animal shelter, and everything else is appositely resized for incineration in the oil drum that has helpfully consumed so much rotten wood already.

Within a few hours, the animal shelter's exterior had been remodelled and its contents reorganised, and now stands ready to receive a delivery of firewood in a week or so. In shifting trees, pallets and other bits of rubbish from one side of the shelter to the other, I came across two surprises; a dead rabbit under a pallet and my instant squeamish reaction to it. Trying to live out here and not being able to handle dead wildlife is never going to work, and it took me about thirty seconds to realise that. So, armed with gloves and fortified by some loud Bon Jovi from the garage speakers, bunny went down in a blaze of glory in the hedgerow. I'll check tomorrow to see if he was wanted dead or alive by any of the usual predator suspects. If he's still there, then at least we ain't strangers anymore.

The second chapter of this story will begin as soon as we know that Ted has either agreed or been forced to bring the condition of the drainage at Stone House up to the standard that he expressed it was in the contract of sale. At that point we will start our plans to convert the wood store that sits snugly against the back of the house into my new office. An island for one that became a home for two is becoming a funny farm for three.

Deferred Success (4th December)

Binfield's, a local garden furniture company, recently unearthed the frayed and brittle remains that once constituted my tether, or to be more precise, the end of it. When we left London, we put our garden furniture and equipment into storage during our stay in Gloucestershire, and then brought it out when we arrived here. Having removed the last of the wooden sheds that littered the garden about a month ago, we decided to erect our greenhouse alongside the existing one that Ted left us. I constructed the frame while Barbara and her sister, who was visiting at the time, brought out the carefully wrapped glass panes from the garage, and I began to piece together the delicate puzzle. Unfortunately we found that a few pieces of glass and some of the fixtures had either gone missing or been broken in the move and so I turned to my friend Google to source a local supplier for what we needed. Luckily I had the original manual, and was able to track down the local agent for the manufacturer of our particular greenhouse.

After several attempts to raise them on the phone the next morning, I was greeted by a monosyllabic grunting man who was able to make me understand that the person that I needed to speak to was not there. I asked when I might call back, and was told simply "Saaaa-ght-er-gnoooome", which I took to mean in the afternoon. I did ring back in the afternoon but no one answered. I repeated the process the next day, and this time the grunting man said that his colleague would be in on "Wyanz-zer-deeee", so I wondered if he might take my number and leave a message for his colleague to ring me back on Wednesday."Woooy? Whatt-eyew wornt?" he bellowed down the phone. Worried that I had totally misunderstood their website, I said "I beg your pardon, this is Binfield's isn't it? Your website says you are a garden centre". After a worryingly long pause, during which he presumably thought about my question from a number of angles, he replied "Yearrrze", and so on the verge of giving up I said "Well, I want to buy something from you". Something evidently registered, as he then took down my number and said I'd receive a call back.

Eventually a lady from the company rang and from the original instruction manual I was able to give her precise measurements and original part numbers for all the bits that we needed. I asked her to let me know when she received them, and I would pop down for payment and collection. After two weeks had passed without hearing anything, I thought I'd better call for an update. Cunningly seeking to avoid the monosyllabic man, I waited until the next Wednesday afternoon to ring. "Uooo-eeeee erdunn foo?" he answered, and my heart instantly sank. I toyed with the idea of hanging up, but tried again and successfully managed to leave a message for his colleague to return my call. Eventually we spoke on that Friday, and when I asked her when she expected delivery of the parts she replied helpfully "Oh heavens, they've been here for a week". Sensing victory was at last within reach, I said that I would come down the next day, but she stopped my in my tracks by saying it "wouldn't be convenient". After agreeing that collection would be the following Saturday, I hung up and considered the matter settled.

Amongst our plans for the following weekend was a short shopping trip to Malvern, so we drove past Binfield's on the way. Well, we tried to, we think we did, the map agrees with us and it may be that we even came quite close, but we ultimately failed. There was no garden centre called Binfield's at the postcode given on their website, and we could not get an answer from their phone. We did find a large open-air market doing a roaring trade in Christmas Trees, and Barbara asked a chap if he knew where they were. He pointed past the market towards a dirt track and said "Up there. Green Land-Rover". We duly drove up the road, and at the end found a silver Citroen parked next to a fishing lake, and a large lady making bacon rolls in a hut. Barbara asked her if she could help, and she pointed back down the way we had come saying "keep going straight and it's the barn on the right". For the next fifteen minutes we slowly drove around every barn on the entire site and found no Binfield's, no Green Land-Rover, no greenhouse supplies and no sign of life. We continued on to Malvern and I was left to wonder how, in this world of the internet, telephone, satellites, media and customer service training, was it possible to snatch defeat from the jaws of such an easy victory?

It was curiosity rather than customer service that brought Binfield's and I together in the end. The lady I had been dealing with evidently got tired of the clutter in her office and found our telephone number scribbled on a bit of paper on her desk. She called the other day asking when I would be collecting it, and during our brief conversation I managed to extract accurate directions. To her credit, she sounded neither irritated nor impatient, and to mine, I thanked her for her time and effort. However, when I got package home the next day, I found that they had sent the wrong size glass and the wrong specification retainers.

I immediately issued a full recall on my thanks, and promptly replaced them with curses. I then changed tack and located a hobbit-like glazier who works out of an industrial estate in Malvern, and must be about a hundred and twelve. Reassuringly, he used far more syllables than the man from Binfield's, and I was grateful to understand all of them. He then produced exactly what I needed, made to order in less than twenty minutes. Google may be 21st century, but for 20th century old-fashioned companies, there is always 'good old yellow pages' to rely on. The greenhouses now stand shipshape and ready for Barbara's potting season next year.

Wychbold Heartbeat (11th December)

Wychbold is the site of the Droitwich Transmitting Station, the most powerful long wave transmitter in the country, and from where BBC Radio Four is broadcast throughout the UK, as far as Western Germany and apparently quite some way into the Atlantic Ocean. As a technological dinosaur that survives on an old-fashioned diet of specially crafted glass valves, its days are numbered. In an attempt to prolong its life, the BBC bought all ten such valves that remain in existence, and once they are used up the transmitter will fall silent for good. For now though, the 700 foot high structure sitting alongside the M5 and consisting of a giant T-aerial suspended between two masts remains a beacon to many, and to us here at Stone House in more ways than one.

I travel a great deal for work and have been an insomniac for many years. Those of you who spend weeks away from home in the way that I do will be familiar with the 'first night in a new bed' effect, which almost guarantees a grumpy start the following morning once your body has been re-calibrated by an unfamiliar mattress. If you add to this the increasing number of hotels that have removed tea & coffee making facilities from their rooms in an economy drive, and the further irritation that those that haven't can often forget to replenish supplies, the problem can be aggravated.

It is therefore one of my greatest and most reliable pleasures, when staying in some hotel, bed & breakfast or faceless training venue, to regularly climb into bed with Ritula Shah at night, and then doze until Charlotte Green* slips under the covers with me the following morning. Such intimacy with either of these dulcet-toned women would not be possible, were it not for the transmitter tirelessly feeding 198 kHz to my battered little travel radio at night.

It happens that Wychbold is about twenty miles from Stone House as the crow flies, and the two supporting masts are lit up by a series of red aircraft warning lights at night. In poor weather they are obscured from view, but frequently during the hours of darkness they are clearly visible across the fields to the Northeast, gently pulsing and shimmering due to the atmospheric conditions between us. Like the broadcasts, the lights at night are a constant and reassuring presence; an anchor that gives a sense of continuity.

Often I will see them close up from the car, when returning late at night or heading off early in the morning; the twin columns of light burning brightly as I pass by on the M5 only a few hundred yards away. Cloud cover permitting, when flying into Birmingham, I can easily pick them out against the pinpricks of sodium light that carpet the West Midlands at night. As the plane makes a structured series of left hand turns from the north around to the southwest in preparation for landing, the intersecting light trails of the M5 and M42 guide my focus. When I catch sight of them on my travels, I'll often wonder if Barbara has just passed by a window at the exact same time and noticed them winking at her too. When I see them from home, I enjoy the feeling of safety they give.

A transmitter is perhaps a strange thing from which to derive a connection and emotional support, especially as we have only recently moved here; but I have been comforted by the broadcasts sent from this transmitter for many years, and to me it's a bit like finally meeting an old pen-pal and discovering that they are as impressive in person as they are on paper. I know I shall miss the towers when they one day go, but until that time, whether their impact is in my ear, my view or on my route, this illuminated pair of steel lattice masts are to me the Wychbold Heartbeat.

Ritula Shah and Charlotte Green were, at the time this letter was written, regular news presenters for BBC Radio 4's The Today Programme and The World Tonight.

Mistletoe & Wye (18ᵗʰ December)

We are looking forward to our first Christmas here at Stone House, and the last before Baby arrives. Next year there may well be screaming, soiled nappies and projectile vomiting to accompany the glögg and pepparkakor, so Barbara has decided that we will enjoy this one as selfishly as we can. Our five-year-old Argos Christmas tree is still in useable condition (it's even started realistically shedding its plastic needles now) and all the decorations have survived the move intact. We rearranged the living room to make space for it, and recently spent an evening hanging decorations and I must say it's never looked better. Swedish Christmas lights shine from the windows, *adventsljusstake* stand ready to light each Sunday night and Barbara's mother will be here to share the holiday with us. It will be a week of wonderful cooking smells filling the house, brisk short walks around the field in the crisp air, card games and long fireside chats, and it's sure to help us put this year to rest and focus on the many delights that await us in 2012. Peace and goodwill to all. Or rather to most, as for a select few we openly wish a number of sleepless nights first.

Recently I have had less time than I would like to give to general garden maintenance. Specific jobs like building the greenhouse, altering the animal shelter and keeping the drainage system in operation have meant that cutting, tidying and raking have all had to wait. With luck I should be able to get some of it done over the festive period, and this would please me no end as the last of the leaves to fall this year are littering the grass and giving the place an unkempt feel. With the trees now bare, it has become apparent that one of the crops we produce in abundance is mistletoe; the rather pointless parasite that can live on over 200 species of tree, and be completely ignored for 364 days of a year. It thrives most commonly on varieties of apple tree, and in front of the house stands an old 'Lady Emily', which is ageing in its own right and being steadily encouraged on its way by the sheer weight and hunger of the mistletoe that feeds on it. This tree, and about four more in the orchard are completely overgrown with the stuff, and when I first discovered this, I thought we had found a potential small cash crop. According to the National Trust, the UK crop has declined by an average of 70% in the last 60 years whilst demand has remained steady, so I had greedy visions of a lovely end-of-year treat paid for by a few days work with tree loppers.

I went to visit the local florist in town and temptingly explained my situation to him, expecting him to sign me up on the spot as his number one supplier, grateful that I had come to him first. He listened to me with a polite smile and then, when I'd finished outlining my plan, promptly burst out laughing. Once he'd finished wiping the tears from his eyes, he pointed out to the driveway at the back of his shop and said with a big grin "See that pile? That's mine and I've got four times that at home". In turns out that reports of the crop's demise either have been greatly exaggerated or this area is bucking the trend, and whilst we can indeed earn a small amount of cash from it, we're going to have to work much harder for it. The Wye Valley is one of the most mistletoe-rich areas in the country, he explained, and he went on to suggest that if we cut the crop during November next year, bundle it and take it to the wholesalers in Birmingham at the start of December, they will buy as much as we can sell.

With my brain starting to plan how we will earn at least one slap-up meal from our mistletoe next year, I returned home only to find that in a twist of fate too delicious to be planned, some neighbours of ours had stopped by to pop a Christmas card through the door while I was out. On the doorstep to go with it, tied together with a beautiful red ribbon, was a large sprig of mistletoe. I've hung it by the front door, and I smile every time I see it.

Even though this is only a slight setback, it has a reassuringly familiar ring to it. Over the years, my relationship with plants that I neither care for nor like has been totally consistent in its impact. They simply thrive under my withering contempt, whilst the most noticeable quality of those on which I lavish attention is their determination to end their feeble existence as quickly as they can. There was a time that I threw a quarter of a potato into the compost bin in our garden in London, and was rewarded with a bumper crop some months later, whilst the corn I was fussing over ten feet away expired shortly after the husks began to develop.

If only I were able to consider mistletoe a plant of beauty, hawthorn bushes elegant and weeds alluring, then I would be able to create a horticultural Nirvana using little more than my disdain and the occasional length of twine. It's the same story where diets are concerned; if only I didn't actually like houmous, cheese had the calorific properties of carrots and celery actually tasted of, well, you know, anything at all, then I'd have the body of an Adonis in exchange for minimal effort. Whilst learning to love mistletoe is too big a leap for me, I may alter my stance a little and come to respect it as the useful bearer of little profits. Some change is good, whilst some resistance to it is necessary, as otherwise the next cover of Country Life magazine may be a photo of wilting dandelions in the grip of a grinning Michelin Man.

Without doubt a fresh perspective in the New Year about mistletoe and many other things will help in a number of ways, but until then Barbara and I are going to enjoy our latest game of seeing how far we can get from the front door before we have to stop for a kiss.

The Christmas Present Participle (24ᵗʰ December)

Well, it's Christmas Eve, and we've walked, talked, eaten and spent some time showing Barbara's mother the surrounding sights. It is quiet and still here in the rolling hills of Herefordshire, and it's been a wonderful time of reflection and planning. Barbara and I share as many similarities as we do differences, and as you might imagine this is something which can either add a frisson of excitement or a drop of angst depending on the situation. When we first met, my idea of organising a holiday involved teletext and a credit card on the last day of work, while she, on the other hand, visibly paled if she didn't know the departure gate twelve months before going to the airport. Compromise and context, as ever, have been the key to a healthy relationship thus far, and in most matters equality and fairness is the obvious way forward.

In the past, when Barbara and I had discussed the idea of having a family, we had often agreed that we would not want to know the sex of the baby until the birth, imagining that the surprise would be better. Since September, Barbara has changed her mind quite quickly and determinedly, and as she is doing more than the lion's share of the work, I was well aware that equality wasn't fair and compromise wasn't possible in this matter.

Yesterday we all went to the hospital for the 20-week scan in the full knowledge that we were going to ask. Delightfully named the 'Anomaly Scan', it's the one in which they count fingers and toes (check), make sure all the vital organs are in good shape (check) and reassuringly point out that the baby's bladder is full (check). Despite the full range of technology at the disposal of the NHS (I was utterly amazed to be able to see the chambers of its heart in colours to show the blood flowing in and out), I had no idea that the gender test simply relies on the baby's willingness to spread its legs. Now, I'm not one to refer to anyone's unborn child, let alone mine, as 'fast and loose', but it seems as though on this occasion I might as well. When Barbara asked if she could tell us the sex, the sonographer easily encouraged the baby to roll over onto its back with the ultrasound, pointed at the screen and said "I'd be very surprised if it wasn't a boy".

Having seen our son and judged him to be a little wriggling thing with an impressive bladder, we went for a celebratory coffee and a quick shopping trip to buy him his first piece of clothing as a keepsake. As we were browsing through endless blue and pink garments, I was reminded of our differences over holiday planning. We'd found a compromise that encouraged us both to embrace the other's preference of planning or spontaneity. Clearly, in this situation, we'd need a different solution, and so I had planned for Barbara's will to take precedence over mine. It was a total waste of time as it turns out, as finding out has been far more enjoyable than I had thought; it has nothing to do with me feeling restricted by an early decision and everything to do with us savouring endless possibilities together.

We have no idea what colour our son's room will be, and we don't really care either; I think I've got some spare green paint in the workshop, and if not there is always the B&Q end-of-line bins. We are equally pragmatic about his wardrobe, as he will wear the mixture of girls and boys clothes that we have already been kindly given by generous friends, family and freecyclers. Come to think of it, given that his mother wears nothing but Doc Martens and his father often wears pink, it's probably quite appropriate. Even in the twenty four hours since we found out, all the things that we have spent time thinking about probably won't happen exactly the way we plan; I am not sure it even really matters what plans we may have for him, as he will no doubt surprise us with his taste, his temper, his will and his preferences. There's even a 20% chance that he will be actually be a girl. In short, we don't know anything until we get to May next year, and then we'll find out for sure how much more we don't know.

Dwight Eisenhower once said; Plans are nothing; planning is everything. And maybe with the holidays that we took, Barbara and I might have missed a trick as they could have benefitted from at least some planning on my part.

On that note, I am now going to reconsider my belief that I am not hungry, as I'm fairly sure I can find room for a wafer-thin mint. On my way to the kitchen, this plan may change into a slice of cake, perhaps a glass of wine or I may abandon it in favour of some fresh air. No matter what it ends up as, I shall enjoy it. Merry Christmas!

Darwin Farmin' (1st January 2012)

Now, I honestly don't know who was more stupid; him for doing it, or me for letting him. I'm sure that if we'd sat down over a pint and calmly thought about it, we would have both come to the conclusion that it was a completely daft idea. I can't even enjoy the relative comfort of hindsight, as my total lack of common sense on this occasion calls into question whether I should be allowed to tackle other tasks requiring similar levels of intelligence such as boiling a kettle, operating a toothbrush or putting my pants on. However, given that I am still alive and he continues to have a job by dint of the fact that I'm too embarrassed to say anything to his boss, I feel that this post should serve as a learning opportunity and so I share with you the following piece of advice: Do not under any circumstances have your septic tank emptied in winter. Such a bold statement clearly needs some qualifying in order to help you to make the link between this simple household task and total stupidity, but if you bear with me I'm pretty sure I can help you out with this.

Septic tanks are passive biological treatment plants; they just quietly work around the clock and you need do nothing except empty them when they are full. In December ours was nearing capacity and so, using Google, I found a company not too far away and spoke to a chap on the phone about it. Once he had established where we were, which involved the usual banter about the Pink Pub and whether or not I was a Wolves fan, it was a matter of confirming access. I described the gates and path through the orchard to the field, and that he could park the lorry within about six feet of the tank. I also pointed out the nature of the land here; sitting on a gentle hilltop as we do, any vehicle will have to contend with inclines, albeit slight ones. "Hmm, I'm not sure", he said and proceeded to voice caution about taking a 15-ton lorry up an incline of long, wet grass. "Well, how about leaving the lorry in the road? You could run pipes straight alongside the house to the tank that way". He seemed more enthusiastic about this idea, but when I calculated that he would need at least seventy metres of pipe he said it was a non-starter. Then, after a pause, he said "Tell you what; I'll ask Bryan to pop by and have a look, as he only lives up the road from you and it'll be him doing the job anyway. If he thinks he can get the wagon in there, then that's what we'll do." I said that would be fine, and requested that he let me know afterwards so we could decide our next move.

I received a phone call early one morning about a week later from a very bright and enthusiastic sounding man. After a few moments trying to work out who it actually was, Bryan from the sewage company said with great cheer that he was on his way to empty our tank. When I protested meekly that I was waiting to hear back about whether or not it would actually be possible at this time of year, he hushed me with a reassurance that it would be absolutely fine, backing up his confident assertion by proudly stating that he was a keen 'off roader'. Forty-five minutes later, he showed up in a fourteen-wheel sewage tanker, complete with flashing lights.

He waved vigorously from the cab as I approached to unlock the gate which allows direct access from the road to the orchard, and he swung the lorry through the opening and got about fifteen feet into the field before the wheels starting spinning. With a grin about as wide as the Amazon Delta, he stuck his head out of the window and pronounced himself a bit thick for not engaging the all-wheel drive. Whilst the alarm bells in my head stood silent, I grinned feebly back, and after a number of crunches, some grinding and an emphatic thud, the lorry proceeded across the orchard in a more sedate manner, passing through the next gate into the field. By the time I had closed the gate to the road and walked back up to the field, the tyre marks on the ground clearly showed that he had reversed halfway down the field towards the corner where the tank is and had then thought better of it. The deep cuts in the earth were straight, true, and proof that he was lucky to get back to the hard standing outside the animal shelter.

At this point, all of the evidence pointed towards the fact that this large and cumbersome lorry was not going to improve its already precarious situation by taking on the extra weight of eighteen months worth of sewage, but strangely neither Bryan nor I seemed to give this thought much time; with him presumably focussing on his wages and me hungry for the peace of mind that an empty tank would bring. He happily connected twenty or so metres of pipe to the back of the lorry and dumped the end into the first chamber while I made him a coffee. He then flicked a switch and we both retired to lean on the fence in suitably manly poses. While the lorry took on board two thousand litres, we consumed our coffee and exchanged small talk about off-roading. He said it was fun, that he was experienced at it and had a number of vehicles that he had bought for the very purpose. His only regret was that his parents had forbidden him from using them in their field at home, and judging by what happened next, it was a wise decision on their part.

Once he had disconnected all the pipes, put them away and we had taken care of the paperwork, I thanked him and he was ready to go. I stood by the gate holding it open, and from his position it should have been a simple matter of driving forward to clear the animal shelter, so that he could reverse a quarter turn to the left and then head straight through. It all started normally enough; he inched the lorry forward and as soon as the rear wheels left the hard standing, they found the soft mud and lost their grip. I imagined that a plan B would be appropriate at this point, but Bryan's off roader instinct kicked in, which meant that plan A on steroids clearly seemed the better bet. He then began a process of reversing to the end of the hard standing, and accelerating forward as fast as he could. It was a bizarre sight to watch a 15-ton lorry do an impression of a salmon swimming upstream. Even more bizarre was seeing Bryan's smiling face each time the lorry came to a standstill opposite me while lumps of mud were flung out far and wide behind it; "Nearly there, one more go should do it. By heck, this is fun!"

After five minutes or so he sheepishly admitted defeat and stepped out of the cab to survey his handiwork. I racked my brains for what I might have in the barn or shelter that we could place under the wheels to give them purchase, but came up with nothing. Then, having considered the situation carefully, he came to fully understand the problem by realising that his lorry was in fact not an ATV. "By heck, I've got it!" he exclaimed in excitement "I need more speed, but I haven't got the traction so I'll use gravity instead." I wasn't really sure what he meant, so just I stared at him vacantly. I think my stare then turned from vacant to helpless via incredulous at what he did next.

He climbed in the cab, revved the engine and shot off in reverse back down towards the septic tank. As he left the hard standing, he started turning the lorry and accelerating even more. I swear I saw a look of panic cross his face, and I could do nothing but run after him as fifteen tons of metal, water and excrement disappeared around the animal shelter and hurtled backwards across the field in a wide arc like a giant pendulum, with mud and grass flying up on all sides. Finally it came to rest in a flat area in the middle of the field, the engine idling. Bryan's cheery disposition had completely evaporated, and were I a gambling man I'd have bet a tenner that the aroma in the air wasn't exclusively from the back end of the lorry. It was like that scene at the end of the film *Duel* when Dennis Weaver is about to play his last hand, but rather than a Dodge Dart all I had nearby was a rotting chicken shed. I just wanted him gone and I didn't care how.

From his position Bryan was able to track slowly across the field on mostly flat land, squeeze through the gates and finally disappear down the road leaving a pair of muddy tracks as far as I could see. Over the winter I'll use the tractor to smooth the ruts he made, in the spring fresh grass will cover the exposed earth and from the mantelpiece my Darwin Award will remind me of my New Year's resolution to keep jobs like this for the summer. Happy New Year!

Tilley Tales (8th January)

I can't remember when I didn't know what a Tilley Lamp was; the paraffin pressure lamp invented at the start of the 19th century and whose latest design, the *Stormlight* has remained unchanged since 1964. As a young boy spending time in the cold and wet northwest of Scotland, I spent many evenings clinging to the heat and light it produces, and frequently was given the job of pumping it up to maintain the pressure on which it relies. To this day, I find there is nothing quite so cavernous as the silence that immediately follows the muffled pop of a Tilley being extinguished. We had one as a fancy when we still lived in London, but we rarely used it as Barbara didn't care for the noise, smell or complicated process of ignition.

It came into its own when we rented a small house in Gloucestershire for a year, so much so that we bought another when we realised how indispensable it had become to our comfort. Staying warm in a house that had more in common with a colander than a cottage, and that was equipped with an ageing central heating system fuelled by LPG very quickly proved to be a futile struggle. Shivering at the end of our first quarter, we calculated that it would have been almost the same cost to heat the house if we had simply burned bank notes in the grate, and so we decided to save the boiler for hot water and stay warm as best we could using paraffin, wood and thermal clothes. Throughout the very cold winter that we spent there, we each kept one of the red lamps by our sides, and they burned all day and every day without missing a beat. Being asked to compensate for a draughty house with a poorly-vented fireplace that struggled to heat much besides itself was a tall order, but the fact that they came close to achieving this shows that they can punch well above their weight.

Despite being lucky enough to be connected to the gas mains, the boiler at Stone House is also ageing and extremely inefficient. Its replacement, whilst important, is not as urgent as other things and therefore must wait in line. Therefore, since the onset of winter, the Tilley Lamps have been back in action. In the seven or eight years that I have owned and used one, apart from replacing mantles and refilling the tank, I have never once carried out any maintenance. This fact became all too apparent in December, as first one and then the other succumbed to a build up of carbon deposits, and there is no half measure with a Tilley; it works right up until the point that it doesn't. The relatively warm weather at Christmas meant this had little impact, but now that the balmy weather has once again given way to stormy winds and dropping temperatures, I'll be typing in mittens unless I get them working again.

With no moving parts except for a stopcock, they are mechanically as simple as they are brilliant; a reservoir of paraffin is first pressurised by a hand pump. Then, when released, a tiny stream of fuel is forced through a heated metal pipe causing it to vaporise. At the top, it mixes with air inside a chamber, and is then deflected down through a burner where it ignites as bright white light against a mantle, and combustion having begun, the lamp now produces a ball of searing heat and brilliant light. With a full tank and enough pressure, it will last a whole day, and can easily heat a small room or take the chill out of a larger one. They are impervious to rain or wind, are as happy indoors as they are outside, and perfectly safe if used with enough ventilation to ensure that there is no build-up of carbon monoxide.

The rather fiddly ignition process requires first making sure the reservoir is pressurised and then preheating the vaporiser, which is achieved by clamping a sponge soaked in methylated spirits around its base and igniting it. Once the mantle is lit though, it takes over from the preheater in maintaining the temperature of the vaporiser, and so the clamp can be removed. The only tricky bit is judging when the vaporiser is hot enough to release the paraffin stream, and it's a case of trial and error as each Tilley will have its own particular tipping point. You quickly learn though, as releasing the paraffin too early will result in the lamp doing a very passable impression of a large oil rig flare, complete with black smoke and acrid stench.

Competing for space in the workshop with an increasing number of started-but-not-finished projects, I took them both apart, cleaned each and every piece and rebuilt them. As the engineering of the vaporisers needs to be both precise and reliable, I replaced both of them and now the mechanisms are as new. I have fettled them with new mantles and polished glass, and once again there is one burning behind me as I type.

In a house that is literally at the end of the line for gas, electricity and telephone, we need to be prepared for seasonal power cuts and storm damage. Barbara and I have always been fans of candlelight, and therefore keep a healthy supply of tea-lights, candles and firewood.

For me though, when it comes to sourcing light and heat when other options falter, the Tilley holds a very special place. It burns as brightly in my childhood memories as it does in our lives today; a wonderfully practical invention that I find romantic, economic and effective. I am grateful for not only the light and heat that it produces, but also the reassurance that I take from its constant and comforting white hiss. If you've never experienced an evening in the company of one with a good book and a glass of wine, I highly recommend it.

Midnight Moonlight (15th January)

As a rule that generally holds true, most dogs will turn around a few times before they lie down. There are also some who seem overly fastidious in how they go about this, displaying what may be the canine equivalent of OCD in the process. They will start afresh a number of times after interrupting themselves with some snuffling, pawing or generally scratching around in what I assume is a dedicated effort to make the perfect bed complete with hospital corners and turndown treat. Finally there are those, usually of advanced years, who will get part-way through their first turn before their conscious mind seems to evict this instinct by the scruff of the neck, leaving them free to get on with the important business of lying down quickly and with the minimum of fuss.

I lack this predisposition in any form, but I sometimes wonder if it might prove useful during those times when I am fidgety, generally unable to relax or sleep fitfully at night. Last Monday evening was just such a time; I didn't have a good book to hand, there was nothing I found interesting on television and rather than relax on the sofa in front of the fire, I was gripped by an urgent need to do something.

Utterly at a loss as to what bit of mending or improvising I could possibly do at nine o'clock in the evening, I went looking for inspiration and got as far as the utility room. When I opened the door it was almost as if the lights were already on, and glancing out of the window I could see the entire vegetable garden and field beyond was awash with brilliant moonlight. In an instant, I rushed up to my office to collect the camera and tripod and sailed through the door, waving goodbye to Barbara on the way. I glanced up and towards the west, noticed that the thicker clouds were mustering their forces somewhere over Leominster, and decided that I would enjoy and record this beautiful atmosphere until the moon disappeared.

Crossing by the garage, I headed to the gate that leads into the orchard, an area that rabbits seem to love at night for some reason. During the day you never see them for fear of airborne predators, and it is mostly the playground for a reticent resident pheasant. Sometimes when I come home late at night and pull in to the driveway, the car headlights will sweep across the grass like a searchlight and pick dozens of them out in a scene reminiscent of The Great Escape. As we plan to create vegetable runs in this field one day, Barbara and I know that we will have our work cut out to deter them from grazing on our crops, but we are nowhere near building that bridge, let alone crossing it. My approach sent them racing for cover in the hedge at the far end, and I raised one foot on the bottom bar of the gate and stared up at the night sky. I haven't wanted a cigarette so much as I did then in a long time.

Most of the novels that I have ever read contain moments like these when the protagonist has seminal thoughts; fundamental life-changing realisations about who he is or what he needs to do; all set against a beautiful backdrop of nature that later becomes a symbolic memory for that important watershed.

Having previously found when mowing the orchard last summer that I lack the resources to multi-task, such a staged moment is impossible for me, as when I see a beautiful view I just gawp at it. A real glassy-eyed, slack-jawed, lights-on-but-nobody-home stare. I think that's about it really, although absent-minded heavy breathing and a bit of drooling may also occur, but you'd have to check with Barbara about that. I think that once my brain is tasked with processing an image that it finds appealing, it's a case of 'all hands on deck', and little is left to take care of everything else. And since everything else includes maintaining vital bodily functions, things like lifestyle changes or career decisions are simply not going to get a look in. It's probably a good thing that I didn't have a cigarette.

As the cloud cover thinned and the stars shone brighter, I headed up into the big field and crossed to the highest point in the middle. I have never been good at navigating the heavens, with the possible exception of being able to find the North Star via The Big Dipper. I think it's the astrological equivalent of being able to play chopsticks on the piano; not all that impressive, but amusing enough for a few minutes. From where I stood, I had the widest uninterrupted view of the horizon from the Malvern Hills in the south through east to the Linton Downs in the north and across towards Leominster in the west. I contemplated sitting down to enjoy the moment, but suddenly fearful of what I might sit in, I stayed standing, and after a while slowly meandered diagonally across the field down towards the house, studying the north eastern horizon as the clouds began to thicken.

I'd been wandering around in the moonlight with absolutely nothing on my mind and for no reason whatsoever. I'd seen rabbits in the orchard and I'd seen one on the moon, I'd heard owls hooting in the distance and Margo's dog barking at the night air. I had neither sought nor encountered any life-changing conclusions, and my life was more or less exactly as it had been about an hour before. I went back to the house to find that the fire was still warm and my bed beckoned as the moon slid behind the clouds.

In the morning when I woke up, I realised that I felt more relaxed, less fidgety and I'd slept better too. Perhaps it's because I had taken the time to turn around, snuffle and paw the ground. Maybe it should be a dog's life.

Coming Home to Roost (29th January)

It has always been our plan to share Stone House with animals that are useful in providing either food, company or land maintenance. Approaching our first six months here, we know that we have thus far only shared it with local wildlife, and so yesterday we began to put that right by collecting our first three chickens. A picture postcard of such an event might show a trio of fit and healthy birds clucking away, any of which could be cast as a cover model for William Kellogg's best known cereal brand, but the reality is somewhat different as we did our best to collect, calm and befriend three rather straggly looking ex-battery hens.

Following the household mantra of reduce, reuse, recycle, we conducted a good deal of research into chicken husbandry, and have discovered a wealth of useful advice and support from the British Hen Welfare Trust. With over twenty million hens in the UK busily producing raw materials for all the breakfasts, groceries and desserts that are eaten each and every year, profit margins dictate that there are a huge number that reach the end of their profitable lives long before they end their natural ones. With a vision and purpose that seems to spring from the pages of Loren Eiseley's 'The Star Thrower', the BHWT attempts to save from slaughter as many of these unwanted birds as possible, and annually secures a peaceful retirement for around 60,000 of them in households like ours.

Having constructed a chicken house, fox-proof pen and free-range area last year, we contacted them and offered to re-home some birds at the beginning of this year. Just last week, we received an email saying, "your girls will be ready for collection on Saturday", and so we set off bright and early having completed all the jobs on the check list. We would need a cardboard box of a certain size with holes cut in it for transportation, a particular kind of food to help them in making the switch from battery hen feed to a more varied diet and, given that they have only ever known eighteen hours of artificial light per day in a small metal cage, plenty of patience to help them adjust to their new life.

We arrived at a farm near Coventry to find a truly well oiled charity machine working flat out. You were given an arrival time slot based on alphabetised surnames, and two lanes marked with road cones directed your car to the collection point where novices were given plenty of advice and old hands were waved on through. After our induction, two chatty young ladies selected our birds from a brood of over a hundred whilst reassuring us that watching hens was both more exciting than watching television and a probable sign of mid-life crisis. I paused to wonder if keeping chickens could be as effective at helping me cling to my fading youth as getting a motorcycle, trendy haircut and lover half my age, and quickly concluded that the chickens would almost certainly be safer, look less stupid and require far less energy. We then plonked them in our pre-prepared box, bought some ex-battery hen food before exchanging thanks and heading off home.

As we drove back down the M42 and M5, the birds were very quiet and we had been warned that they would be in shock, having only been rescued from the battery farm that morning. The occasional cluck could be heard at lower speeds, but for the most part we heard nothing and imagined that they were already cuddled up and on first name terms. Once we left the smooth motorway and began negotiating the numerous roundabouts, sweeping curves and twisty bends along the A44 from Worcester, the birds seemed less happy as they audibly skidded from one side of the box to the other, clucking in irritation. I'm not sure who was more relieved when we finally pulled into the driveway with the car smelling and sounding like a proper farmyard.

Carefully following the instructions, we took each bird from the box, affixed a coloured ring to their left feet to help with identification, and then introduced them to their new home by, well, you know, stuffing them through the open outer door. We left the inner door to their enclosure open as well, hoping they would quickly walk down the ramp and start exploring their new patch complete with watering and feeding stations. For about fifteen minutes they stumbled around inside the house, tripping over the roosting bars, pecking at the walls and behaving almost exactly like we did once when faced with the complexity of the New York City subway system. At this point we thought it best to leave them be, and had we not noticed one of them starting to eat the wood shavings that covered the floor of the house, we probably would have.

I know that termites thrive on eating wood, but chickens do not so far as we know, and so we took the decision to 'encourage' them outside. First I opened the outer door in an attempt to shoo them into the run, but succeeded only in scaring them up into the nesting boxes. Remembering that these birds had only ever known a living area marginally larger than the ground they stood on, it seemed clear that they felt no need to wander and the only way to get them outside was to open the egg hatch and pluck them out. One by one they were first cornered and then scooped out, and finally all three were walking around their enclosure learning to distinguish between weed and feed whilst presumably wondering what on earth daylight was.

We left them alone for as long as the light lasted and, come dusk, we went back to guide them back inside their house. Having left them as meek and mild animals, we returned to find a gaggle of feisty birds that probably would have given Colonel Saunders a run for his money. I imagine that any local farmer watching me running around inside the pen trying my best to catch three confused hens would have had a good laugh. Every time I tried to grab one, she flapped her wings, hopped over my hands and scooted to a different corner. Barbara suggested a more determined grabbing technique, and after a further ten minutes effort, we finally had the birds back in their house.

Already we had noticed their different personalities starting to emerge, and it didn't take us long to think of names for the noisy one, the bossy one and the rather dim one. Once the door was shut, there followed a further fifteen minutes of indignant clucking, flapping and scratching during which we assume bunks were assigned, cleaning rotas were drawn up and the pecking order was established. As we went back down to the house we celebrated the fact that Stone House, once home to just Barbara and I, was now becoming a proper smallholding thanks to the arrival of Jordan, Jodie and Jade; three skanky and rather ragged looking birds who, we hope, still fancy the occasional lay.

Hedge Fun (5th February)

I may well be wrong, but as I understand it hedge funds pretty much guarantee a profit by spreading their risk and investing in your life at the same time as betting on your funeral. As private investment entities, they can avoid many of the regulations that other funds are subject to and usually make huge amounts of money whatever happens. I apologise if my simple understanding has insulted any hedge-fund managers. If it has, may I suggest you consider the upside: my explanation would have been flavoured with the subtle hint of personal experience if you worked in the insurance industry. Be that as it may, I am intrigued by a single event being valued in opposing ways.

Over the last few months I have enjoyed playing with my array of petrol-powered tools. Whether it's slicing through a tree with a chainsaw, strimming the grass around the well or racing around the orchard on the tractor, it's an activity that ticks two of my favourite boxes; noise and destruction, and it also allows me plenty of fuel for my daydream of being a hunter-gatherer.

Just before Christmas on a drab and dull Tuesday, I was working in my office when I heard a series of loud squeaks and banging metal in the road outside. At the foot of the driveway, in a slowly settling cloud of dust, was a sight that suddenly transformed me back in time to being the kid at school who suddenly lost interest in all his toys when it transpired he didn't have the latest must-have game that the cool kid in the class was playing with.

Farmer Harris had stopped by, and he had brought with him his tractor equipped with the most fantastic accessory; the adult agricultural version of Merlin, Simon and the Rubik Cube all rolled into one. I turned completely green with envy, and immediately promised myself an entire evening devoted to looking at second hand prices on eBay for one to fit my little tractor.

Farmer Harris is a ruddy-cheeked octogenarian in the rudest of health who lives a mile or so down the road, and has looked after the hedges around our field in exchange for taking the hay from it for a number of years. As our focus will be more on infants with two legs rather than four for the foreseeable future, this is not an arrangement we are keen to change at this time, and so we had been expecting a visit from him at some point in December. I greeted him, let him in and carried on working whilst keeping half en eye on his progress around the field.

During one of his rest breaks I took him a mug of tea, and as I approached his tractor I noticed two things. Firstly, they are absolutely huge when you get close; utterly massive. Secondly, he had named his tractor 'Emma' as evidenced by large yellow lettering on its engine housing. As someone with an old Saab named 'Holly' whose maintenance, preservation and polishing is my hobby, I felt an immediate kinship with him and judged that it would have been rude of me had I not offered admiring comments about her chassis, bodywork and overall appeal. I think I even might have stroked her bonnet appreciatively whilst asking what I felt were appropriately knowledgeable questions.

Emma's must-have accessory is more properly known as a heavy-duty flail hedge-cutter, and it is the most devastating tool I have ever seen in operation. As I walked away with empty mugs, Farmer Harris climbed aboard, fired up the engine and set the flail going. Good God, I have never seen shredded hedge fly so far and so fast. I must have been fifty feet away when I started to run; yet I was being pelted with bits of high-speed hawthorn until I got to safety behind the garage. I looked back in awe as man and machine ripped through the top of the hedge as efficiently and effectively as you would cut through paper with a kukri.

When Farmer Harris had finished, we exchanged pleasantries about weather, local news and whether he might want to use the field for his rams during lambing season, and he went on his way home. As he disappeared down the lane, he turned to give me a toothy smile while waving his right hand. He very much had the air of a man who was happy with his lot: he had done a hard day's work, was going to enjoy his short drive home over the rolling hills before presumably tucking into a well-earned meal.

I locked the gate and returned to the field to survey the new, sleeker landscape. Now West Malvern would be clearly visible at night, and the view from the house into the field is far more open. Feeling envious of the tractor's power and impact, I suddenly regarded my tools as rather puny while I paused to study the long row of Leylandii that link the house to the garage; my big winter job that I had already been putting off for a number of weeks. I wondered if it would be as easy for me, and if I would head home happily after going ten rounds in the ring with it.

As I looked at the defensively study trunks, the entwined network of branches and the densely thatched canopy, I knew that although I wouldn't be investing in it's future, I was certain that a bet on its quick demise wouldn't exactly be the easiest money I'd ever make.

Bête Noire (12ᵗʰ February)

You can run, but you can't hide. Or you could just sit in a corner, close your eyes and say 'Nyah nyah nyah' until you go blue in the face. Given that Barbara and I have probably got several years of that to look forward to from May, and prompted by Farmer Harris' recent visit, I decided that it was about time to stop trying to hide from one of the jobs that has been on my to do list since we arrived; the Leylandii hedge. I'd already attempted it in November, and given up after a day as at twelve feet high and forty feet long, it is a worthy enemy with excellent defences. Having lived near this type of pest for many years in different places, I have come to dislike it for a number of reasons. It produces an enormous amount of sticky sap, it grows into an incredibly dense tangle of wood that yields little for the fireplace and the sheer pace at which it grows means you can't turn your back on it for a minute.

Having put it off for long enough, I realised that if I left it until the end of February, the birds would start nesting in it and then in the months that followed it would start its growing for the year and my problem would exponentially increase. I chose the week between Christmas and the New Year, being a typically quiet week, as the one in which I would start my planned attack. Waging a war against a tree of this kind would both require careful planning and plenty of energy to combat its famed resilience. Briefly I toyed with the idea of calling up the US airforce and asking if they had any Agent Orange left, and thinking better of that I wondered whether I could pay Farmer Harris to bulldoze it with Emma. Reasoning that he would not be best pleased at having his Christmas dinner interrupted, I accepted that the hedge and I were going to have to engage in hand to hand combat, and I fancied my odds in the way that I fancy marmite.

In all honesty I did think about a refined approach using some judicious pruning and skilled cutting, but after about five seconds I remembered that no one expects The Spanish Inquisition, so I rejected those ideas in favour of fear, surprise, a hopeless inadequacy and an almost fanatical devotion to noise and destruction.

I yanked the chainsaw out of the cupboard, brimmed the tanks with oil and fuel, sharpened the blades and fired it up. In a dense cloud of two-stroke smoke and in a manner inspired by countless scenes from movies in which the hero cuts a path through a dense jungle, I attacked the hedge at shoulder height as though the chainsaw were a machete. Twigs, branches, leaves and cuttings flew about my head and to keep my energy up I swore out loud at the hedge with each thrust; "Take... that... you... useless... piece... of..."

There was more than enough hedge for me to exhaust my entire vocabulary and invent quite a few new words too. After about an hour and a half's swearing my arms were aching, my legs were sore, I had amassed a number of cuts to my arms and face and it was all too clear that my initial offensive, although having made a dent in the hedge, was noticeably far from Blitzkrieg! In an effort to reassure myself that all was going according to plan, I called a temporary ceasefire to allow time for a warming and restorative coffee.

I studied the battlefield, and as I could sense my enthusiasm again on the wane, I wondered if there was a Plan B that I could switch to. I briefly considered reviving my previous idea of dousing the whole thing in petrol and standing back while it burned. Sadly, given the short distance between the hedge and house, I judged scorched earth policy as too risky and dug deep to find what dregs of resilience I could.

Coffee break over, I turned up the garage speakers even more and set back to work as my iPod shuffled randomly through its contents. Some songs proved more conducive to warfare than others; Bryan Adams' 'Summer of '69' really helped me cut through the more stubborn branches and foliage, while Beethoven's 'Pathetique' really didn't. Mind you, both of those seemed fantastically effective when compared with the Bee Gees who starting singing a bit later on. I don't know about you, but I find it utterly impossible to walk normally when I hear 'Stayin' Alive', so you can imagine how much of idiot I looked waving the chainsaw about while strutting alongside the hedge in my boots, overalls, gloves and goggles. And I was singing along too.

So far the job has taken Barbara, her mother and me a total of eight days, and it isn't over yet. Once cut, all the branches had to be dragged to the animal shelter to be first dried and then separated into wood for the fireplace and wood to be disposed of. The larger logs will need to be split and dried for two years to make sure no sap remains to damage the chimney, and the smaller ones will be stored for use as kindling. The leftover twigs, branches and leaves will be burnt and then scattered as fertiliser. For the moment though, it is piled high in the shelter providing homes for all manner of birds, rabbits and other wildlife.

Having waged a long and arduous campaign from which I emerged victorious over a formidable foe, my joy is subdued and my sense of victory incomplete. One day, hopefully in the not-too-distant-future, there will be a long wall built along the roadside boundary of Stone House, and its arrival will be the signal to take up arms once more and open up the views from the house by razing what remains of the hedge to the ground, consigning it to history forever.

Edward Albert Jones (14th February)

On Friday last, we had a phone call from Farmer Harris' wife, Margaret, who informed us that despite rallying after a spell on life support over Christmas and the New Year, Ted, the former owner of Stone House, died last Thursday after a short illness. Our thoughts are with his brother and sister who survive him, and we hope his passing was peaceful and without pain.

As I wrote about previously, within a month of taking over the house from Ted last July, we had discovered various defects in the drainage system which he had deliberately omitted from and misrepresented in the Enquiries Before Contract document, which forms part of the agreement of sale. After uncovering the truth with some detective work, interpretive surveys and statements, we contacted his solicitor to ask him to pay for the replacement of the main sewer, and the alteration of the outflow from the septic tank, which he himself had constructed some forty years ago. Although based on the original architectural design that he had shared with our surveyor, beneath the ground we found a highly creative interpretation that valued nimbyism far above neighbourliness, to say nothing of common and sanitary sense.

As our focus is needed on more important things for the foreseeable future we have left the matter with our solicitor and, apart from the routine management of the current system and dealing with electrical and drainage contractors, have given the matter little thought since.

We will now deal with his estate, and when the dust settles after agreement is reached and repairs are concluded, the matter will be forgotten. He will be remembered in the years to come; firstly for his carefully designed 1970's Porn Bathroom, a real work of art that had a number of authentic touches including dark red shag-pile carpet, soft up-lighters, carpeted whirlpool bathtub, gold spotlights and a number of strategically placed mirrors.

And secondly for his prophetic, and now rather ironic welcome to the area when he handed over the keys to us on the day of completion:

"Well, you see, this is Herefordshire. If you lend something to someone, you have to go and

get it back and if you borrow something from someone, you have to fix it before you can use it."

As you wish Ted, but in my time and on your dime.

Eau Dear (19th February)

I'll never know how Captain Lawrence Oates got the courage to leave his tent near the South Pole on March 16th 1912, having just uttered the immortal words "I'm just going outside and may be some time", but I do accept that sometimes circumstances can conspire to make inaction impossible.

During recent months, on account of her pregnancy, Barbara has joined me in the unpredictable world of insomnia. In a middle-aged portrait of the utterly bland and average, we both usually go to bed at a 'sensible' hour, read our books for a short time and then switch off our lights before rolling over into the land of nod. For a few hours we enjoy a variety of slumbers from the blissful to the fitful, before nature's alarm clock rings. We then privately spend anywhere from a few minutes to sometimes several hours caught in a bitter internal dispute between the warmth of the bed and the call of the bladder. After the less embarrassing conclusion, calm is rarely restored and the rest of the night spent in duvet-twisting restlessness. Whilst for me this is bread and butter, for Barbara it is a new and wholly unwelcome experience.

The cold snap at the beginning of February provided our warm bed with numerous opportunities to try gaining the upper hand in these negotiations, sometimes giving the call of nature an almost unnatural run for its money, but thankfully so far continence has an undefeated record. Temperatures outside have recently been as low as -10° resulting in crisp mornings, icy conditions and some beautiful crystal displays in the conservatory. The overnight temperature inside the house has fallen as low as 11° on some nights, and the idea of spending the entire day in bed has been a very real and tempting prospect.

Nothing lasts forever of course, and the weather forecast told us that we would have a few days respite before a further cold snap arrived from the east. Passing the thermometer at the foot of the stairs on my way to bed one night the other week, I noticed the outside temperature slowly rising and I lulled myself to sleep with thoughts of an approaching summer of new parenthood framed with hot sun, cold beer and Bob Marley.

Predictably enough, sometime before 5.00am I was in the bathroom as usual staring at the Wychbold Heartbeat and all was absolutely normal. Except that, on this occasion, it wasn't and in my bleary-eyed torpor I couldn't figure out why. There was a noise somewhere over my head; an unfamiliar noise... a bit like a sort of hissing. It seemed to be coming from... the hallway. OK, right, we're getting closer now. There was a hissing noise in the hallway. A snake? No, it can't be a snake; snakes are cold-blooded animals and any snake around here would have frozen to death long ago.

Like a ship emerging slowly from a fog bank, the answer came to my mind. It was the water mains pipe that feeds the header tank in the loft. But, why on earth is the header tank being filled at 5 o'clock in the morning? Had the chickens secretly put themselves in a night-time hot wash to avoid freezing? A second boat emerged a bit quicker behind the first, and I realised there must be a burst pipe somewhere. Careful not to disturb Barbara, I felt around the bedroom door, grabbed my dressing gown and headed downstairs as quickly as my sleepy legs would carry me. There was no evidence of a leak anywhere, but the noise from the water mains was louder and remaining constant.

Ted extended and improved Stone House over the forty odd years that he lived here, and as a result there is a maze of plumbing everywhere. A number of taps are on the outside of the house, the garage has a sink and a washing machine, and even the Cider Barn and animal shelter have water feeds. Somewhere there was a burst pipe that had been thawed into full flow with the rising temperatures, I had to find it and I had to find it now.

It was 5.15am, dark and the thermometer read 1°, so I gritted my teeth, pulled on my boots and stepped out of the utility room into the night air. The snow crunched underfoot as I edged around the corner of the house to check the outside taps. Both were fine, but as I approached them I could hear gushing water coming from the direction of the garage. Relieved that the house seemed to be clear, I went back to fetch my keys and crossed to the garage in the moonlight, which revealed that in my hurry I had put on Barbara's pink striped bathrobe instead of my grey one. Feeling grateful for the fact that traffic seldom passes along the B4220 at night, I neared the garage and could see a dark patch on the ground outside the side door where the snow had melted. I opened it and was greeted by a curtain of water; the pipe had burst right above the doorway and, channelled by its foam insulation, was drenching the back of the door, the radio, fuse box and light switches.

I opened one of the front shutters and got in without having to take a freezing shower, but couldn't see a thing in the dark so ran back to the house, remembering that the water mains stop cock was on the wall of the kitchen behind the fridge. When I got there, Barbara had come downstairs to find out what on earth all the fuss was about, and greeted me by enthusiastically admiring my choice of wardrobe. Between us we pushed, pulled, yanked and teased the fridge out far enough so I could get my hand in the gap to close the stopcock. After three clockwise twists, the hissing noise stopped and was replaced by the beautiful quiet of a Herefordshire dawn.

Back in the garage, I found that the radio and iPod were completely soaked through and sadly beyond repair, the flooded cement floor was happily draining under the door and the electrics seemed intact. I located the inlet valve for the water and closed it so that we could switch the house back on, and then investigated the source of the problem beneath the insulation: a split, caused by water freezing, of less than one centimetre in length.

Later that day, it took me just five minutes and less than ten pounds to cut out the burst section and replace it with a copper sleeve, and I considered it an extremely cheap way of learning to keep the outside water switched off unless it was needed during winter months. With luck, and a respectful nod to Captain Oates, I hope it may be some time before I go outside like that again.

Fire in the Hole (26ᵗʰ February)

Remember the A-Team? In the eighties, they went from one scrape to another helping poor souls to whom the more normal channels of assistance were closed. In almost every episode, there came a point when they had been cornered in a deserted mineshaft and faced certain capture or death. Invariably one of them would grit their teeth and whisper something like "Remember that time when we were trapped by an entire army in Panmunjom that wanted to kill us repeatedly until we were extremely dead, and we had absolutely no way out?" The other three would knit their brows, scan their memories and slowly smile in recognition. Then, in a pop video montage set to the theme music, they would quickly build an armoured vehicle out of a dustbin lid, rusty nail and crisp packet before escaping in the nick of time. Phew! Who expected that? Apart from all the car chases and explosions, it was their apparent ability to make something out of nothing that was so appealing, and in my own way I like to think that we can sometimes do the same here.

Parts of Herefordshire and Worcestershire frequently top the BBC's table of 'coldest temperature in the UK last night' and so the ability to light a fire is now an essential skill. It's also something that I have traditionally been completely rubbish at, as I grew up honing my ability to push the advance button on a boiler instead. Daft as it may sound, sometimes I've even struggled to light firelighters, although that may be because they were bought from Lidl.

This lack of skill was highlighted perfectly during the cold winter that we spent in Gloucestershire, where I battled with a poorly designed and badly vented fireplace. At the time I assumed it was all down to me, and I spent many evenings shivering while the glowing embers of my fire-lighting confidence extinguished along with most of my efforts.

Despite the poor equipment that I had been using, this was something that I was going to have to learn to do both consistently and well, especially as we now have one of the most brilliantly designed fireplaces you can get. Thankfully, this winter has been much easier than last, and even though Barbara and I had already become great friends with our bellows, I am pleased to report that my ability is slowly evolving through persistence, a little creativity and a slight but discernible pyromaniacal streak.

Some basic truths about lighting fires are that it can be a complicated and messy affair. Wood takes a long time to dry out, good kindling is hard to find unless you buy it for a pretty penny and firelighters are expensive. Add these up, and you get one large problem in need of a solution, and even though the SAS base at Credenhill is only up the road, I have yet to find a crack commando unit hiding at Stone House.

Luckily solutions come in all shapes and sizes. Like most people, we use a normal amount of toilet paper and kitchen towel, and have built up a healthy supply of cardboard inserts.

Normally these would be put into the recycling along with everything else, but now they are an essential ingredient to our survival just like the crisp packet that was so crucial to the A-team. A few miles down the road from us is a timber yard, where large trees go in and small logs come out, a by-product of their work being a huge mountain of sawdust. I approached them last autumn and asked if I could have some, they told me to "fill my boots" and so I loaded up the car with a couple of large Ikea bags, and brought them back.

In late September last year, using an idea I'd seen before, the scene was set for me to produce a large arsenal of toilet-roll sawdust firelighters. In my mind the cardboard inserts were steel canisters and the sawdust was dynamite, and whilst humming "Dum, dum-de-dum, dum-de-dum-dum-dum-dum, daa-da-da-da-daaaaa" I found some masking tape and started a production line. A simple, if time consuming and repetitive process that involved taping one end of an insert, filling it with sawdust and closing the other end. The finished article looked more than a little like something that *Face* and *Murdoch* would have produced to get out of a sticky situation, and I had visions of lobbing one over the hedge and ducking while chewing on a fat cigar.

The first time we used one, it had almost no impact on the fire that I was trying to light. With my daydreaming role-play seriously under threat, I set about finding the solution with appropriate zeal. Was the sawdust damp I wondered? No, it was fine. Was it just that sawdust doesn't burn so well? Surely not; it's wood isn't it? Well, it seems that sawdust doesn't burn as well as I'd hoped. In explaining the idea to our neighbour Andrew (who appropriately enough calls me 'Mr P' for fear of mispronouncing my name), I learned that he uses sawdust to bank the sides of his fire to keep it low and make it last longer, so it's clearly something that most people use for precisely the opposite purpose that I had in mind.

Andrew may pity the fool who thinks he can use sawdust as a firelighter, but through experimentation I have now found that if you inject the tube with a teeny-weeny little bit of paraffin first, you get quite a different result. I love it when a plan comes together.

Chicken Psychology (11th March)

The author Douglas Adams once said, "Human beings, who are almost unique in having the ability to learn from the experience of others, are also remarkable for their apparent disinclination to do so." I completely agree with the second part of that statement, but I think he may have missed the mark slightly on the first by not distinguishing between having the ability and actually using it. Judging from my own track record, that of others and what I've seen outside at Stone House over the last month, I'm pretty sure that humans and chickens have a great deal more in common than just a good stir-fry.

Thanks to my good fortune I am not a single-celled being existing for a brief moment in a small clump of pond-scum before being eaten, and that means I can spend time watching chickens and noticing how absolutely vile to each other they can be. A week or so ago I spent half an hour in the chicken run, and observed exactly the same sort of behaviour that you might experience in a playground, pub, boardroom, classroom, nightclub, home, motorway, office or family dinner.

Jordan is the undisputed leader of our little brood of three. She doesn't question it in the same way that a Ferrari driver doesn't if waiting at a traffic light next to a Ford Fiesta and Vauxhall Corsa eagerly revving their engines on either side. She just raises an eyebrow, smooths her hair in the mirror and stares at the road ahead knowing that it's over before it's begun. If either Jade or Jodie approach her when she is eating, she just looks at them and they retreat. No need for shouting or bare-knuckle fighting; it's as if she simply says, "Excuse me, but I think you'll find these seats are taken." and there's nothing more to discuss.

Jodie is the runt in every way you can imagine. For weeks she had less feathers, less body weight and less courage than the other two; when she raised her threadbare wings to flap them you could see that she certainly wouldn't be appearing in a KFC near you anytime soon. She mostly spent her time in the coop, cowering from the others or being chased around the yard if she dared to venture out for water. Unfortunately we have learned that this is how it is for chickens, particularly when they settle in to a lifestyle without the restrictions of artificial light and metal cages. I had been advised to make sure some food was available inside the coop for her during the daytime in case she never made it out. Just like many people, Jodie is the victim of bullying. But it's the startlingly familiar way the bullying manifests that I find so utterly fascinating, as it made no sense at all on a physiological level, but total sense psychologically.

Jade is the bully and has proved it by demonstrating her cowardice time after time, but she has also proved that she is capable of learning from her own experience. When they first arrived, all three were scared of us, but Jade in particular has learned a number of things. She has learned that we bring food, and so now runs towards us when we approach. She no longer shies away as we move around the pen, and has discovered that bootlaces and fleece zippers are quite tasty. She has also learned that there are two places to get water and three to get food, and knows where they all are. Most importantly, she has learned that Jordan is in charge and Jodie isn't, and she has had a distinct need to use that knowledge to continually reconfirm her own place in the hierarchy.

With metronomic regularity over a number of weeks, rather than eat from a vacant feeder Jade would approach the one where Jordan was, who then promptly but casually told her to get lost. Aware that her status had just tumbled, Jade would then rush right past the other feeder and into the coop where Jodie was, and rebuild her self image by scaring the poor thing up into a nesting box, cornering her there and ostentatiously eating from the small tray of food. After two beakfuls of corn and a power trip lasting a minute or so, she felt her status was once again high enough to face the outside world. With an about turn and a generous poop in Jodie's face, she would then leave.

This repetitive cycle was clearly not driven by a need for food, warmth or any other of Maslow's physiological needs. I suspect it was all about Jade's self esteem which would appear to be almost entirely dependent on being inflated by Jodie's grovelling after being impaled on Jordan's supremacy.

If this interpretation of Jade's behaviour is right, then chickens too come with all sorts of baggage in different shapes and sizes. Some know who they are, some don't need, want or care to know and others are only happy in those brief moments when they can confirm their status by grading themselves as being above or below others.

Perhaps humans aren't quite so unique or remarkable after all.

Health & Safety (18ᵗʰ March)

In 1970, Barbara Castle (the Secretary of State for Employment and Productivity) introduced the Employed Persons Health and Safety Bill. In the same year, the US Government did something very similar and the carefree sixties were well and truly over on both sides of the Atlantic. In the decades since, the now snappily named Health & Safety at Work etc. Act (sic) has continued to lay down the law in all manner of situations to a nauseating level of detail. Having done so, it then proceeds to allow everyone to interpret it pretty much in any way they see fit.

Such is life when you attempt to standardise the length of a piece of string it seems, and things not easily categorised as unhealthy or unsafe are presumably gathered under the rather handy term of etc. Rules for these are then defined by someone at the HSE, as evidenced by the example that if 10% of a workforce in an air-conditioned office complain about the temperature, they are within their rights to expect their employer to do something about it; but if that number is only 9%, then it's up to them to go and buy a fan or a heater.

It would seem therefore that this well intentioned and unenforceable law remains just that; a large body of work that grows ever more dense by the day through its effort to codify common sense at the level of its lowest common denominator. Most people, myself included, refer to things as "probably" in contravention of it, or "likely to cause a problem" with it precisely because we don't actually know. No one does from what I can tell, but this enormous grey area is also a highly fertile land for ideas and innovation, as I think I proved a few weeks ago.

I love using tools, especially the loud petrol-powered ones that Arlo Guthrie would probably refer to as 'Implements of Destruction'. I can never have enough of them and, truth be told, I have one or two that I have absolutely no use for. However, it has become clear since moving to such a remote and rural location, that there actually are a few more that I could really use, but in our current list of priorities Mamas & Papas rightly trumps Black & Decker without question. Trips to B&Q these days are firmly focussed on indoor matters, and all thoughts of routers, angle-grinders and reciprocating saws are swiftly quelled.

Last autumn, our neighbour Andrew kindly gave us a huge amount of wood to use as kindling, sourced from a furniture company in Hereford that puts all its offcuts and rejects in large bins behind its factory. With a long-standing agreement that allows him to help himself when he needs to, Andrew has a healthy supply in his barn and has kindly shared his bounty with us. Most of the wood comes in the size and shape of kitchen cupboard doors, which I think you'll agree are not entirely appropriate to use as kindling without resizing.

So far I have used a number of tools for this job; none of which have been ideal. First I used a chainsaw, which is quick but very much a case of overkill as it results in a large pile of splinters and jagged edges. Next, a sledgehammer which is exhausting as I have discovered pine to be notably resilient and far more flexible than I had imagined. Then I tried a jigsaw which proved very good, but only for certain cuts that can be clamped and that are narrower than the depth of its blade. Finally, I scraped the bottom of my creative barrel by using a hammer and chisel.

Never, in the field of woodwork, has so much noise been made by so many tools to so little effect over so much time. One day I shall tell my son that there was a time when a circular saw gave the pram he's sitting in a good run for its money.

As with all things like this, necessity is the mother of invention, and so began a cunning plan that would achieve the desired outcome at the expense of common sense as described by Health & Safety guides (and anyone else, for that matter). I needed a saw that could cut cupboard doors first lengthways and then in to sections. In an ideal world I would have a bandsaw, and in a less ideal one, a circular saw. In my world there were only a jigsaw, vice-grip, a healthy disregard for rules, time and Merlot.

I am reasonably competent at crossing roads in light traffic, and by combining this confident belief in my observational abilities with stuff that was lying around the workshop, I created a bandsaw by clamping an old jigsaw upside down in a vice-grip and locking the power on. A crude but highly effective design, this jury-rigged bandsaw also boasted great flexibility by not having any annoyingly restrictive parts like protective guards or optic shut-off switches, and provided I could distinguish between the wood, the blade and my fingers, all would be well.

Using this device, now patented and marketed as the Et Cetera Compliant Bandsaw, I transformed six cupboard doors into three weeks' worth of kindling in less than ten minutes; one for each finger that I still have attached to my hands.

Having fought for the health, safety and common sense of equal pay, anti-apartheid and breathalysers, I'd like to think that were she still alive today, Baroness Castle would recognise that some omelettes are worth breaking eggs for.

Chimney Fire (25th March)

Last Thursday evening Barbara was busying herself with paperwork on the sofa, and I was up in my office endlessly noodling over a simple job that really could have been signed off, sent out and invoiced for long ago. One of the true joys of living out here is that every now and then I can recapture a little of the feeling that I had in the summers of my childhood, when time seemed to stand still for hours on end; and this was just such an evening.

Suddenly there was the most deafening noise coming from our bedroom across the hallway from my office, a roaring that I imagine a sand storm in the Sahara must sound like. Barbara instantly muted the television, and we shouted to each other in one of those clear and concise conversations that gets to the heart of the matter in seconds. It went something like this:

"What's that?"
"Buggered if I know, but it's coming from the bedroom."
"Well, it's coming from down here too."
"Fuck."

I ran downstairs and outside where the roaring noise was even louder, and looked up towards the chimney. I was greeted by the most amazing sight, both beautiful and frightening, of a flame jetting some five or six feet out from the top of it. I don't know about you, but I'm used to flames being wafty romantic yellow things, but this looked and sounded for all the world as if an RAF Typhoon had nosedived into the roof with its angry red afterburners pointing skywards.

Barbara called the emergency services while I set about closing the fireplace doors and shutting the vents, as all I could think of was to stop the air supply. Mercifully as soon as both these jobs had been done, the afterburners died and the noise abated. It seemed like the fire was going out by itself, and although a good deal of smoke continued to billow from the chimney, we felt back in control of the house. From the garden we could see blue flashing lights making their way up the hill from town a few miles away, and it was now a case of waiting for the experts.

Several minutes later, six fire-fighters arrived outside with a fire engine that bristled with ladders, huge amounts of impressive paraphernalia, and what I was sure was the lighting rig from a Pink Floyd concert. Road cones were deployed, compressed air hissed from various vents and within thirty seconds enough hardware had been set up to make sure Stone House would be the local talking point for at least the next six months. In truth, all the activity seemed a bit over the top, and when the chief later admitted that our call had come through at the halfway point of a rather dull PowerPoint presentation on 'safely handling dangerous equipment', a few pieces of the jigsaw did fall into place.

The chief, an amiable chap called Julian, ambled down the path with a big grin on his face and asked for an outline of what had happened. He appraised the situation, sent two men up onto the roof, two more to the back of the house and then came inside with a colleague. Furniture was moved around, and at that point Barbara became marooned on the sofa, torn between either watching the television or two burly fire-fighters in full kit on the floor in front of her. It was a completely unfair contest really.

We learned that the chief knew the house very well, and had been a work colleague and friend of Ted's for many years. As he and his colleague poked their noses up the chimney, they were in constant radio contact with their two colleagues on the roof who were poking their noses down it at the same time. They confirmed that the entire chimney was lined, that the house was safe and then prepared to clear it of smouldering debris. As he closed the doors to prevent burning embers from dropping out onto the floor, he reassured us that all would be well by saying "Don't worry; Ted was a stickler for doing things properly." Barbara murmured into her fingernails, and I studied the creases on the back of the sofa closely.

The duo on the roof began rodding the chimney, sending showers of embers down into the grate. Of all the materials to not use in a burning chimney, I would have thought that wood might top the list, but not for these chaps who inserted length after length of bamboo in an effort to dislodge burning resin and tar. It seems that chimney sweeps over the years had not been particularly efficient, and they estimated that quite a few years' worth of flammable creosote had built up in the pipe bends, and the flue on the chimney stack itself had narrowed to less than half its original diameter.

After a while, the noise of dropping embers slowed to a trickle, and they judged it safe to open the doors and start removing the ashes and tar from the grate. With a declaration of being very house proud, Julian and his team cleaned up every last speck of ash and soot, and made sure that no traces were left behind them. Barbara and I thanked them, saw them out and decided that we would drop something off at the station for them next week.

Now that all the excitement was over, we discussed the evening's events before settling down to enjoy what remained of the evening. I slowly became aware that there was something very familiar about the strong aroma from the chimney that filled the room, and it was beckoning me. As the television screen receded, my mind left the room and took me back almost thirty years in time, crossing three thousand miles of ocean as it went. It surfaced in the small study of a green house in Maine, where numerous black and white photographs hang on the walls, every surface is covered with books and papers, and where I watch my grandfather bury his pipe in a large tin of Edgeworth tobacco before lighting it and filling the room with its wonderful smell.

No Loughing Matter (9th April)

We have not managed to involve ourselves in local life as much as we would have hoped since moving here, which is a shame. Clearly Barbara's pregnancy and mobility, and my peripatetic job are factors in this, but we have gone to a number of Harvest Suppers and always make time to stop and chat whether it be with the local farmer, contractor or publican. Even so, almost every community activity that we hear of revolves around the local church and fundraising for it, and keen as we are to be a part of local life, we are not comfortable with the hypocrisy that our presence in their church would be. Perhaps, through a lack of shared values, our life here will prove to be one of happy and peaceful co-existence rather than complete integration.

Driving home a few weeks ago, Barbara spotted a sign just by the turning into the B4220 from the Hereford Road. It read *Loughing Match*, and gave a date not too far ahead. With spring in the air, we were excited to think that there might a community activity near the house; something fun and outdoorsy to help everyone blow away the winter cobwebs. But before we could even start to figure out what it might be, we first had to establish how to pronounce it. Neither of us knew the word nor what it meant, and our reliable friend Google seemed petulantly tight-lipped on the matter.

Barbara favoured a rhyme with 'dough', which didn't hit the spot for me, so I suggested that it should sound like 'tough'. She wasn't too keen, but when I told her that I loughed her very much, she agreed to my version. Warming to my theme, I started wondering if our village might play host to Herefordshire's answer to County Clare's famous matchmaking event held every September in Lisdoonvarna. After all, the localities are similar enough even though no one has yet written a song about Stanford Bishop.

On the first weekend of spring, lough was very much in the air as I headed out early in the morning on some errands. The sun was already shining with strength, the clouds were high and hazy and it felt only right to take the convertible out of its winter wraps for the first topless jaunt of the year. We had planned a busy weekend of outdoor activities; vegetable planting, chicken house cleaning, taking some baby bump pictures, perhaps a lunchtime drink on Bringsty Common and this, my early morning recycling trip. On my way back from Malvern, I was passing Garlick's farm, and almost drove into the roadside ditch as I did a double take at what I saw.

Obviously the sign we'd seen previously had seen better days, and this was the Ploughing Match that it referred to. From what I could tell as I passed by, the event comprised of a hundred or so ancient tractors slowly ploughing up and down some fields, while various spectators squinted, pointed at and presumably commented on their progress. There had to be more to it than that, so I decided that we would come back later on and take a closer look. I continued home, now giggling as a particular Monty Python sketch had surfaced in my mind, and I could hear Michael Palin shouting "Right! Anyone not happy with my little plan of marching up and down the square?"

Once back home, I told Barbara what I had seen, and we agreed to drop in during the afternoon. After a number of jobs had been done, we turned up at the entrance to the field, parked and headed down to the action. Numerous tractors still tracked back and forth across a number of fields, and it even seemed like some were racing each other; albeit very slowly.

We spied a note pinned to a gate between fields and wandered over to it hoping to shed some light on what appeared to a cross between farming, modern art and mindless loitering. We found only strict sounding rules that clearly told us what competitors couldn't do, but precious little information about what they should do, so we continued on our quest for answers.

Standing in a group of men rubbing their chins knowledgeably, we spied an official looking chap in a hi-vis vest and decided that he would be able to help us. He studied us as we approached, taking in the vast gulf that lay between us and everyone else on site in terms of age, wardrobe and dentistry. I asked him if he might explain what was going on, and then realised that I had inserted my foot into my mouth when he fixed me with a stare and said; "ploughing". I explained that we were new to the area and to rural living too, and would appreciate it if he could give us a bit of history to the event.

When it comes to my attention span, experience has taught me that my eyes are far bigger than my stomach, and so my well intentioned gesture of interest proved predictably hollow. He described in nauseating detail the widths of different kinds of furrows, the types of machinery that could be used to make them, the variety of soil conditions present, the very strict rules and the number of events that take place around the country. I listened politely for as long as I could, making our excuses when he paused for breath, as Barbara's silent giggling was threatening to set me off too.

So, there you have it. A ploughing match is a group of farmers who meet at weekends to pit their skills and vintage farming equipment against each other to secure the trophy for best furrow in a bewildering number of categories. No doubt there would be many a story to tell over a pint later that day, and it seemed like a well organised event that brought some colour to the area on a glorious spring day.

As we drove the short distance home, I wondered if somewhere in the world accountants meet up with their Casio FX-3's and tally long columns of figures at high speed, or if electricians have a porcelain fuse festival with the winner being awarded the pliers of honour. So far as I know they don't, and therefore this Ploughing Match may mean that that we have more in common with the locals than I had thought. I too love my work enough to devote significant parts of my weekends to it; it's just that it had never occurred to me that it might be a recreational activity too.

Our first view of Stone House in January 2011

The Living Room (with Ted in the armchair)

The Dining Room

The 1970's 'porn' bathroom

The vegetable plot

One of many sheds

The Orchard

Celebrating our arrival with a glass of wine in the field

Exchanging Pheasantries (21st April)

I consider the pheasant to be the most ridiculous creature I have yet met. Sometimes, when I watch Gerald, our resident Mongolian Ringneck pheasant, wandering around the orchard from my office window, I see an ill-equipped creature trying to navigate haphazardly through what I presume to be a relatively simple life, and often failing to quite a noticeable degree. Walking seems to be too much for him at times, he clearly has the memory of a goldfish and whatever brain he was born with must have come with batteries not supplied as he lurches from one mishap to the next, showing not the slightest inclination to learn from them. I once watched him trying to mate, and the object of his affections deserved a lifetime achievement award for accommodating his efforts without ridicule.

Possibly because they remind me of my adolescent years, I feel very protective towards them when it comes to the local pastime of hunting, and the available evidence suggests to me that they haven't a hope in hell. Compare them with the fox or rabbit; equally hunted animals in this part of the world, and both worthy adversaries whose downfall at the hands of hunters requires a degree of planning and stealth. The fox is as wily as the rabbit is fast, and through cunning and agility they can keep their predators at bay for hours at a time.

Over the last eight months I have observed Gerald on a number of occasions, and concluded that pheasants must be the easiest animal to hunt because neither skill nor precision seem to be required for the job. If you happen to come across a wild animal, you would normally expect it to run, hide, fly or anything else to get away from you. Gerald emphatically won't, preferring to wander in vague circles whilst performing an excellent imitation of a doddery pensioner holding up impatient commuters as he rummages in the depths of his bag for a bus pass. All fluster and precious little result.

Now having studied them for a while, I am starting to believe that the pheasant is actually far more intelligent than I had thought. Just take a leisurely Sunday afternoon drive around these parts, and I promise you a pheasant will drop what its doing in order to run across your path before long; drawn inexorably to danger like a moth to a light bulb. In the last few days alone, I could easily have brought home six or seven. Well, the remains of them at least, and I flatter myself that quick reactions are all that prevented Barbara and I from tucking into pheasant fritters last night. However, I suspect it's mostly due to the pheasant's deep understanding of human psychology and being well versed in Sun Tzu's The Art of War.

Every time one of these silly birds darts into the road in front of me, my first instinct is something along the lines of "Oh my! Pretty bird with long feathers! Mustn't kill it!" as I screech to a halt. The bird clearly expects this, as its reaction seems to be "Ha! The idiot stopped! Now I shall taunt him!" and then, rather than evasive action involving wings, it turns in the exact direction of my travel, and starts trotting ahead staying firmly in front of me no matter which way I swerve; annoying road-hog that he is. They are impervious to shouting or horn blowing, and my utter fascination at this suicidal behaviour prevents me from running them over.

I'm not sure if they adopt the same approach when a gun rather than a vehicle is trained on them, but I'd like to think they do. As soon as you spot him, he first surprises you by running directly into your line of fire, and then just tires you out by running from Land's End to John O'Groats several times over. Their survival is ensured through a clever mix of stamina and the total absence of challenge; it's like hunting Forrest Gump.

All of this leads me to wonder why Pheasants ever evolved as birds. They do come equipped with working wings, but for some reason seem loath to use them. A loud noise is normally more than enough to make your average bird take to the air, but pheasants traditionally require beaters by the dozen to get them airborne, and even then their undercarriage never retracts as they start looking for a landing strip within seconds. On a number of occasions I've seen Gerald penned in for hours by fences and hedges that he could easily fly over; once staring mournfully at a hole in the hedge big enough for his girlfriend to pass through but not for him. He looked utterly inconsolable as she headed off for a night on the town without him. Feeling sorry for him, I opened the window and yelled "for fuck's sake, fly!" but it didn't help and he continued dithering in circles for quite a while after. Their dislike of flying can sometimes get dangerous on the road outside Stone House. They seem to be creatures of habit and like to cross from the top of the orchard into the field opposite, and they predictably do so at a leisurely pace with no hint of the green cross code. Motorcycles are completely ignored as they swerve past, as are cars which usually stop and then sedately follow them for a while. However, when a lorry fully laden with most of Old MacDonald's produce bears down on them, they seem to know that psychology is no match for eighteen wheels at speed, and launch themselves over the hedge very quickly in a flurry of flapping feathers. Pheasants playing chicken? Now that's what I call sport.

Chilling' in our Crib (29th April)

With the incessant rain of recent weeks the garden has become an impassable quagmire, the road a rising river and the chickens now prefer free styling to free ranging. The local farmers love this weather as the land has been crying out for it for months, and with its arrival our rural resolve has mostly dissolved. We are once again city dwellers sitting on the inside of the glass staring morosely out over the grey landscape wondering if it will ever end. When it does, we'll come out and play again, but not before; I've even run out of weather-based banter with which to ambush Tony the ever-cheerful postman.

Looking on the bright side, this time gives us a chance to take stock before looking forward, and with our last ante-natal class finishing last night there is little left for us to do now except practise massage and relaxation techniques, enjoy a meal out à deux, engage in nesting activities and wonder how things will change from the habitual to the unrecognisable.

Over the last five or six months, Barbara has been absolutely indefatigable in her efforts to gather all the paraphernalia that we are going to need from mid-May onwards. This feat becomes even more impressive when we compare what we actually paid with what we would have, had we bought things new. And if that weren't enough, she has done all this with her foot in dire need of its next operation, my frequent business trips and no nearby friends on whom we can rely.

Whether from an auction website, thoughtful acquaintances, a note in a shop window or a car boot sale, she has been able to secure absolutely everything that baby will need from prams to pumps and all manner of things in between. In addition to this, friends, colleagues and family members have been unstinting in their generosity, and now the back of the garage, the lean-to and the spare bedroom are crammed with goodies from the very old to the brand new; some having arrived from as far away as Sweden, the United States and Australia. Now, at the end of April, only two things remain on her list of things to get.

There are a number of factors that drive this thrift; our lifestyle choice and the current financial climate being two of the most obvious ones, and an equally attractive consideration has been the enjoyment we derive from creating something new out of something old. Of course when it comes to precious lives one must be careful, and there are some things on which we will not compromise, but in the main we see no harm in thoughtful economy even when it goes against the tide of common advice. We have found that a great deal is written about the danger of using second hand car seats, for example; one never knows what sort of treatment they received beforehand. Yet no matter how appealing this argument may sound, it evaporates when you apply the logic that these same seats are often fitted, as they will be in our case, to cars that have had three or four previous owners.

Some items that we bought were in dire need of attention, either structurally or cosmetically, and these were excellent weekend projects where we could spend hours rummaging around the workshop finding old bits of wire and pots of unused paint with which to transform them into a piece of retro-chic. One such effort was the crib; a veteran from the early seventies judging by the cartoon characters that adorned it. When we collected it from the chap in Malvern who was giving it away, it came in pieces, was missing various bolts and did not completely inspire us with confidence.

It looked rather bland and sorry for itself, and so Barbara decided that as well as fixing it, we should liven it up. Constrained only by the rule of what we could find rather than blue for a boy and pink for a girl, we searched the length and breadth of the workshop and came up with some cream paint and a tin of red that was leftover from the on-going restoration of the breeze house, and she set to work by the chicken enclosure while I went foraging for some suitable ironmongery.

It would be true to say that I do the lion's share of the handiwork around the house, and Barbara does the vast majority of the cooking. Whilst we may conform to gender stereotypes in this regard, we like to think we buck the trend in our approach to both. Cooking and fixing should be undertaken with utter abandon and a total disregard for any rules, and so it was that paint was liberally applied to the crib in a few hours while I prepared various bits of broken lawnmower and other sundry items to fix it all together.

The result is colourful, possibly a touch on the loud side and probably not what the original designer had envisaged. As it will not be required until November or thereabouts, our plan over the summer is to decorate it with pictures, stickers and other bits and pieces. In time, baby may add a few more of his own choosing, but for now it remains a blank canvas in need of a mattress and an occupant.

As the rain makes way for the sun and the summer, as soon it surely must, baby will arrive and there will be no more chillin' in our crib for quite a while. For the moment though, as I look out over the front lawn where our occasional ducks Nanna and Ambrosius are waddling around in delight, the rain seems just perfect as it purposefully washes and rinses everything in these final weeks, leaving Stone House freshly scrubbed in readiness.

One Giant Leap (7th May)

The great feat on July 21st 1969 by the crew of Apollo 11 is one of those moments by which eras are defined, and Neil Armstrong's wonderful quote and those grainy images are indelibly marked on the consciousness of almost everyone over a certain age that I know. Back in the early 1970's when I was at primary school, it was Neil Armstrong and not Michael Jackson that made moonwalking cool, and occasionally my friends and I would pretend to take that one step down from the bottom rung of the ladder, pronounce those words, and then wander around the lunar landscape of the playground in a manner that was probably somewhere between bad yoga and John Cleese's 'Ministry of Silly Walks'. It's just one of those childhood memories of no consequence that I am reminded of when I see that clip shown on television or, oddly enough now, when I have to work in the vegetable garden.

Stone House boasts a wonderful vegetable garden that nestles on the slight slope between the garage and the garden; a trapezoid plot that we hope is large enough to produce a healthy amount of food over the course of a season. Our future plans involve converting half the orchard into a much bigger area for this purpose, but for now we are happy to use the existing one which was created by Ted a number of years ago.

We have found, as he did before us, that Herefordshire soil has its own very particular qualities, chief among which is an extremely high clay content. So rich in these minerals is the soil, that it can turn the ground to concrete in the summer or a Glastonbury-esque mudbath in the winter, and we are glad that Ted went some way to tackling this problem by putting in a rubble base, a herringbone system of drainage pipes and adding what must have been many tons of compost.

To help matters even more, our neighbour Andrew generously gave us free access to the manure pile he keeps at the edge of his land, and as well as liberally adding this to the soil over the winter, Barbara and I now feel well qualified to share with you exactly how much muck you can fit in the back of a Skoda with the rear seats folded down. The answer is "a lot", and once you have brought it back you'll need to spread it over the soil so the nutrients can work their magic. This can either take hours of back-breaking work, or about half an hour's messing around with a rotavator; hardly a tough decision in my book.

The rotavator is yet another fantastic piece of petrol-powered machinery that looks like the result of a one night stand between a lawnmower with no tyres and one of those things that council workers use in order to paint white lines in the middle of a road. Utterly daft in appearance, it is also deceptive in performance. Sadly it neither revs highly like a chainsaw nor makes a throaty noise like a tractor; preferring to softly *put-put-put* whilst wiggling gently.

The first time I used it last September, I had absolutely no idea what to do with it and the manual was typically reticent on the matter. I briefly toyed with the idea of going back to Homebase and asking the teenage shop assistant if he had any tips, but preferring to save what little face I could, I reasoned that it shouldn't be too complicated. I lined it up at the edge of the heat-baked, weed strewn earth, fired it up, released the clutch and waited to see what would happen.

Slowly, but with incredible force, it started chewing its way across the ground, leaving deliciously dark and crumbly soil in its wake. Where the soil was loose, the weight of the engine forced it down until the blades found purchase, and it gently climbed ahead and back up. Where the soil was hard, I discovered that all I had to do was simply dig my heels in and hang on for dear life, while the blades marched on the spot until the soil gave in. Weeds were dug up, soil was loosened and within less than half an hour the entire vegetable plot looked ready for a guest appearance on Gardeners' Question Time.

So brilliant is this machine, that it was the catalyst for one of the truly inspired decisions that Barbara and I have made since moving here. We would grow our vegetables in rows spaced just a little wider than the track of the rotavator, and weeding throughout the season would be accomplished by the simple act of driving the rotavator up and down in between each row. Earning a cold beer on a hot day should always be this easy.

Having hopefully freed up a great deal of our time from the boredom of weeding, it will no doubt be given over to defending our crops from hungry wildlife, so we plan to sow them their very own special vegetable garden in the hope that they leave ours alone. We now look forward to a long hot summer of tending the garden while it yields onions, garlic, carrots, radishes, rhubarb, cucumbers, courgettes, potatoes, corn and a variety of herbs.

Whilst the idea of using the rotavator to weed with extreme prejudice adds to my personal enjoyment, the last laugh I leave to the Herefordshire clay which takes only a few seconds to attach itself to my boots in large and heavy clumps as I walk behind the machine. After a few small steps it becomes more of a struggle to lift my feet as my boot size swells to around twice its normal size. Progress, although comical, becomes increasingly laborious and this results in more or less the exact same gait with which my friends and I impersonated Neil Armstrong all those years ago.

Stuffed Chicken à la Remorse (13th May)

Some people know when to stop eating and some don't. Over the years, I have enjoyed a rich and varied relationship with food which has resulted in a number of waist sizes. The same is true for animals; whilst most cats will pick at their dinner over an evening, your average Labrador can't even chew once before swallowing and will sometimes wobble from dinner bowl to basket seeming to wish for a quick slurp of Pepto-Bismol on the way. None of this, however, compares with the relationship that chickens enjoy with worms.

A few months ago Barbara and I were focussing on getting the vegetable garden ready for spring. Part of this meant creating a small corner for herbs, and we felt that it would be nice to separate each plant using rocks taken from an area adjacent to the garage. We spent an afternoon huffing, puffing, digging and dragging in order to move these large and heavy stones into position, and our efforts were rewarded with the creation of a small rockery herb garden just next to the strawberry patch.

At one point during the removal of one of the larger stones; a task requiring sledgehammer, crowbar, shovel and a significant amount of swearing on my part, we disturbed a large and juicy earthworm that immediately began burrowing its way back underground to safety. Barbara suggested it might be a nice snack for the chickens, and so I grabbed it before it could make its escape.

The chickens typically graze from dawn till dusk on a plentiful supply of layer pellets, a standard feed that provides them with all the nutrients they need. They supplement this with grass and whatever grubs they can find on their own through endless scratching. When we tossed them the worm we had found, it was Jodie who spied it first and made off with it in a hurry. The other two immediately tried to ambush her, and for the ten or so seconds that it took Jodie to swallow it, it looked for all the world like a fight outside a nightclub at 3am.

So pleased was Jodie with her treat and so crestfallen were the other two without one, that we immediately went back and started digging for two more. Before long we had unearthed them, took them back and were careful to make sure that each bird had one. Previously we had found they really enjoyed small chunks of melon, but we had never seen this kind of reaction before and so Barbara was very pleased to find that the local pet store sold dried mealworms.

As an occasional treat, a small handful of these thrown on the ground will send them into fits of ecstasy as they hunt, scratch and peck their way through eight of ten of these tasty morsels. Standing at the fence and shaking the tub now elicits the Pavlovian response of bringing them to your feet from wherever they are.

On Friday afternoon Barbara and I had agreed to take advantage of the dry and warm weather to take a slow stroll around the field to inspect our perimeter and see how much growth the rain had caused. As we crossed from the house she asked me to wait while she gave the chickens a worm or two, and disappeared into the garage to fetch the plastic tub.

No sooner had she shaken it once or twice than her captive audience arrived at a speed that would have worried Usain Bolt. Ever the tease, she held the tub out over their heads and shook it some more, presumably to make sure their digestive systems were operating at fever pitch. This was clearly too much for Jade who launched herself upwards, zeroing in on her target with a great deal of flapping. Barbara was completely taken by surprise, the result being that about half the tub rained down on the chickens who must have thought they had died and gone to heaven.

What followed was an avian hoovering match in which Jordan scored more points than the other two put together, but this didn't seem to matter as they all ate their fill and then spent an eternity scrabbling around the same area in case they had missed a morsel or two. I don't think chickens burp, but if they did they would have let rip in unison at that point I'm sure.

We thought no more about it until the morning when we went to let them out for the day. On opening the door, the usual rush to get out, poop and head for the feeders was somewhat slower than usual and only two were in the running. As Jodie and Jade did their best to stagger in a ladylike fashion to the feed shelter, it was all too apparent that Jordan hadn't made it out of bed. A quick peek in the house revealed that she was still rolled up under her duvet with a cold towel against her forehead whilst presumably muttering, "Oh my God, what have I done?" Half an hour later, she did make it outside, albeit in a rather unsteady fashion, and it was very apparent that all was not well in her world.

She was, it would be fair to say, little more than an orange and white fluffy ball from which a fevered head protruded at one end, and diarrhoea projected at the other. She spent hour after hour perfectly still with her eyes frequently shut in concentration as she battled bravely to undo the damage of the previous day's gluttony. By now, Barbara and I were very worried; how on earth could we be trusted with an infant if we were unable to look after a chicken?

Sadly there was nothing we could do, and we spent the day checking on her progress from time to time whilst offering encouraging words like "Greedy Guts" and "Mrs Creosote". Thankfully, she correctly interpreted these as signs of love and support, and redoubled her efforts to reduce her BMI to something more manageable. Later, when she waddled to bed, we weren't sure if she was going to make it through to the morning, as she had been in pain for at least twelve hours and presumably most of the previous night.

This morning, as the door slid back, all three came pelting down the ramp and disappeared in the direction of their food and water. It seems therefore that 36 hours' discomfort is all that is required to recover from an episode of staggering overindulgence, but from now on we shall be much more careful when handling dried mealworms in their presence.

Schadenverwirren (20ᵗʰ May)

A German compound word created by combining 'harm' and 'joy', schadenfreude is used to describe a feeling of pleasure that can be derived from the misfortune of others. The word has no English equivalent unless *epicaricacy* is to your taste, and a great number of humans, regardless of their origin, are prone to the occasional bout of it. As the spring begins to get into full swing, a form of it is increasingly occupying my thoughts.

Typically, it can be experienced individually as a hidden pleasure, and usually only publicly when part of a partisan crowd. At some sporting events it is very much the form, and seems to be what fuels a significant proportion of television scheduling. Generally the enjoyment of it in private is something that people won't rush to admit to for reasons of propriety. This duality is unfair so I will now own up to mine, thanks to the stretch of road that passes by Stone House, although bewilderment at the misfortune of others is a more accurate description of what I experience.

The B4220 is a minor road linking two trunk roads that meander in westerly directions from Worcester; eight glorious miles of tarmac that twist and turn their way up hill and down dale, through hamlet and past farm, all the while affording stunning views of the Herefordshire and Worcestershire countryside on either side. Apart from local traffic, it is a favourite destination for petrol-heads and keen cyclists, the latter capturing my attention from time to time.

Stone House sits almost exactly halfway along the only bit of straight road to be found on the entire eight-mile stretch, which also happens to be on a steady incline. At the top end of the straight is a sharp, blind corner on which the Pink Pub stands, and the bottom feeds into what can only be described as a corkscrew (motor racing fans familiar with the Laguna Seca raceway will know just what I mean). All in all, it is the perfect place for anyone wishing to explore acceleration, deceleration and the edge of grip.

When we lived in West London, driving a car was a highly risky activity in which a noticeable percentage of those doing it were selective about when and where certain laws could be ignored, whilst expecting other road users to heed every last one fanatically. This made them just as dangerous as the cyclists and motorcyclists who acted with the same myopic conceit, and the only difference between them all was the severity and speed of the impacts each could withstand.

Thankfully, out here, it is largely different: using the roads in the country tends to be a much gentler pursuit involving less surprises, generally better manners, and the occasional frustration being mostly restricted to tractors and livestock. This absence of road rage means that other emotions can rise to the surface, as the majority of incidents are self-inflicted.

You might think that I derive pleasure from the Darwin Award-winning motorcyclists and motorists who frequently ignore the 'sharp bend' warning sign and depart the road opposite the Pink Pub, where they sail through the ever-pruned gap in the hedge like lemmings before burying their machines in Farmer Giles' furrows, but you'd be wrong. I think their attempts to remove themselves from the gene pool are tiresome rather than joyful, and if their efforts must continue, I sincerely hope that they do so without causing harm to anyone else.

My occasional interest lies with the cyclists, who are drawn to this area in their droves. Lycra-clad groups frequently meet at local pubs, head off in various directions to enjoy the scenery and later reconvene at another pub to refuel and compare notes. Whilst this is markedly different in so many ways from urban cycling, there is one thing that never changes; I have rarely seen a cyclist in any setting with a look on their face that is anything other than sheer agony.

In a cruel twist of fate, probably due to route-planning advice given by touring companies like Wheely Wonderful Cycling of Ludlow, only about 5% of the cyclists that pass by Stone House do so from the south. This results in a high pitch whoosh as they hurtle past at forty miles per hour, spitting bugs out through gritted teeth, and bracing themselves before rearranging their lunch as they whip through the corkscrew.

Unfortunately, the remaining 95% approach from the north, and with enormous quantities of panting, huffing and groaning they take quite a while to pass by, their enthusiasm, drive and adrenalin having already waned at a lower altitude. It's like listening to a collection of first serves from a fifth set tie-breaker on Wimbledon's Centre Court.

If I am outside as they draw abreast of the gate, most will usually notice me looking at them with an expression of bewilderment on my face. In a waste of valuable energy some will attempt a grimace, others will manage to say something like "Zwoff-gnnnnnnnn! pshht-lrrrrrrrrgg!" in time as they bear down on their pedals, and a charming chap once gave me the finger. Conversely, those who have already decided to push their bicycles up the hill on foot usually give me a cheery wave and a smile.

It's not their misfortune that I take joy from; it's their fortune that bewilders me. Therefore with my tongue in my cheek and my hat raised, I offer you a new word; Schadenverwirren.

Driving Without a Licence (2ⁿᵈ June)

There is a very different feel in the air at Stone House now; a new range of sounds, a wider spectrum of smells and a totally new sense of purpose. With a new member joining the cast here, it's as though spring has really, finally and truly sprung. In sympathy over the last two weeks, the field and orchard have yielded an enormous amount of hay from the first cut, the hedges have expanded in all directions, and the weeds are enjoying a time of prosperous growth.

It has been nine months since we knew our lives would change, and from the beginning it has not been plain sailing with a few upsets and worries along the way. Thankfully the early ones soon passed, and as our confidence grew Barbara spent many months enjoying her pregnancy. As her bump got bigger word spread in the local community of an impending arrival, but no matter how much we discussed our future it still somehow didn't feel real. We often confided in each other that it would probably sink in after the birth, and in the meantime we decided to enjoy noticing the small changes as the weeks passed.

In addition to the enormous quantity of web-based research that Barbara carried out, we decided to join our local NCT group and attend a course of pre-natal classes. At the time, I remember going along to the first class thinking that it would be an evening tea party in which information freely available on the Internet was shared in someone's front room. In many ways I was proved right, but we still committed ourselves and took the opportunity to ask as many questions as we could. Aside from the obvious learnings about birth, feeding and neo-natal health, it also appeared that I made the teacher rather nervous due to having a similar profession, and so I have also learned that it's probably best not to facilitate a facilitator. Or maybe just not me.

The course gave us our first sense of reality. It was no longer just us and a bump; there were five other couples and five other bumps with due dates spanning less than six weeks and a whole array of concerns, fears and experiences. A completely unlikely mix of twelve people all brought together in search of some support, guidance and reassurance for what has to be the most extreme event for so many reasons. With hindsight, the course is the one thing that kept me sane when all else failed in the heat of the moment.

Even before we got married, Barbara and I had discussed numerous aspects of having children; from whether or not we should, through to what we would call them if we did. At some point in between these two ends of the spectrum, it was deemed highly likely by every medical expert that we have ever dealt with, that Barbara would most probably not carry a child for a full term for a number of reasons. This, and the isolated location of Stone House, were the driving factors in my refusing work during the first part of May. As Murphy's Law would have it, we spent most of May up to, including and past her due date kicking our heels and waiting for something to happen. As it didn't, we amused ourselves with barbecues, house cleaning and our camera instead.

Already now, just over a week later, it feels like a century ago that Barbara's waters broke, signalling the beginning of the 72-hour marathon that would result in the arrival of our son. No book, no class and no conversation could ever have prepared us for this period of time, and when it came down to it we were operating purely on instinct and didn't really know what we were doing. We still don't, and we are slowly coming to grips with the fact that this feeling may last quite a while.

After the waters in the very early hours of Tuesday morning, there came an eerie pause which we fully expected to be brief and end in the beginning of her contractions. Nothing happened and having been reassured that all was well, we were told to wait until something did. It didn't, and so we were asked to present ourselves at the hospital on Wednesday for a spell of CTG monitoring in which both Barbara's non-existent contractions and the baby's heartbeat would be simultaneously observed. It transpired that she actually was having contractions, but was not able to feel them. More importantly, each contraction resulted in the baby's heartbeat slowing down quite significantly, but as it quickly recovered each time all was deemed well and we were sent home with an appointment to induce on Friday evening, unless something happened sooner. Anna, a midwife with knowledge as all-encompassing as her compassion, observed, "I think something will happen before Friday" as we left.

Something did happen at 6 o'clock the next morning, and we were back in hospital hooked up to a CTG monitor by 9am with contractions, now very obvious and painful, every three minutes. For the next three hours Barbara rocked on her feet, I provided massage and baby's heartbeat continued dipping in time with her contractions. By one o'clock, we had been moved to a delivery room with contractions every minute, and the scene was set for gas and air, which duly arrived and was greedily consumed. One of my most vivid memories of that time is of Barbara lying on the delivery bed wearing her purple Doc Martens', and I believe I shall enjoy dining out for years with the glib comment of "Did you know that my wife gave birth wearing combat boots?"

By 4 o'clock Barbara had reached the end of her considerable ability to withstand pain, and asked for an epidural. As it took effect some 45 minutes later, the midwife visibly relaxed, and then took one look at me and told me to go and get some food and fresh air. I did as I was told, and fully expected to come back to find Barbara sitting up in bed, numb from the waist down and chatting over a cup of tea about beach holidays.

Returning twenty minutes later, I heard her screams from the corridor long before I got back inside the delivery rooms, and it was clear that her epidural had lasted less than an hour. I never have, nor ever wish to again, see or hear Barbara in pain like that. This was something that neither of us were prepared for, and which had also caught the staff off guard. Between 5pm and 7pm I did not recognise Barbara, her voice, the look in her eyes or her manner. She seemed to be trying as hard as humanly possible to focus on some distant place where no pain could reach her, while her body ran over hot coals that no man will ever know.

Thankfully a large top-up of her epidural took the edge off the worst of the pain, and much to my astonishment she started a conversation with me about how the birth of our second child would be very different. Having already assumed my nether regions would be sentenced to a lifetime of solitary confinement, and believing that a heady cocktail of drugs fuelled her comments, I humoured her as best I could. I didn't have long to think about it as something had happened on one of the monitors, a decision was made not to wait for baby any longer and a large number of people and machines suddenly appeared in the room. I had been warned in my NCT class what the 'blades' were, and so I was reasonably well equipped to withstand the shock when they were unwrapped. What I wasn't prepared for was the force with which they were used.

In obvious distress, our son was delivered by forceps at 8.14pm in Hereford County Hospital on Thursday 24th May, and was immediately rushed to the Special Care Baby Unit where he remained for the next four days receiving the very best care from a superb team of neo-natal nurses and paediatricians who now have our eternal gratitude. At the same time Barbara was kept in the maternity ward where she was treated for an infection and a haematoma that threatened further immediate surgery. The doctors wavered over the need to give her a blood transfusion, but after four days she stabilised, and mother and son were finally allowed to stay together in the same room. It was a further two days before I could bring them home, and for all of us it was an extremely difficult week; one that we record here only to prove to ourselves in the future that it made us that little bit stronger.

We came home at dusk on Wednesday 30th May. Never having driven a child of my own before, I suddenly had no idea of how a car worked. I think I hit every pothole there was, I braked too suddenly yet too hesitantly, and veered around corners far too sharply. Having recently sold my venerable Saab, a model of car that I have driven exclusively for the last twenty-two years, I would like to pretend that my awkward driving style was due to my new-to-me Volkswagen estate car. In truth, my car skills were just as self-conscious and uncomfortable as they had been the first time I ever drove, and it was relief indeed when we arrived home, made it through the front door and had a chance to relax at last.

The moment I stepped through the door with both of them and closed it behind us was wonderful; as if nine months of waiting for it to feel real had at last come to an end. As a part of our lives from now on, he will naturally feature prominently in this book, for which he will need a nom du plume to match ours, and so it is with great pride that I introduce our baby boy who we feel is, in every way, really *Rather Good.*

Village Idiom (10ᵗʰ June)

As a product of an education system that prized measurable mass regurgitation over the vagaries of context and interpretation, I have long parroted sayings without really thinking about them. Hence I now feel rather stupid for never having previously connected the idiom "Make hay while the sun shines" to the fact that you really ought to make hay while the sun shines. By 'ought', what I really mean is 'drop everything no matter what, forget about sleep and don't even think of stopping until it's done', but this may be a local nuance thanks to the weather.

This year, a hot late March made way for the wettest April on record, which then outstayed its welcome until it was relieved by a stunning week in the second half of May. This seasonal kaleidoscope produced incredible growth everywhere at Stone House. The field, which was last cut before our arrival in July of 2011, had been transformed from something that looked like a large lawn in need of a trim into one of the sets for the Hollywood epic Gladiator, complete with waist high stalks waiting for Russell Crowe to wander through whilst staring moodily into the middle-distance.

Fruit trees blossomed, hedgerows fattened and the enormous willow turned from a skeleton of branches into a cascade of leaves in less than a fortnight. Everywhere you looked, spring hadn't just sprung; it was in a fully-fledged rout from the confines of winter, thanks to the extremes of temperature and moisture that enveloped it.

For one week at the end of May, when the sun shone, almost nothing happened in Herefordshire that was not to do with grass cutting and haymaking. Every farm worked together during those days, sharing labour, resources and expertise; we even had a traffic jam on the B4220 caused by a line of enormous tractors having to queue up to get though the gate into Andrew's fields, where they would shadow a meandering combine harvester as it spat ton after ton of grass cuttings into their trailers.

I've never seen hay made before, but in the last hot weeks of May, on the occasions that I was home, I watched Farmer Harris take his payment for services rendered by driving a variety of machines around the field and the orchard. Hay sells for about £2 per bale in these parts, and our three acres of grass produced something in the region of eighty or ninety bales. With that kind of money at stake you might think that it would be a case of cut it, bag it and flog it as quick as you can, but that would be to consider hay for its financial as opposed to its real value.

First the grass is cut and then it is left to dry out for a few days in the high heat of the sun. Watching a tractor decimate three acres of grass in less than an hour is quite an impressive sight, and I was all for clapping my hands in delight until vibrations caused by a very close pass behind the animal shelter reduced my carefully stacked woodpile to a heap on the ground inside.

As I inspected the field that evening, I also noticed that the gate between it and the orchard had been removed, it's hinge posts leaning at an unfamiliar and rather precarious angle. At over eighty years old, Farmer Harris' eyesight is perhaps not what it was, and it would appear that navigating several tons of tractor through narrow openings, or close by buildings can be a rather hit and miss affair.

A few days later, he returned for the next step which I think must be the inspiration behind shampoo adverts for men all over the world. It's very similar to what they do to their hair while they twinkle their teeth at the camera; a sort of tousle with a bit of a 'juj', except rather than using perfect fingers to do it, you use a twenty foot wide scarifier on the back of a tractor. He looked like a man rediscovering his playful youth as he raced up and down the field flinging grass far and wide behind him to make sure it was aired, dry and ready for baling.

He stopped for a quick chat before heading home that night, and as I always have great difficulty understanding most of what he says, I judged it prudent to say nothing about my woodpile or the gate. Instead I responded to the squeaks and whistles that constitute the bulk of his vocabulary with polite agreement and the occasional wave of my arms, and this seemed to satisfy him and send him on his way.

The penultimate part of the haymaking process was the most enjoyable to watch; Farmer Harris dragged what can only be described as an oversized art-deco toaster around the field, which would eat its fill every few minutes and then pause to give birth to a beautifully formed bale of hay. It was rather like watching a large chicken slowly waddling across a field, squatting every ten paces and depositing an egg.

When I got home the next day, his son had already turned up with a hay bale lifter and taken their bounty away on a flatbed trailer. The field and orchard had been transformed, and in a matter of a few days they had harvested almost half the winter feed they would need for their flocks which seemed to me a very good investment of their time.

As I walked around that evening in the hot sunshine, I noticed that the fence posts had been repaired and the gate put back on its hinges, but the woodpile was still scattered all over the ground inside the shelter. While wondering which idiom might apply best, I switched on the outdoor speakers, grabbed a cold beer from the fridge and set about re-stacking it with a smile on my face. If you want something done, and all that...

Traditions and Toposcopes (22nd June)

At the age of ten or thereabouts, I sat down one morning at school for the weekly assembly and prepared to listen to the headmaster's wife make her usual worldly, motivating and educational address. She opened with the following salvo: "The only good German is a dead one". With my background I naturally felt targeted, but even at that age I understood the reasons why someone of her age and experiences might make such a statement, however fatuous it may be.

The lasting impact of her address has been that the judging of something as good or bad simply due to a biological or geographical accident is a complete anathema to me. In the years since, this has been summed up beautifully for me with a quote by Shimon Peres: "Most people prefer to remember rather than to think". He uses it on occasion to explain some of the political difficulties that he deals with on a daily basis, and for me it is the best way that I have yet found to sum up what I consider to be the utter irrationality of nationalism and other circumstantial fanatic loyalties.

I'm not against fanatic loyalty at all; it is simply a strong preference. It's just that all too often it masquerades as *Identity*, using its blinding irrationality to fuel pointless generalisations that are rooted in inherited memory rather than thought. Thanks to my headmaster's wife I will always choose to call the whole thing off rather than argue the toss.

The first weekend that I brought Barbara and Rather home from the hospital was a gentle, strange and totally wonderful experience. Our thoughts were completely focussed on him and his needs, so much so that we completely forgot about the Diamond Jubilee celebrations that were taking place at the same time. By the Monday of that bank holiday, things had settled a little bit, and whilst catching up on the news I discovered that the Worcester Beacon, perched on the highest of the Malvern Hills, was going to be lit that night. With a clear view of it from the field, and stories of how the beacon could be seen for twenty miles and more, I thought I would take an evening walk to catch some fresh air and watch a bit of the spectacle.

To get the clearest view, I stood by the hedgerow on the far side of the field, and looked some eight miles towards the Southeast. After the deluge of rain on Sunday, I was glad to notice that although completely overcast, it was at least dry. On the crest of the hill, I could see flashbulbs peppering the night sky as hundreds of people had gathered around the toposcope built there for the last Diamond Jubilee in 1897. I imagined them singing and celebrating, and as I am not a particular fan of the Royal Family, I was content to congratulate them from afar.

I could tell that the moment to light the beacon had arrived when the flashbulbs on the skyline increased to a frenzied peak. I craned my neck to see if I could make anything out, and as the pinpricks of light began to lessen in number, a steady orange dot became faintly discernible. The beacon was lit, and I felt sure the crowd cheered, recited the national anthem and shared a moment of warmth and unity.

In a beautifully choreographed moment, for some underscoring the momentous occasion, and for others overshadowing it, the clouds parted perfectly to allow a full, yellow and sagging moon to appear directly above the beacon. It appeared majestically, danced slowly for about a minute, and then slid gently behind the clouds for the rest of the night; it's multi-faceted point having been made.

As I wondered back to the house, I started thinking of Rather and what choices he might make in his life and how already, at the age of only three weeks, he faces pressure from people who are keen to make him like the same things they like. Stronger and potentially more corrosive than what hobbies, games and teams he is encouraged to like, he is certain to at least be influenced, if not conditioned, by his parents' views and values when it comes to things like responsibility, the law and equanimity in dialogue.

No matter what choices he makes, and which ones become traditions and beliefs that he ends up celebrating and holding dear, Barbara and I hope that the views from his toposcope are those of his own thought rather than the memories of other people.

Holy Moly (8th July)

The allied soldiers who attempted a mass escape from Stalag Luft lll during World War Two inspired one of their number, Paul Brickhill, to immortalise their story in the 1963 film 'The Great Escape'. Considered by many to be a classic film, it is a tale of good pitted against evil, of overcoming seemingly insurmountable odds and, ultimately, a series of agonising defeats snatched from various jaws of victory.

In a drama based on real events where life and death dance with each other closely for almost all of its impressive 172 minutes, there is little room for light relief. Nonetheless, I like to imagine a short scene set a little before the story starts in which fact, fiction and drama mix. In it Dickie Attenborough thoughtfully muses to his fellow conspirators: "Darlings, you know, my brother always says moles are frightfully interesting animals". Later that night, David appears in his dreams and chides him gently in his breathy voice; "Richard, I do wish you'd listen to me sometimes; I actually said voles". Given that the film uses a large amount of artistic licence, I see no reason why this scene cannot one day be inserted into a Director's Cut prequel. Such a scene would resonate with the inmates later in the film, providing them with the same sort of 'Aha' moment that we have had at Stone House.

With most things in life, it's the little things that can make a big difference. And so it is that one consonant can be all that lies between victory and defeat, between freedom from tyranny and a punishable offence, and between a broken leg and a nice English lawn.

Moles are furry creatures equipped with enormous front paws that are ideally suited for digging. With two thumbs on each paw and the ability to survive on less oxygen than most other creatures, they can burrow from Land's End to John O'Groats in less time than it takes me to make a cup of coffee, and are the bane of farmers and gardeners everywhere. Thankfully there are a myriad of options on offer to dissuade them from their favourite pastime of destroying lawns, plants, vegetation and crops by, well, killing them.

Despite appearances, moles are not nocturnal; simply preferring to work when other animals don't. They are business-like creatures that tend to travel from A to Z using the shortest and most efficient route. Unfortunately, they mark the entrances and exits to their tunnels with little mounds made from the earth that they extract, and these also act as beacons to hasten their downfall. Clearly inspired by these irritating pests, the prisoners in the film excavate their tunnels in the same way, but ingeniously improve on the moles' flawed technique by dispersing the soil subtly and some distance away from their tunnels; thereby removing any evidence of their clandestine work.

Voles, as their name might suggest, are very similar to moles in that they happily burrow under the ground from A to Z, but with some important differences. Firstly, they need a higher oxygen content in the air that they breath, which means their tunnels are perforated with ventilation shafts at B, C, D etc. all the way to Y, rather like the New York Subway. Secondly, they don't mark every Tom, Dick and Harry with a helpful marker beacon, and this means that they can convert a lawn from a verdant smooth surface into booby-trapped minefield capable of snapping your ankles several times over.

These are not necessarily problems in themselves, but a third and potentially insurmountable one does present itself if you ask a professional to help you get rid of these unwelcome visitors. It turns out that you can't unless you pretend to have a cold or a speech impediment. We found this out when we called in a pest control specialist to deal with a wasp nest that came to life during an unseasonably warm week in March. Having searched high and low throughout the Cider Barn for the nest, Mr Rentokil was unable to find anything, but was keen to earn his call out fee by asking us if we had anything else he could exterminate.

Barbara and I seized on this generous offer to ask him about the hundreds of holes that cover the land around Stone

House. We showed him a particularly pock-marked area near the greenhouse where walking can be a dangerous affair, and said, "we're not sure, but we think we have a problem with voles, and this area is the worst. Can you do anything to help?"

He looked at us sharply and said "Nothing if it's voles; they're supposed to be protected. I wish you'd said moles." I asked him why, given that they were just as destructive and greater in number. He smiled and said, "Because they're cute and furry, but remember I did say they are supposed to be protected..." Nudge nudge, wink wink, say no more.

Autour du Moi, le Deluge (15th July)

Life at Stone House continues to change as the three of us try to settle into new routines. Rather has recovered completely from the distresses of his first week, and is now an energetic infant with all the usual behaviours and daily developments you would expect. One of the recent ones is that he can occasionally shape his mouth into a grimace at times when he is not passing wind, and we therefore expect to see his first real smile very soon.

Having been wrong-footed by his late arrival, I was back at work within two weeks of his birth and we have been so grateful that Barbara's family have come and gone with clockwork regularity to help her cope with nappies, sleepless nights and colic. Unusually my work has been predominantly abroad for the last six weeks, meaning my Saturdays at home have involved hurried kisses, cleaning bottoms and packing. As a result the piles of unopened mail in the office are threatening to block the view from the window, and the unchecked vegetation on all four sides of the house is similarly poised to block out the sun.

Or rather it would be, if there were any sunshine to be seen, and as we are currently enjoying the wettest summer on record, it isn't. Now that I come to think of it, with the exception of the last week of March and that of May, it has rained almost without pause since February. It wouldn't be too far from the truth to say that the only times that I have seen the sun this year have been at 30,000 feet.

This has meant that the land has been untended since May, and this weekend I decided that some maintenance was in order lest we let the jungle take over, so I went out for a recce on Friday to prioritise what needed to be done. Trudging across the orchard, I looked down and noticed that it had become a paddy field. The water has been sitting there for so long now that either new waterborne wildlife has arrived, or the existing inhabitants have become amphibian.

The water table has worryingly risen into the back of the garage, the hedge around the field has reached over twelve feet high in places and there are some gargantuan weeds appearing everywhere. In addition to all of this, the grass has become thick, lush and very long. Even if it were dry, it would present a challenge for both the mower and the tractor, which are not the youngest you have ever seen.

Yesterday I chose to attack the hedge that runs from the road alongside the house to the field; over seventy metres of hawthorn hedgerow. It is one of those jobs that I have always hated, and I cannot imagine a time when I won't. When dealing with hedges before, I would plan my breaks according to time: first the sides, followed by a coffee and then the top, followed by a beer. Now my breaks are taken when the petrol runs out and I need to let the machine cool before refilling.

Even if I do say so myself, I have done an absolutely terrible job and it now looks worse than if I were let loose on a bonsai tree with Vidal Sassoon's entire armoury. I have left a message on Andrew's answer-phone asking if I can have access to the field on the other side next weekend, so I can try to remedy the worst of it, but I suspect it will remain a weeping eyesore until Farmer Harris turns up in December to give the hedge its annual short back 'n' sides.

With today being the last rain-free day forecast before my eightieth birthday, I really had to tackle the grass. After a morning trip to Malvern for supplies, I donned my overalls, topped up the tanks and wheeled my ancient lawnmower into action. Right from the start, the going was tough and the results were pitiable as the grass put up almost unbeatable resistance.

Soggy grass cuttings clogged every nook and cranny on the lawnmower, and I counted thirty-eight full loads that had to be emptied. To make matters easier, I dispensed with the time-consuming round trip to the compost pile with the wheelbarrow, developing instead a new country dance that involved standing in the field and pirouetting with the grass-box at arms length. Time after time I sent the contents in a wide arc over the long grass where, in time, it will decompose.

In a little over three hours I had cut all the grass areas around the house, the verge along the road and the chicken enclosure. My aching muscles were telling me to call it a day, but the field and orchard still beckoned and at least I would be able to sit down on the job.

A further hour and a half was spent on the tractor doing lengths of the orchard and laps of the field. In places the grass had grown so thick that I could smell burning rubber from the belts as they forced the blades to keep turning. Almost half of each lap was driven through standing water; the rear wheels churning the grass into mud in their efforts to maintain forward motion, the blades blending the grass and water into a mint coloured froth before ejecting it from the vent.

One day I will invite a marketing person from Honda to come and witness the punishment that a twenty-year-old tractor can withstand.

Taking Stock (22nd July)

It's now been one year to the day since we arrived at Stone House on a grey and rainy afternoon, and as we begin our second there seem to be many reasons for us to take stock, refocus plans and celebrate with gratitude. Naturally the most obvious is the arrival of Rather, who continues to delight us and prevent us from sleeping in equal measure, but there are others of varying importance and impact.

As the Weather Gods would have it, today was a rarity: a beautiful, hot, sunny and endless summer day. We spent it catching up on outdoor chores, visiting the car boot sale in Ledbury, pottering, and this evening we feasted al fresco whilst enjoying the sun's warmth. We celebrated our year with a barbecue and the promise later tonight of some of the soft and sweet raspberries from our garden.

It has been a year of settling in and getting to know Herefordshire from scratch, and both through the local area and our NCT group we have started to make new friends. It has also been a year of continued frustrations with Barbara's foot and associated legal manoeuvrings, but we hope that the latter will have concluded by this time next year. Lastly, it has been a year of adjusting to a very rural existence, and as we slowly learn to be more practical we sincerely hope that not everything that starts life as black & decker will end up as araldite & gaffer too quickly.

In short, one year on from the start of this upheaval and new beginning, we are exactly where we would wish to be without ever having been able to imagine it previously. Using the equation that averages all things good from all things not, we find our sums very much adding up in our favour and with each passing day our resolve and sense of peace increases.

And for the day's icing, Barbara returned from the supermarket this morning with a bottle of what I now consider the most perfect wine called 'Barefoot'. Given that it combines my favourite grape with my preferred dress code, all we need now is a little Bob Marley and a big hammock!

Industrial Evolution (29th July)

On Friday night I watched the opening ceremony of the London 2012 Olympics, and it was an excellent reminder of just how much creativity, playfulness and resilience there is in this country. In many ways I felt humbled by the spectacle, and almost entertained a thought that were we still living in London, we might have tried to find a way of getting tickets for the night.

Like all good dramas though, it portrayed life without any of the boring bits, and so I remained content to be at home. When I went to bed, my thoughts were occupied with Brunel and the Industrial Revolution, the vast catalogue of Arts and a celebration of the Individual.

It's one thing to move from London to deepest Herefordshire in search of peace and The Good Life, and it's another to fully embrace all that it involves. After a year here, Barbara and I have learned a great deal about some things that the BBC wisely chose to leave out of their sitcom, and we feel certain there is much more to come. Mercifully, a few things are far easier that we had imagined, and one of these things is making jam.

There can be no doubt that jam making on an industrial scale requires all manner of specialist equipment, a good deal of additives for extra flavour and consistency, and is only worth doing if you exploit the economies of scale. That's fine if Tesco's Value at 80p a jar is what you are after, and there is much to be said for it. But if you want something a little better, and probably healthier, all you need to do is chop up some fruit and boil it with some sugar. The only other thing you need consider is what to put it in, and it couldn't be easier to log into freecycle and find someone nearby who is desperate to be relieved of the twenty jars they have been forgetting to recycle for the last six months.

We are lucky to have inherited a long row of raspberry bushes that borders the vegetable plot, and last year Ted had plucked them all before we moved in, so we had no idea how good they were. In September, Barbara set about pruning them using Google's advice. This involved, as far as I can remember, cutting all the branches and stems back to about two feet high and hoping for the best. The result was approximately forty feet of ragged and rather dead looking twigs that managed to survive the winter, and then responded well to the wet spring; becoming green, bushy and doubling in height by the start of the summer.

When several hour's worth of picking, boiling and decanting raspberries to make jam is compared to the three seconds it takes to pick a jar from a shelf and pop it in your trolley, it is easy to see why all this might be seen as boring, eccentric or unnecessarily laborious. In its defence I can only say that with the significant amount of hours that many labour saving devices have allowed me to reclaim over the years, I appear to have done nothing new or different.

One of Barbara's pipe dreams is to sell what she produces in some shape or form, and both my appetite and waist are testament to how good with food she is. Perhaps she will ply her wares from the back of her Skoda at car boot sales or maybe one day from a stall at a farmer's market, but it is early days and as the more cautious and methodical half of this relationship, Barbara will without doubt take time to let her dream evolve.

Last year we attempted to make jam with the plums from the orchard, and were successful in making two jars that lasted about six months. This year we produced on a slightly larger scale, and if Barbara's dream is to become a reality a number of things will need to happen including honing our skills, creating new and larger growing plots, better tools and some sort of a business plan.

We would also be well advised to look at our current harvesting process, which is modelled on the one for me and one for the basket method. I suspect we could double our production capacity without too much effort, but it might halve our fun.

For now though, I feel it is a good start to have produced almost twenty jars of delicious raspberry jam, all individually made with love and no artificial ingredients. As an amusement, we have also come up with a brand name and label derived from the artistic licence of this book and the reality of our life here.

Red's Rather Good jam will be consumed over the coming months and also given to friends as favours. And so as others strive for gold medals, this nascent cottage industry stands as our individual contribution to the Olympic summer of 2012.

Good Old Yellow Pages (5th August)

If practise makes perfect but familiarity breeds contempt, then I need to choose carefully which adage best describes how I feel about my new-found expertise in unblocking sewers. As we discovered less than a month after moving in, Ted had been deliberately dishonest about the condition of the private drainage system during the sale, afterwards becoming vague at first and then defensively protesting his innocence when the extent of the problem inevitably came to light. Now that I have spent a year 'up to my arms in it' on a weekly basis, I would willingly hold his nose in it if I could.

As he appeared none too keen to enter into a conversation about it, let alone come to any sort of mutually agreeable settlement, we started a calculated and strategic effort to wrest from him the money needed to both replace the clearly collapsed sewer and to install a soak-away that he had considered totally unnecessary for the better part of forty years.

As we already had intimate knowledge of some of the peculiarities of the United Kingdom's legal process, we suited up for battle silently, methodically and very thoroughly. In other words, we planned to make sure that so much shit would hit the fan, more than enough would stick.

As the new kids on the block, we had no recommendations for anyone local that we could ask. Furthermore, we had no idea of what would be involved in such a structural and potentially large job, and so we turned to the Yellow Pages. We placed a call to those chaps in Day-Glo pink and told them that it was just possible they could save our lives. They responded by turning up with their fancy van and hi-tech equipment, and started sucking their teeth immediately. By repeating the phrases "whatever it costs" and "money is really no object" several times, I managed to ensure that their eye-watering quote was almost three times higher than anyone else would come up with.

With butter that refused to melt in our mouths, we duly despatched a letter through our solicitors; Sue, Grabbit & Run. It was a polite but firm request for Ted to make good his promises. It comprised of independent expert witness advice, a few diagrams, some complex physics and measurements, several photos, the equivalent of some legal chin rubbing and Dyno Rod's quote. This would, we hoped, pulverise a nut with a sledgehammer whilst planting a seed, and therefore we were not surprised to hear nothing back for a while.

As with all games of Chicken, the hardest part is knowing when to blink, and after a number of weeks, we began to waver and wondered if we should check whether Royal Mail had been the weakest link in our chain. It hadn't been, and before we planned our next move we heard on the grapevine that Ted had died after a short illness.

We eventually received notification that our letter had indeed been received, but that it would be dealt with as and when other more pressing matters concerning Ted's estate had been finalised. It would take many months for t's to be crossed, i's to be dotted and fees to be earned, and so I busied myself with exploring private drainage options and getting less stratospheric quotes from a variety of local firms.

I was also perfecting the technique of clearing the 30-metre length of pipe, of which only 7 had not collapsed over the previous 40 years. There were a number of different methods requiring a variety of approaches and time, and all were equally unpleasant. Towards the spring of this year, I had refined the process into what I considered was the best way, and it was possible to clear a severely blocked drain in less than five minutes without breaking a sweat. I shall spare you the gory details, but suffice to say that it is an improvisation inspired by events at Fukushima, and perhaps Dyno-Rod could learn a thing or two from me.

Finally in March of this year, I received a four page letter from Ted's solicitors; Bodgit & Scarper, in which they outlined their thoughts. In no particular order of importance, they suggested that I was a nasty little chancer looking for a quick buck, that I really ought to engage better professional advice if I was going to survive in the adult world, that it was a low shot to attempt to sue a dead man and that I would be well advised to look up the meaning of the phrase 'Caveat Emptor'.

Somewhat taken aback by the tone, I continued wading through their legal diatribe until I reached the fourth page. There I found, whilst maintaining their client's innocence and stressing his unimpeachably good character, they concluded that they would be prepared to offer half the amount shown on Dyno-Rod's grossly overweight quote as a gesture of goodwill.

Given just how innocent they insisted Ted was and how distasteful and opportunistic they felt I was, it was not made clear why they felt the need to offer me a five thousand pound bung simply out of the goodness of their hearts. I accepted it regardless, noted that the architecture of their resolution stank of the DNA that the legal profession shares with politics, and engaged the services of a local drainage contractor without further ado.

Good old Yellow Pages. They don't just help with the nasty things in life like a blocked drain, they're there for the nice things too, you know.

Knowing Your Onions (19th August)

Charles Talbut Onions was a grammarian and lexicographer, and the author of the Shakespeare Glossary. This book, first published in 1911, is one that I spent many hours searching through during my three years at drama school, often in desperation. Sometimes in rehearsals a director would ask me a question like "so why does Parolles liken virginity to a withered pear?" Not having the faintest idea, I would dive into my copy of Onions (as it was commonly referred to) in the hope that whatever information it offered might somehow improve my performance. It never did, and the truth is that I rarely understood what Shakespeare was on about. Consequently the sum total of my acting in any of his plays was little more than an improvised combination of clenching my buttocks, speaking in my best telephone voice and attempting a bit of complex mental arithmetic in order to look thoughtful.

Herefordshire seems a very long way from the boards I once trod and the bard who still confuses me, and one of the truly delightful aspects of working the land is that you don't always need to understand why so much as know how. With regard to this, I have so far found the three most valuable resources are the Internet, common sense and elbow grease. It just so happens that a good example of this is the journey, from cradle to grave, of another kind of onion.

To start, you need to know how to plant and care for them, and Google told us to plant them in October at a depth of 5cm in 30cm intervals. This roughly equates to taking a step and shoving one into the earth as far as your forefinger will go, and that's about as scientific as it needs to be. Once this is done, all you need to do is make sure they have water and try to keep the weeds away. From October until March or April very little tending is needed, and as the green shoots start appearing it may be worth doing some general tidying around them, but that's about it.

The next step is to harvest them, and this is where Google is not too precise about the timing. Or rather, it is very precise in that it offers a great many conflicting opinions, and in the end we gambled on our instinct. I suspect that we pulled them out of the ground a few weeks later than we should, and as a result we have in the region of sixty or seventy rather enormous red and white onions. Despite their size, I can attest to their delicious flavour both raw and cooked.

We are not sure how long they will last, but we have been advised to keep them in a cool and dark place, and with any luck they may last through the winter and well into 2013. As the Cider Barn is probably the best place to store them, we needed to learn how to plait them so they could hang from the ceiling joists. Learning to plait is very much like understanding Shakespeare as far as I am concerned; if I read about it, I am left in the dark. However, if I watch it, I'll get it. For this reason, we are grateful to a YouTube video that shows just how easy it is to plait a length of onions.

With six plaits of varying length and quality now hanging in various parts of the Cider Barn, I believe Barbara and I have given a reasonable account of ourselves as smallholders in this instance, and look forward to improving our technique over the coming years.

In time we may come to learn why certain things happen in certain ways at certain times, but we're pretty sure that knowing how to make the best of it all will almost certainly be more useful when it comes to smallholding. It's hard to say whether we'll ever 'know our onions', but even Parolles would have to admit that our food producing cherry has well and truly been popped, and the wettest summer on record has resulted in just a few withered offerings on our Conference Pear tree. Never mind though; all's well that ends well.

Selective Affection (27th August)

Our neighbour, Andrew, is an avowed animal lover with very strong views, and scant regard for anyone else's. Although he keeps no livestock or pets, he feeds anything wild that he can including foxes and badgers, and the birds flock to him like the pied piper every morning in the field by his house. Since we have known him he has been looking after a one-winged crow and an orphaned wood pigeon "until they are well enough to release", and employs a complex system of nets and shrouds to prevent them from leaving. Evidently also a net curtain twitcher, he once gravely admonished me for not stopping my car on my way to work in order to move a flattened pheasant to the side of the road out of respect. When he saw that we were keeping chickens, he smiled ominously and said, "you do know that my foxes will try to get them, don't you?" He stopped smiling abruptly when I said, "Of course; that's their job. And it's my job to stop them."

In June we popped over to share a coffee and cake with him at his invitation, and were admiring his house and grounds while he was inside boiling the kettle. In particular, Barbara commented on a series of metal structures suspended from various trees and fences just by the kitchen. He said that they were to keep away "those bastard Sparrowhawks" that kept trying to eat the smaller songbirds that came to feed by his kitchen. He then explained that as these predators typically come swooping in low over his hedges, he had carefully positioned protective shields so that they would plough into them if they didn't abort their attack run. Barbara challenged him innocently; "Oh, but I thought you liked all animals?" Despite reiterating that he did, it would seem that he is just like the rest of us in being arbitrary about which animals he likes, which he doesn't and then selecting the data he needs to back up his choice.

I was reminded of this the other day, at the conclusion of a game of hide and seek between me and Mr Toad, that started a few weeks ago when I finally removed the rotting wooden floor of the last shed by the greenhouses, and in so doing accidentally demolished Toad Hall. I don't know how long he had lived under it, but given that the shed had been there for a good twenty years and toads can live even longer than that, it may be that his tenancy had been since birth.

When I first uncovered him and he made his presence known, I left him to his own devices thinking that he would simply pack his bags and thumb a lift elsewhere. I was mistaken. Perhaps he is old and frail, maybe he has poor eyesight or it could be that he is just rather unadventurous, but a few days later I found that he had rehoused himself a few feet away under a wheelie bin by the house.

It may well have seemed an ideal pied-à-terre, but he hadn't reckoned on the fact that his new home was mobile, and being exposed once a week was probably going to become very tiring for him. I expected he would move on again on rubbish collection day, but the next day he was still there when I returned the bin on my way past to the garage.

Had he ventured even only slightly from his position, he would have found a hedgerow fifteen feet away, and the vegetable garden at a further thirty feet, both places offering a far more varied and plentiful diet than the occasional passing earwig he was possibly going to get where he was. As he had shown absolutely no inclination to move, I decided to drop what I was working on and rehouse him then and there.

Using the essential toad-moving-kit of a piece of wood and my hand, he was quickly relocated to the herb garden where he would soon meet his new neighbours. As they are a lively community of beetles, slugs and worms, I hope he will find them rather appealing and spend a good deal of time chatting them up and then eating them. I have no idea if he'll like it in his new home or if the shock of the move will kill him, but I reasoned that he stands a better chance there and so I headed off feeling virtuous, loving and rather pleased with my efforts.

As I stopped in the workshop to collect what I needed to complete the job I had started earlier, I became conscious of my highly selective behaviour and began feeling a little ridiculous. I had just spent the best part of twenty minutes rehousing one single animal that hadn't wits to look after itself, and I was about to invest half that time killing thousands of other animals that had been frustrating me for months by transporting earth into a cavity that in time was going to cause me a problem.

Far from being an animal lover then, I am an animal user given that my affection is mostly available in exchange for what I get in return. I kill ants because they carry earth into the manholes that unchecked would cause a blockage to my sewer, but I encourage toads as I know they will eat the slugs in our vegetable garden. Neither is Barbara a true animal lover, as any spider around here would tell you if it lived long enough, but she enjoys the chickens as they provide amusement, eggs and an endless supply of excellent compost accelerant.

And it's not just something that happens on a personal level. Differing opinions everywhere are enshrined in national cultures through legislation that decrees which animals you may keep or kill for pleasure, which you may poison for convenience, which you may eat and which must be left to do as they please.

But, as selective and different in our affections as we all clearly are, I hope we can agree about the fly that arrives through an open window and immediately spends the next half an hour banging its head into the glass trying to get back out again.

Someone to Watch Over Me (2nd September)

From time to time over the last year, friends and colleagues of mine have remarked that the decision Barbara and I made to give up our urban life of comfort for one of rural remoteness has seemed more than a little eccentric, and perhaps we weren't really sure what we were doing. There have also been one or two comments made locally that echo this sentiment, and never far from mind is one of my favourite lines from Peter Ustinov's autobiography; "What more irrefutable proof of madness can there be than the inability to have a doubt?"

Whether sane or not, it was a decision made quite soberly and one which we have yet to regret. Any obvious doubts might arise from the fact that we have had to forgo a number of benefits; the income from a London-based executive position, proximity to friends and ease of travel to name but three. Even if there had been worries in these regards, smoothing them should be easy as we are continually told by the media that living in the country is so much cheaper than a city. This isn't the case by a long shot, and we can confirm that living in Herefordshire is slightly more expensive than living in Hanwell, so we count ourselves lucky that our aspirations are not wholly based on financial success.

However, I have felt something once or twice that has given me pause for thought: the isolation which can sometimes remind me that there is no one to call in an emergency. In more poetic and wine-fuelled moments I fancy we are being pioneering and edgy in our own way, but on other evenings when the line between solitude and loneliness blurs, that same edge can feel like a precipice, as we now live without anyone to watch over us. To fuel any uncertainty further, my work can often take me away for a week or more at a time and there is little that I can do from hundreds of miles away.

Perhaps these feelings are what drew me to a statue back in the spring. We had seen it on numerous visits to The Hop Pocket, a local craft centre where you can easily lose a few hours on a lazy Sunday afternoon browsing for bric a brac and tasting local cider and perry. Every time I saw it, I felt it was offering me a safe place beneath its outstretched arms; its hands holding any problems at bay. We now know that it is actually a piece of bronze mail order art called Olympic Man that is supposed to represent the focus and precision of a coiled spring. Obviously I prefer my own interpretation, and it was our gift to each other to celebrate Rather's birthday.

With no history to compare to his present circumstances, Rather is naturally unaware that the world presents any kind of a challenge beyond food, sleep and poop. So far he has a generally calm disposition with few outbursts, and is very much given to frowning deeply in quiet and dribbling contemplation. Like any infant, he automatically trusts everything around him and will in time, no doubt, learn to be suspicious of his surroundings through his daily encounters with them.

Before then he needs someone, specifically us, to watch over him. Those of you with children will know how everything in our lives has changed as he spends not one minute unsupervised when awake and every minute worried about while he sleeps. This level of focus and concern will only increase when he starts to crawl and his curiosity helps him to discover how many sharp and dangerous things there are at Stone House.

One of the challenges for us is to keep some sense of the couple that we used to be before he arrived, and with a regular bedtime Rather gives us a little bit of time each evening after he has settled for the night. Thanks to the generosity of Barbara's mother, our Angelcare monitor constantly watches over him for us, keeping track of the ambient temperature, sending us an audio and video feed and always ready at a moment's notice to alert us if his breathing becomes troubled for any reason.

With this peace of mind, we have an hour or so to press the parental pause button and unwind over a glass of wine before turning in for the night. As we sleep, the monitor stands guard and when Rather stirs in the small hours, there is just enough of a soft glow in the room for him to make out a dark outline on the headboard of his crib. One day he will recognise it as the face of Bob Marley, the man who gave him his middle name, and whose spirit we hope also watches over us all.

Who Pays the Price? (9th September)

This letter is the final chapter in a long running saga about raw sewage where no one really knows what's going on, business avoids responsibility, the media wants a story and the residents spend too much time up to their knees in it. Partly in jest and partly as a tribute, I have named it after a case study that I have worked with for many years and for which I have a new found appreciation. It is also the second stage in the quest to provide Rather with a room of his own, which began last autumn.

It has taken thirteen months to get our private drainage system sorted, and thanks to two local contractors and a fat cheque from Ted's estate, Stone House now has a functioning and hygienic drainage system that is efficient and as kind as possible to the local environment. There still remain one or two minor aspects to iron out, and these are in hand. As well as being a very steep learning curve, project managing this contract has also changed my mind about the annual rates charged by water companies.

It's clearly a crime that so much fresh water is wasted through under-investment and a crumbling network of poorly maintained pipes that bring us water, but I'd like to make a plea to those of you who are connected to a mains sewage system to recognise that it's usually a case of out of sight, out of mind when you flush; and paying for something that you don't acknowledge the complexities of will always rankle.

With this rather technical entry that outlines the extent of what we have had to realise here, I like to suggest that the part of a normal water bill that is generally not moaned about is rather good value. The clever bit, as I've discovered, is that the while your fresh water arrives under pressure, the whole drainage and sewage removal and treatment process, whether public or private, stays far cheaper and easier to maintain than it could be by carefully exploiting gravity.

The first stage is to put some distance between you and your waste for obvious reasons. The main sewer connecting our house to its septic tank had collapsed many years ago, meaning frequent and regular blockages. As it was dug up, it became clear that not only had it failed completely, but sadly the seeds of its demise were sown the very day it was installed. Now it has been replaced with a modern plastic one, and the weekly unblocking routine should be a thing of the past.

The pipe needs to be laid at a very precise angle because, and there is no nice way of saying this, you want solids and liquids to travel at exactly the same speed. If the angle is even slightly out, the whole set up is redundant as either nothing moves or you get a similar phenomenon happening inside the pipe that you see offshore just before a tsunami; fish, normally suspended in water, are left high and dry on the sea bed by the ocean retreating faster than they can swim.

Once safely through the main sewer, everything arrives at and drops into the second stage; the septic tank itself. An invention of almost 200 years ago that is simply two adjacent chambers connected by a filter, it uses time and gravity to separate solid from liquid, the former being unable to pass through the filter into the second chamber. The liquid in the second chamber must then pass from the tank and be gently fed back into the earth via a soak-away system, the solids that remain requiring annual removal by a professional contractor.

The third stage is the soak-away where the liquid is returned to the ground. Rather than going to the bother of installing such a system, Ted chose to connect the outflow from the septic tank to the storm drains on the road outside, and simply mix his household waste with rainwater. As a result we had to start this stage from scratch, and this is where we found that the topography of the land worked against us.

Stone House sits at the lowest corner of its plot, and so a new trench had to be dug uphill and a pipe and pump were installed to carry wastewater from the septic tank up across the field to a new chamber. By gravity it then flows into the soak-away, and from there back into the soil, eventually re-joining the water table below.

The pump was going to need a power supply, and we quickly found that no electrician was prepared to touch Ted's existing wiring and fusebox, which would not have looked out of place on Khao San Road in Bangkok. We had always known that the house would need to be rewired sooner rather than later, and so we consider it a bonus that it had to be included in this project.

The soak-away itself is a five hundred foot trench dug five feet deep and two feet wide that distributes wastewater over a surface area so large that it avoids creating a bog and can be naturally filtered by the soil. The trench is filled with small stones on which rests a pipe, the bottom half of which is made rather like a colander. The pipe needs to be absolutely level so that it fills evenly with wastewater, which then seeps down into the stones below. Both pipe and stone are then covered with plastic sheeting, and the earth and topsoil are replaced above so that it is hidden completely from view.

Due to the nature of soil, and in particular any soil with a high clay content, soak-aways can never be guaranteed. In time, the gaps between the stones may become clogged, causing it to stop working. Whether this happens in a couple of years or more is anyone's guess, and when it does we'll need to add more sections of fresh stone and new pipe to keep the system working and to prevent flooding.

With this work now complete we have levelled the earth, reseeded grass and find ourselves in possession of an enormous mound of excavated earth from the building of the soak-away which we shall keep for future landscaping projects.

When compared to the workload of the last year, it should simply be straightforward annual maintenance and monthly monitoring from now on. However, if I could exchange all of the above for the price of a typical water bill that included connection to a public sewer, I would do so without hesitation.

Déjà Vu (16th September)

In the last few weeks we have seen a little more than usual of Farmer Harris as the big field yielded its second crop of hay for the year. Preferring to take a chance rather than arrange a mutually convenient time, the first I usually know of his arrival is the clatter and rattle of one of the ancient tractors from his collection on the road outside, and I often wonder how many times he has turned up and found no one home. After a toot of the horn and a wave, I open the gate to let him in, we exchange a few words about the weather and local news, and he carries on with whatever job he has planned.

He and his sons eschew the more modern tractor and farm machinery for reasons of practicality and enjoyment; their farm being spread across a great number of separate smaller fields like ours. The state-of-the-art leviathans that most farmers around here use would be almost certainly be a case of costly overkill, added to which his son Jacko derives great pleasure from tinkering around with their old machines to keep them running sweetly.

To my complete surprise the other week, he came to finish the hay with some wonderful old machinery being towed behind a tractor of his that I had not seen before, but instantly recognised from my younger years; the Ford Series 4000 from the late 1960's. It is this model of tractor that my grandfather used on the land where he lives and worked in upstate New York. It is a bullet-proof three-cylinder workhorse that pulls, pushes, cuts and drags almost anything you ask it to without ever skipping a beat. His was the one on which, with a beaming smile in 1979, he encouraged me to take my first accompanied and then solo driving experiences under his watchful gaze and infectious laugh.

Enjoying my brief moment of nostalgia, I studied the lines and creases in Farmer Harris' face as he pointed out the dents, oil leaks and crude repairs that added to the tractor's undeniable charm. I wondered how long he had been working the fields in this area, and so I asked him if he was from these parts. "Oh heavens no", he cried, "I'm from Bockleton."

163

Smiling at our obviously polarised views on what constitutes a great distance, it seems he had moved here from all of twelve miles away in 1938 at the age of eight, and had started working shortly afterwards. He spoke fondly of the time when the now dismantled Worcester-to-Leominster railway brought hop pickers to the area by the hundreds, and went on to describe how prisoners from the second world war were drafted to work the land. With a twinkle in his eye, he concluded our brief chat with a considered comparative comment about the working styles of Germans and Italians before climbing back on the tractor. Then, with a chuckle, he headed off to the field dragging his ancient hay making equipment as he went.

He started off by criss-crossing the field and raking the hay into long rows ready for the next stage, and then paused while I offered him some tea and one of the few plums that the tree has given us this year. Next he attached the baling machine and set off once more. It whirred and clanked as it chewed the hay, weaved it into a bale and finally spat it out into a large metal frame that was dragged on the ground behind. As soon as eight bales were in the frame, a lever was tripped and one complete layer was left behind on the ground, ready to be piled up into a stack during the final stage.

Several hours later, the field was a fresh minty green carpet, and the scent of the four or five haystacks that dotted the landscape was almost irresistible. I'd never climbed up a haystack as a child, and as Farmer Harris was preparing to leave, I was tempted to ask him if he would mind if I did. Instead I helped him with the last bit of clearing up and we exchanged a little more idle chitchat about old tractors and driving lessons. Then, and as his tea was calling from down the road, he disappeared as fast as the old Ford would take him.

Every Little Helps (23rd September)

We live twelve miles from the nearest train station, eighteen miles from the nearest big town and eighty miles from the nearest city and airport. With distances like this and no public transport we have increasingly become reliant on Internet and mail order shopping, although we have yet to fully embrace the supermarkets' home delivery services. You shop and we drop a vague approximation of your order was the level of choice we had in London, and it's hard to imagine Ledbury or Malvern will offer anything different.

Obviously this is part of the deal that we made when we moved here, and we are both pleased and relieved that we still do not miss any of the conveniences that London offered us. The local town, some five miles away, has one Chinese delivery service and four restaurants which pretty much fit the bill with our dining out habits. Even the pangs for Dominos Pizza and Subway have finally subsided after two years of cold turkey.

The only possible exception to this might be that we can no longer pop to Ikea on a whim to buy the hundreds of tea-lights and dozens of pillar candles that are our staple diet every year when the days get shorter. The prospect of a winter without these is as daunting as the idea of driving 160 miles just to buy them, and so a creative approach to this purchase will be needed. The list writing, detail-focussed among you will instantly know that the obvious solution lies in planning ahead and combining journeys, something which I find a challenge probably because it carries the faint whiff of multi-tasking.

So necessity being the mother of invention as it invariably is, Barbara decided to invent a new method of food shopping by flagging down a passing ice cream van that was heading home from tempting children at the local campsite. It was during one of the last warm days in August, and she had spotted it coming up the lane behind the field, its sign clearly visible above the hedge. Her instincts told her it was likely to turn right at the pub and come past the front of the house and, like a bear waiting for a salmon, all she had to do was stand by the road and look hungry with pleading eyes. Luckily for us it did come our way, but it sped past at great speed before she made it to the roadside, and so our hearts sank as our 99 flakes flashed before our eyes and disappeared.

However, the eagle-eyed driver had spotted Barbara's desperate waving from the lawn, and presumably in an effort to wrest as much profit from the sodden summer as possible, had stopped and done a u-turn before pulling up at our gate a short while later. It took Barbara a good five minutes to inspect the menu and make her selection whilst chatting to the vendor, who turned out to be a local who ran this and one other van with her husband. On her recommendation we both chose an oversized ice cream that ended up in our mouths, on our faces and down our fronts in more or less equal measure.

We were thrilled to discover that an isolated position allows you a vantage point from which to ambush and lasso passing food when you get hungry, and we thanked her with obvious delight. As she drove off I couldn't help but wonder if she might make a point of slowing down and playing her chimes as she passes us in the future, and, more importantly, whether or not the same trick could be made to work with lorries from Majestic Wine Warehouse.

Jordan, Jade & Jodie; our first three hens in January 2012

An angel flies in to Stone House in February 2012

Farmer Harris trimming the hedges in February 2012

Sunrise and mist by the Cider Barn in March 2012

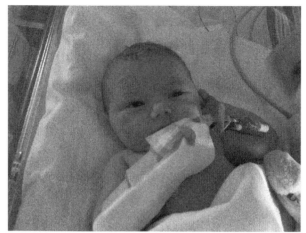

Rather Good on 24th May 2012

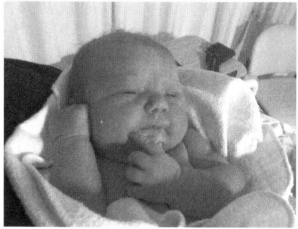

Jolly Good on 18th November 2013

The bench from A Walk in the Woods in April 2013

Barbara taking a 5am stroll with coffee in July 2013

Earth, Wind & Fire (7th October)

I grew up on a strict diet of no television and a steady supply of books. The shelves in my room were lined with typical children's titles by Laura Ingalls Wilder, E.B. White and Enid Blyton. My imagination was fuelled by these stories, and as a result I have a vivid and romantic idea of what outdoor life should be like. In my dreams, the heat of Blyton's summers mix with the playfulness of White's adventures and this mixture is set against the sheer scale of challenge and possibility from the prairies of the American Midwest.

Life, as we know, isn't quite like it is in the movies or the books and even though Wilder's are autobiographical, I am unlikely to either meet or succeed against the odds that Charles Ingalls faced on almost every day of his life. By comparison, mine has so far been a life of luxury, excess and soft hands and I imagine I shall continue to consider myself a bumbling amateur on the gentler slopes of a learning curve. This feeling is never more acute than when I see someone doing something that I can't do, doing it with ease and doing it with more equipment than I have.

I have learned to light a fire with relative ease, and having once lit one beneath the central heating oil tank at my parents' house many years ago, it could be said that I have an attraction to fire that, although strong, stops short of outright pyromania. I cannot, however, light a fire in the rain using green wood. But the man who owns the field on the opposite side of the B4220 can. What's more, he gets to do it on a huge scale using a JCB digger to pile up enormous amounts of branches, cuttings and undergrowth. It's not just the wood around here that's green, I can tell you.

During the winter of 2010, Barbara and I discovered how hard it was to use a fireplace with a chimney that didn't draw air, and last year we tackled the problem of trying to get heat from a fire made with damp wood. Clearly I am making progress in my fire lighting skills, but with my neighbours able to produce something that Aeneas would have easily noticed from his ship as he sailed away from Carthage, I am now hungry to climb further up the slope of my learning curve.

Leaving aside the removal of fences and trees in preparation for future land development, Stone House produces enough green waste on an annual basis to make recycling it logistically impossible. Even if we were able to transport it, the cost would be prohibitive and so I now understand why farmers continually burn throughout the autumn, and it's something I need to learn to do safely.

As usual, I turned to Google, reasoning that if it could tell me how best to mount an insurgency using fertiliser and sticky back plastic, it must be able to tell me how to light and control a fire in the wet. It did, and armed with a large tub of Vaseline and some cotton balls stolen from Rather's nappy changing table, I set out the other day to test the instructions.

I planned everything from what I would burn through to where I would burn it. I chose some dry wood that I had stored for a few months to start it, and had several mountains of cuttings to pile on top once the fire had got going. Four cotton balls wiped in Vaseline were all it took to get going, and as soon as the fire took hold I realised my mistake: I had carefully studied how to start it, but not how to control it once it was going. Nor, it seems, have I much common sense at times.

Lighting an outdoor fire on a day with winds gusting up to 30 miles an hour in no way can be described as sensible. Add to that, my location was right between the Cider Barn and the Animal Shelter, meaning the wind swirled every which way in a highly unpredictable fashion. The fire was manageable in its early stages, but after I had piled quite a bit of vegetation on top, it dried out very quickly and the flames trebled in size coming very close to the Cider Barn. It quickly became clear that managing it was going to require reflexes and acrobatic skills that I don't, and probably never could, possess.

On the positive side, the wind made the fire burn at such an astonishing rate, that it didn't last long at all. On the downside, as it burnt and started to create ash; the wind picking up glowing embers and distributing them pretty much everywhere within a hundred foot radius. For about twenty minutes I ran in large circles like a wheezing hippo, stamping out hot embers as they rained down on the grass.

It calmed down after I had run for what seemed like a marathon, although it was probably less than half an hour. The wind continued to remove the ash as soon as it formed which kept the coals glowing brightly, and before too long what had started as a pile about ten feet wide and seven feet tall had been reduced to a small pile barely wider than a foot or two. I returned to the house in a sober mood, feeling lucky to have learned yet another valuable lesson without having caused any lasting or irreparable damage. Hopefully that will continue to be the way of my world.

Seasonal Affective Order (14th October)

Anyone looking down from an aircraft flying high over the British Isles on a sunny and cloudless day will see for themselves that there are more shades of green to be found here than almost anywhere else in the world. When viewed from a closer vantage point, much of this country is quite staggeringly beautiful; whether you are standing on Holkham Beach in Norfolk, meandering along the Gower Peninsula in South Wales or taking a river cruise through the heart of London late at night.

However, I find the beauty of these places conditional on the presence of decisive, or even extreme weather. Hot sunny days seem to bring the best out of British cities, and stories showing pale-skinned office workers wearing sunglasses and sitting in parks during their lunch breaks are a staple diet for news programmes. Equally, the picturesque beauty of The Cotswolds, where Barbara and I spent a year, is as stunning in the heat as it is at ten below freezing, which it was for almost a whole month during the winter of 2010. Sadly, none of these places are able to thrill me on a dull, windy and wet day, which is a shame given that this forecast is arguably the most accurate for the majority of the time.

With the possible exception of the Malvern Hills, the countryside around Stone House lacks any of the obvious beauty of these other places, and the cities of Worcester and Hereford, whilst perfectly pleasant, functional and accessible, have little about them that feels vital. However this area has one particular quality that, in my experience, it shares only with the Highlands and Islands of Scotland; the ability to be just as beautiful in average and indecisive weather as it is in extremes.

Granted this may just be because it's now our home, but every once in a while I turn a corner and am confronted with an ordinary view that takes my breath away, just as I was the other morning. I saw no grand scale, no glorious architecture and no remarkable natural features. Just the Cider Barn, the large tree next to it, some wooden fences and a bright rising sun burning off the morning mist.

I am not exactly clear on the meteorological reasons for mist and fog, but I seem to remember it's something to do with cold air hitting warm ground (or possibly vice versa). Whichever way around it is, those circumstances had conspired to produce a stunning view at sunrise as I went to let the chickens out. As they clucked and fussed in the mud around my feet, I stood perfectly still for five minutes or so, doing absolutely nothing except drinking it in.

The strength of the sun is now fading from one day to the next, and as I left the chickens to their feed, I saw that nature clearly knows this and no animal is currently busier than the spider. It's as though they know the insects are getting fewer in number, and this has resulted in a flurry of activity wherever you look. Every gate, every tree and every shrub and hedgerow glistens with their dewy webs in a mad dash to take advantage of nature's end of season sale.

Such is their rush that there are almost no vacant places left to build a web, which has meant that their efforts look rather ramshackle. Along the boundary between the vegetable garden and the field, I started to count the individual webs that covered the hedge and got bored once I had passed seventy. On the terrace outside the Cider Barn, the bustling arachnid shanty town continued and it was like a shop window the day before Halloween with each and every section of the wire fence decorated by a web, made highly visible by the moisture in the air.

The industry of these animals seemed to be bordering on the frantic, matching the hectic pace of local harvesting. What had previously been nothing more than irritating pests creating a higher than normal need for indoor dusting at a certain time of the year, had become an occasion for outdoor delight, although I fear we are many years away from Barbara describing a spider with such generosity.

With the exception of those at discount sofa shops, all sales must come to an end. Soon the insects will disappear and the temperatures will continue to drop as we head inexorably towards winter, and the cycle will then begin again. As I wandered back inside to a hot mug of coffee, I reflected that Autumn, once little more to me than the Summer's epilogue and Winter's prologue stewed together in water with leaves, had finally proved itself to me to be a season of value in its own right.

Plan B (21st October)

With the growing season all but at an end, my outdoor efforts are now directed towards maintenance and preparation for next year. Specifically, this means that at the moment the grass and vegetable garden are blocking out everything else on my radar. For many months of the year, the grass is a constant time thief that I cannot ignore, and having asked more of it that it could give this summer, I lost the services of my tractor for most of August while parts of the engine were replaced. As a result, I have concluded that I really do need something up my sleeve to make sure I never again allow my temperament to be controlled by the absolute certainty that grass will grow. Thankfully it will soon not need any of my time until next spring, giving me a few months in which to come up with a solution. The vegetable garden has, for our first full summer of residency, been remarkably kind to us. With our limited skill, and our focus being very much on Rather, we have still been able to produce a reasonable harvest. Having given little time to the maintenance and upkeep of the plot throughout the summer, we were faced with metre-tall weeds pretty much covering the ground after our harvest. Clearly these would all need to be removed so that I could till the soil, add manure and prepare it for sowing onions and garlic before the winter sets in.

With laziness as my ever-present watchword and Barbara's full agreement, I decided to combine both these tasks and ask the rotavator to chomp its way up and down the garden. I had visions of doing this two or three times in order to be sure that all the weeds were chopped finely and folded into the moist soil, where they could decompose over the winter. How wrong my vision turned out to be.

The rotavator has sixteen blades attached to its axle in four rows about three inches apart, looking a bit like a larger version of the teeth in an normal household blender. I have previously made mention of how sticky Herefordshire mud can be and I also know how strong weeds can be. Through the beauty of hindsight, I can now assert with absolute conviction that between these three facts can lay a perfect storm.

I set off with the sun on my back and a smug smile on my face, and before I had got five feet I could see that the weeds in front of me were being cut down perfectly. What I could not see was that they were being wrapped around the axle and then being cemented into position with mud. Blissfully unaware, I made it about halfway around the vegetable garden before the huge spinning clump of mud and weeds grew too big and jammed itself against the axle housing. Everything ground to a sudden halt with the clutch screaming out for mercy, I cut the engine and allowed a small "oops" to escape my lips. Glancing beneath to confirm that all had indeed gone completely Pete Tong, I wrestled the machine onto the paving slabs at the side of the garden before wandering off to the workshop in search of inspiration. The best I could think of was try cutting through the weeds with a Stanley knife, but it was clear this was futile. With the same air of innocence that a Labrador might employ when leaving the scene of some kitchen crime, I parked the machine back in the garage and disappeared to Spain for a week's work hoping that things might look better when I came home.

Predictably, things look exactly the same on my return, and as yesterday morning dawned bright and chilly, there was no time like the present to carry on with this job. Wondering how I could keep the same problem from happening again, the logical step seemed to be to reduce the amount of weeds in the vegetable garden. I thought this could best be achieved by mowing them down with the recently repaired tractor, which took only fifteen minutes, and I was left with a patch of ground almost clear of all weeds. Ready to start tilling the soil once more, I manoeuvred the rotavator into its starting position at the top corner of the plot, and used a crowbar to prise off the dried mud and weeds that had been wrapped around the axle for the last week. Progress was slow but sure, and my efforts left me ready and raring to go. With a full tank of fuel and higher hopes, I set off again and was pleased to see the blades immediately digging deep into the relatively weed-free soil. After precisely one full lap of the plot, the clutch began squeaking like before and this time even some smoke appeared. As I was sure that no weeds were wrapping themselves around the axle, it could be nothing more than the mind-bogglingly adhesive properties of Herefordshire mud. For once I was right, and the blades had mixed the mud into one wide log. There was nothing for it except to stop and dig it out the every time it jammed.

Clearly this was going to get frustrating and boring in equal measure, and at times like these I seize on any chance to make things easier and quicker. On this particular occasion, this meant minimising the amount of bending over that I needed to do, and so I quickly learned to tip the machine on it's nose to bring the clogged blades closer to hand. What I had not realised was that by tipping the machine in this way, I was also upturning the oil reservoir. After running the engine for a half hour or so, it had properly warmed up and the oil had lost all of its viscosity. On my third or fourth maintenance stop, oil had managed to find itself in parts of the engine where it really shouldn't be. This meant that on restarting the engine, it belched out clouds of blue oily smoke for a few minutes before it burnt off. Even Rather, who spent the morning in his pram overseeing my efforts, looked suitably impressed.

Several hours later, the job was done to an acceptable degree. This is one of those occasions where persistence won over poor skill, and having already overworked the tractor once, it is only thanks to Lady Luck that we still have a working rotavator. We will need to speak with Farmer Harris, or one of our other neighbours, to find out how they manage their soil, but I imagine it almost certainly require the formulation of a 'Plan B' which I find very exciting, as I cannot see how it won't involve new, and probably bigger, machinery.

Under Pressure (28th October)

Hindsight is a wonderful thing, and I am often taken by Woody Allen's thoughts on the benefit of living life backwards. As impossible and delightful as his idea is, I shall nonetheless rejoice in an unexpected, but now totally obvious, benefit of living at Stone House that has only recently revealed itself to me. Someone more savvy than I may well find the following predictable, but they would also have missed out on the frisson of excitement that the discovery brought me, and I am a man who takes his pleasure where it lies.

When we arrived here, the survey carried out on the house revealed that the boiler was on its last legs. Last winter we had it serviced, but this summer when the engineer strongly hinted that he was not far from slapping a 'condemned' sticker on it, we felt we had no choice but to bite the bullet and replace the whole system. After three or four quotes, Barbara and I selected a local company to install a brand-spanking-new boiler which would give us instant hot water and the most efficient fuel economy.

Right from the start we ran into some unforeseen problems that were only obvious afterwards. Almost every property in this area uses either oil or LPG to fire their boilers, as is the norm in rural locations. I say 'almost' as we are lucky to be connected to the mains gas supply, which is a result of two happy coincidences. First, the main pipe that carries gas from Worcester to Hereford runs right past us, and second, Ted rather cleverly approached the workmen during its installation back in the 1970's with a bottle or two of something strong in his hand, and struck a deal to get the house connected.

With the difference in prices and the interruptions to deliveries caused by weather making oil and LPG considerably more expensive and problematic, we feel delighted at our luck, and cross our fingers that it may last as long as possible.

Three young men arrived in the early part of September to start the work, and began by trying to turn the gas supply off. They couldn't and when they looked for a reason, they promptly froze when they saw an odd looking set of pipes jutting out of the ground just by the boundary with the road. It is a governor that converts the national grid gas pressure of 6 bar to the domestic gas pressure of 50 millibar which, to give some context, is a bit like putting a transformer on the side of Sellafield so you can plug your kettle in. It hadn't been touched in years, and had corroded quite badly. So had the emergency shut-off valve on the side of the house, and this meant that neither could be turned off in an emergency.

As soon as Transco had attended and rectified the problems, the engineers started their work and over the course of 72 hours and as many cups of tea and coffee, succeeded in removing our ancient boiler and installing a hi-tech low energy combination one. There was a fair bit of bodging to do behind walls and under floors in order to make the old pipes accept the new system, but they got it done and we now hope to see a significant reduction in our gas bills, especially in the summer months.

My work frequently requires very early morning starts, and having a system that is capable of heating water instantly rather than requiring hours to do so is an obvious benefit. Equally attractive is the cost saving made by neither heating nor storing unnecessary hot water, and with the removal of the old cylinder we have gained a new airing cupboard as well.

With the entire house now being pressurised directly from the water mains, it also affords us a new sense of luxury. Just as with gas, it seems that the water mains in this area operate at similarly high pressure, presumably thanks to gravity bringing our water all the way down from the reservoirs around Rhayder in Wales. As a result our shower has transformed from a pitiable series of drips into the kind of thing health spas boast about in their brochures, and a five minute shower can produce enough steam to fill the whole ground floor whilst leaving you feeling massaged and invigorated all over.

Thankfully it doesn't remove the skin from your back, but it probably would do if the shower head was on the narrowest setting. As a result, we have been advised to fit a pressure-reducing valve, similar to the gas governor, to make sure that all our appliances are not overly stressed and we are isolated from any fluctuations in the mains pressure.

Only now does it seem obvious to me that one of the beautiful things about living in the middle of nowhere is that 'nowhere' is actually halfway between here and there.

Chicken & Mushroom (4th November)

A few years ago I happened to be working in Bristol and staying at what must have been a rather upmarket boutique hotel near the city centre. I arrived on a Sunday afternoon, had a client meeting immediately after checking in and then, rather than explore the local restaurants, opted to have a quick meal in the hotel's restaurant. With a cursory glance I chose the set menu for reasons of speed, and all went well until the dessert arrived in the form of a perfectly spherical portion of bacon-flavoured ice cream. It was green, cold, wet and did indeed taste of bacon. Thanks to this, each of my five senses spontaneously attacked me before, during and after the first and only bite that I took. I managed to swallow it before throwing in the towel and pinning what remained of my appetite on the complimentary biscuits in my room.

Ever since I can remember, I have had a particular relationship with food which means it's all guilt and no pleasure. As a result, I tend to busily scoff rather than deliberately enjoy my food, and have never been very curious about the history of it or the origins of dishes. Recently however, I have spent a little time thinking about the more common pairings of certain flavours; leek & potato, carrot & coriander and tomato & basil being three such examples. It's quite possible that somewhere in the mists of time someone had arrived at these pairings after exhaustive gustative tests, but I now like to think I have evidence to suggest that some pairings are nothing more than natural selection.

One weekend, a month or so ago, I went into the chicken enclosure to clean out their house and change their bedding. It was hard not to notice on arrival that a huge number of mushrooms had appeared overnight, and were so plentiful that it was almost impossible to avoid stepping on them. It was clearly as much of a surprise for the chickens as it was for me, and whilst Jordan dared to inspect them at close quarters, the others kept a respectful distance throughout the week or so that they were there.

A quick recce revealed that mushrooms had appeared nowhere else at Stone House in such numbers; in fact only two solitary and rather sad examples had popped up on the lawn in front of the house, and so I offer this as something approaching scientific proof that mushrooms simply like growing in chicken poop. I conclude that where you find one, it is likely you will find the other.

I therefore would like to propose a theory that once upon a time an unknown hungry diner went out to catch a chicken for their pot, found it as hard to corner one as we do, and accidentally gathered up a few mushrooms during the ensuing successful scuffle. Once back in their kitchen, it was a case of pluck, gut and pop it into the pot, and the mushrooms accidentally went in too. The result was very tasty, and quickly passed into culinary folklore as it is now a cornerstone of the western diet. Whether it's pies, soups or main courses, the pairing of chicken with mushroom is as ubiquitous as salt and pepper.

The next time you find yourself in a restaurant, you will probably have a choice between something artful dreamt up by a molecular gastronomist or a glorious accident of nature. Whatever you choose, I'm sure it will be wonderful, but if cooking is about pleasing all the senses, I shall continue to avoid bacon ice cream at least until I've seen a green pig, and a flying one at that.

Orchard Boot Camp (25th November)

Stone House boasts a rather grand sounding Apple Orchard, which is made up of some fifteen trees that produce anywhere from zero to a gazillion Vilberie apples each year. To anyone who doesn't have the time, inclination or aptitude to make cider, these are a complete waste as they are virtually useless for any other purpose. Thankfully, the wetter the summer, the smaller the fruit harvest; and so I consider this year's almost non-existent harvest a silver lining on the cloud that continues to be the torrential flooding of 2012.

Clearly living in Herefordshire and not making cider is an act of heresy similar in magnitude to that of living in Chelsea and not wearing items of fashion made by Gucci, Prada or Versace, and it would seem that we are destined to swim against the local tide in many respects for a long time. Not only do we not make cider, but as the trees are at the end of their productive life, I have plans to convert the entire orchard into firewood and replace it with something altogether tastier in due course.

The approaching Christmas break from travelling will herald a tree massacre on an unprecedented scale for me, and as I am sure to need help, I shall be press-ganging unsuspecting visitors and houseguests into forced labour. If shameless coercion fails, I will switch to overt manipulation involving leg irons and songs that all start with "I don't know but I've been told, cider tastes like slime and mould".

Preparation and skill being always in short supply around here, I took it upon myself to find out exactly what this sort of work might entail, as chopping down a tree might not be as simple as it sounds. After finishing the hay in September, Farmer Harris had asked if I wouldn't mind pruning the large tree by the Cider Barn so he could get his tractor underneath it next year. I think it's a Lime, but can't be sure as it's somewhat larger than most of the ones I can compare it with on Google Image, and the four large and low-hanging branches that he was referring to looked enormous as well as the ideal proving ground for my amateur tree surgery skills.

With a quiet weekend in October at my disposal, and having purchased a sawhorse and hardhat on eBay, I had all I needed for a day's testosterone-fuelled manliness complete with swagger, sweat and swearing. Fancying myself as every woman's 'bit of rough' during their 11.30am Diet Coke break, I created my stage by wheeling every piece of machinery I could think of that might be useful, and a few that might not, into position on the hard standing between the Cider Barn and the Animal Shelter. I was ready to convert four thirty-foot long branches into firewood and kindling.

Once at the tree, I quickly decided that cutting one of these branches was just a larger version of trimming the stem of a rose. The lowest was a foot or so above my head, and so I duly fired up the chainsaw, lifted it above my head and attempted to 'snip' the foot-thick branch by cutting diagonally upwards. Once I had managed to cut through about ninety per cent of the branch, gravity lent a hand and the branch began to sag earthwards, squashing and silencing the chainsaw as it descended.

I transformed from macho man into spoilt brat in less than five seconds as I pulled, pushed, twisted and shoved the chainsaw in an effort to remove it from the vice like grip of the branch. Oddly enough, whilst throwing a tantrum never got me anywhere as a young child, it worked splendidly well on this occasion, and after a minute-long hissy fit, the chainsaw was released. I am glad that Rather didn't see this display, but I suspect that won't stop him developing a similar trait in time.

The branch was now resting on the ground but still attached to the tree, and to complete the job I needed to get the saw above the cut. All I could think using was a small stepladder, and this indeed proved to be the solution; although not perhaps the best one. I positioned it to give me the best access to the cut, started the saw and clambered up the steps. The combination of my not inconsiderable weight and the softness of the ground conspired to give me only a very short time at the right altitude to cut through the branch. I estimated that I would have sunk to ground level after thirty seconds or so, and I was pleased to cut through the branch in much less time. It didn't take too long to dig the ladder out of the mud either.

Cutting the branches down was one thing, and dragging them to the hard standing where the sawhorse had been set up was quite another. I tried having a tantrum again, but this time it didn't work, and I found that cutting each of the four branches into more manageable lengths was the best way forward. By the time I had finished dragging all the pieces some twenty feet across muddy and wet grass, the day was more than half gone. The sawhorse was remarkably easy to use; a waist-high metal trench on sturdy legs, with a guide to measure the length of each cut and the chainsaw fixed in a hinge on one end of it. I simply sliced through the branches a bit like a butcher shaving thick slices of a ham. Behind me as I worked was stacked the six tonnes of seasoned firewood that we had bought for this winter, and the green wood I was cutting was piled separately in an area next to it. To prevent it causing another chimney fire, we will have to let it season for a year or so before we can use it.

After a long day's hard work, I had produced enough firewood for perhaps a week at best and enough kindling to light five or six fires. Given that I have yet to split the logs, it is hardly economic on any level, but it is strangely satisfying. Regardless of any beneficial impact on my sense of virility, I noted that cutting the whole orchard down was a task not just slightly, but significantly beyond my means, resources and strength. As I nursed my sore back in a hot bath that evening, I wondered if whoever coined the phrase; "you can never have too many friends" had an orchard to cut down. More than likely, I concluded.

Life in the Fast Lane (9th December)

During our year in Gloucestershire we had our first experience with rural Internet connections, but it wasn't until we arrived at Stone House that we really learned what an oxymoron the term 'broadband' can be. Whilst in London, we had never needed to worry as everything from Dominos Pizza to Data simply arrived in a stream at our front door, and all we had to do was let it in. When we left in 2010, we had been signed up to the cheapest package BT offered which, at 3MB, provided more than enough bandwidth for our relatively pedestrian needs. Emails, eBay, news, some browsing and the occasional YouTube video or upload of a large file seemed to be all we ever did, and it was one of those things that never appeared on our radar. In Cirencester we experienced a halving of the speed of the BT Broadband service, but it didn't really affect us too much. The biggest impact was to raise our awareness that it might be an issue given the remote areas in which we were looking to live. During the process of buying Stone House, Ted had warned us that there wasn't even an option to have broadband in the area. We felt sure that the problem could be solved somehow, and in any event there was always satellite broadband even if it was significantly more expensive to use.

On moving in and arranging for BT to connect the phone, I mentioned the broadband problem. After a brief check, they promised that they would be able to deliver a service, and much to Ted's surprise they were right. We were soon online, although the term "broadband" didn't seem quite appropriate, as we were the furthest property from the exchange we were connected to. On the days that it worked, we managed speeds of around 0.2 MB unless a sheep farted in the next field, in which case it either slowed to the point where you could hear the individual data bytes arriving or it dropped completely. On one memorable occasion, a single computer update of 200 MB took over fourteen hours.

When faced with recalcitrant technology, it seems to me you only ever have three options to consider. You can restart the machine and pray, you can kick it and hope or you can give up and weep. With the nearest free wifi at Starbucks over twenty miles away, and just enough sense to realise that replacing crushed routers could become expensive, I soon got used to the familiar sound of Barbara's wail of despair from downstairs, which was code for "can you please re-start the sodding router" when she suffered from browsus interruptus. Whilst never actually solving the problem, restarting it allowed us to limp on in the same way that it is possible to use a car's starter motor to lurch it to the hard shoulder.

With such a gap in the market between the very understandable fact that no company was going to invest their money to lay thousands upon thousands of miles of fibre-optic cable on the off-chance that it might be used, and the alternative high expense of sending data via satellite, it was only a matter of time before an answer was found by developing what can only be described as "wifi on steroids". A few weeks ago, a couple of chaps arrived to install a receiver on the roof of the house. It would need to be in direct line-of-sight with their transmitter, which is situated twenty miles away on the southern tip of the Malvern Hills. As we sit just below a ridge, this could only be achieved by placing it on the top of a two-metre pole and hoisting it above our chimney. It took less than an hour to install, and when it was switched on, it started working instantly. No login and no configuration are needed; it just works as soon as it's on and the speed is, by our standards, absolutely blistering. As mobile phone contracts are now so generous with their minutes, and video calling is the most likely way that I will see Rather take his first steps and hear his first words, we have no further need for the BT landline either.

The net result of this installation is that we now have a 30MB service with no contract from a company that knows us by our first names, and which costs less than half the amount that we used to pay BT for a service that never really worked anyway. Having been a customer of theirs since 1988, I called up to terminate our rolling contract, and as the curtain fell on over twenty years of business with them, I was truly amazed to find out how much of our money they had been holding on account. Now that the surf's finally up, we are eager for action and hot for the game, and we are fairly sure we won't be paying heavenly bills.

Winter Wonderland (16th December)

Having been more or less constantly on the road since early September, it was with a considerable spring in my step that I returned from my last day of onsite delivery for the year this week. I had been in Edinburgh, and throughout my time there had kept a wary eye on both the weather and the airports as the temperature there and at home had dropped below freezing and was stubbornly remaining there.

My journey by plane, train and automobile was delightfully uneventful, and the temperature continued dropping that evening the further from Birmingham Airport I got, reaching minus 6°C by the time I arrived home to find Barbara greeting me with a welcome glass of red wine. There is much work to be done over the next month, but before we can start that, there are visits from relatives and the small matter of Rather's first Christmas to celebrate.

The next day I allowed myself an hour or two of self-indulgent wandering in order to acclimatise to being home for a stretch, to write a mental list of jobs to do, and to take in the beauty that the bitter frost had created. Walking up to the animal shelter to check the amount of wood we had burned so far this Winter, I saw that the cold snap had either killed off or forced all the spiders into hibernation, leaving the remnants of their webs to be transformed from disintegrating strands of wispy silk into robust props that any fancy-dress shop would be proud to display in their windows.

Anything and everything was covered in icy white stalagmites that glistened in the sharp sunlight, swayed gently in the breeze and crunched underfoot. Ground that had been a sea of mud and only navigable in boots since the downpours began in April, had become hard, unyielding and most welcome. In fact, only the chickens were disappointed as scratching around in the mud suddenly required more effort than they were used to.

I wandered along the edge of the field and through the orchard noting the amount of vandalism carried out by our resident moles, and grinned to myself as I had recently learned that the collective noun for moles is a 'labour'. I also saw that there still remained several hundred cider apples to collect, and was pleased to feel them still hard underfoot. I caught sight of a particularly handsome sprig of Mistletoe greedily feasting on one of the ageing apple trees, its berries and leaves framed in ice. We had last year promised ourselves to try to use this parasite as a seasonal cash crop, but through lack of time this year, it remains on the tree looking fat, healthy and festive.

Returning to the garage, it was impossible not to notice our Willow tree that dominates the entrance to the driveway and stands guard against the outside world. It looked to me as though it had been draped with a million strands of tinsel, and I wondered what it might look like with silver and red baubles in its branches. Perhaps one day we will find out.

The cold finally made its way through the layers I was wearing, and I turned back to the house, completing my mental list of jobs as I went. I glanced down the lane; there was not a hint of snow in the air, but the ice crystals were more than enough to make it a beautiful sight. For the next month at least, we shall be happy tonight, walking in a Winter Wonderland.

Tupping Season (23rd December)

'Twas the week before Christmas and nothing was stirring, not even a mouse. Unless, that is, you count the couple of hundred sheep that arrived in the field next door for a week-long ovine orgy that would make Caligula's eyes water. I have learned that sheep are particularly good at two things; eating and dying. If they are not doing the latter they will certainly be doing the former, and the ewes in particular excel at this, as they have nothing whatsoever to distract them. However, should a bunch of boozed-up rams on the pull happen to arrive on their patch, they may find their well-made plans of doing absolutely nothing but eating go somewhat awry.

Over the years I have experienced that Christmas is the season for a great many humans to engage in brief liaisons in the photocopier room or stationery cupboard at work, and except for not needing a shred of privacy, it seems that sheep are of a similar disposition too.

Through my work I am an observer, and my natural tendency is to notice patterns and try to make connections where possible. This means that currently, in the field outside my window, I think there is a large party going on which bears an alarmingly close resemblance to a stereotypical office Christmas party, where the organisation of it is designed to exploit the impacts of alcohol, urge and seasonal amnesia.

The romantic in me would like to imagine that most of the flock would attempt at least a bit of small talk possibly resulting in some common ground being established. Perhaps a bit of chivalrous role-play involving the offering of a tasty bit of grass or a helpful nibble on an itchy flank? This could then result in a rewarding and mutually consensual, if brief, consummation before mince pies and a tuneless rendition of Auld Lang Syne complete with tittering and a nervous exchange of glances.

Such a scenario does not seem even remotely likely as ewes appear to have a thought process that goes something like this: "eat, poop, eat, eat some more, poop, eat, stare at nothing while chewing, eat, eat again, die." The rams' thinking seems to be the same except with an occasional three-second subroutine that interrupts them in the following manner: "eat - [phwoar look at her, shag, pardon me] - eat."

This subroutine is only activated during tupping season and appears to frustrate the rams as much as the ewes, as it prevents them both from eating. Tellingly, the ewes don't stop eating throughout; a sort of "get on with it then, but mind you don't knock my bowl of chips over." The rams, true gents that they are, simply drop their kebabs on the pavement for a moment or two while they get a firm grip, and then carry on as before.

Clearly this ritual has been sufficient to keep sheep from extinction since they crawled out of the primordial slime, and as advanced and developed as I may want to feel by comparison, the rituals that held me captive for a significant percentage of my teens and twenties probably share more than a passing resemblance in their design. However, my memory from the number of years I spent frequenting places like The Redback in Acton on a Friday night suggests to me that more advanced and developed is not necessarily more successful.

So as the sheep next door conclude their hurried and perfunctory liaisons, we will get ready for Santa along with

Prancer, Dancer, Vixen and the rest of the reindeer gang when they arrive tomorrow night to meet Rather for the first time. After a delicious Julbord has been eaten, presents have been opened and the wrapping paper has been properly chewed, it will be time for sheep and reindeer to return home. Then the three of us shall look forward to an auspicious 2013, to the spring and the start of our first full year together. Merry Christmas!

Métro Boulot Dodo (1st January 2013)

As a freelancer I have an unpredictable commute that has varied over the years in terms of distance from my bed; totalling anywhere from three paces to just over eighteen thousand miles on one flattering and completely exhausting occasion. Consequently, I relish those days when I can either work at home or at least close enough to it to allow me to get back at night, however late. I last had a proper home office when we lived in London, making do afterwards with a succession of temporary spaces that have been neither very practical nor comfortable.

Since arriving at Stone House, I have used the small bedroom as an office, and when Barbara fell pregnant a few months after moving in, we knew it would become a nursery. The race was then on to get a number of important jobs done in a certain order by the end of 2012; the timeline being governed by the fact that we felt sure we were going to want to evict baby from our bedroom at the age of about six months. To achieve this, we were going to need some careful planning and project management.

The first step was to reorganise the animal shelter, which we did last summer. This cleared the way for a new office to be created by converting the rather shabby old storeroom which lies against the side of the house.

Eager to press on with the renovations once the unexpected and urgent problems with our drainage system had been resolved in August, we found a builder called John whose work came recommended by friends from our NCT group. Of all the builders that we asked to provide quotes for the work, he was the only one to raise an eyebrow at Ted's previous handiwork, under-promise what was possible and over-estimate its cost.

The storeroom is ideal to be converted to an office, and one day in someone else's hands it will probably be considered a perfect den. Attached to the house, but only accessible by walking through the conservatory, it is private and feels very separate. I wanted a window with a view where there was a door, and where there already was a window with no view, I wanted to re-kindle my enduring love affair with light through glass bricks; a fancy made possible by Barbara's tireless bargain hunting at car boot sales.

One of my biggest concerns was that being the part of the house that was closest to the road, and being built of concrete blocks rather than two foot thick Malvern Stone, the room might suffer from occasional noise pollution from passing traffic. John promised to look into this for me, and when the work started in September he was honest enough to admit to me that he had little idea whether his proposed design would be effective at all.

For over six weeks we lived in a building site as electrics, soundproofing, insulation, glass, radiator, door and floors were installed. The design was tweaked once or twice as unforeseen problems were encountered and overcome, but in the main everything went according to plan. Once the main work was finished, Barbara and I took over with the painting and decorating, and by the end of November only the final woodwork needed to be done.

As soon as the paint was dry to the touch, I began ferrying the entire contents of my office downstairs. Desk, boxes, files, furniture, equipment and the accumulation of what can only be described as 'stuff' from over the years arrived in its new home, ready to be organised. Upstairs, the empty bedroom was now ready to be turned into a nursery for Rather.

Now, as I write this, I continue to be amazed by the insulation which means that I can barely hear the occasional car that passes, and the office remains warm throughout the day and night almost without needing the central heating. With the exception of a little sanding, filling and painting on the woodwork, the office is finished and very much fit for purpose. With 2013 just out of the starting blocks, all that remains is for me to adapt my work so that I can keep my commute short enough to spend a bit more time in it. Happy New Year!

Silk Purse Nursery (13th January)

Having lived in houses, flats and on boats, I have long felt that there is a rule which states that every lodging must contain at least one area that is a jumble made from all the leftover bits and pieces of space that couldn't be used anywhere else. It's a bit like that drawer in the kitchen that contains all the stuff that doesn't have a proper home, and for some reason doesn't get thrown out.

Stone House was originally two semi-detached tied cottages, and when they were converted into one, the dregs of space were gathered up and unceremoniously bundled together into what is now the third, and smallest, bedroom. I remember that when we first viewed the house, Barbara and I poked our heads through its doorway, muttered "hmmm, nice" and moved on without any further thought.

During the conversion some time in the 1970's, a stair box was fashioned in it to accommodate the stairs rising from the ground floor below the bedroom, and Ted had crafted a single bed base that rather cleverly covered it. On our arrival we carefully removed it, but will one day no doubt re-install it when the time is right. On the other side of the room, the roof slopes down awkwardly and, all things considered, there is just enough room in it for one person of diminutive stature to swing a small cat. Despite being the last in line for attention, it does have a particular charm all of its own, and it is a space we are grateful to have.

After six months of Rather sleeping in our bedroom, we had grown used to tiptoeing around in the dark, whispering and the very idea of reading a chapter or two before lights out was a distant memory. With the completion of my new office last November, the way had been cleared for a nursery to be created out of the small bedroom, and with Barbara's customary thrift and creativity, it was achieved at remarkably low cost and in a short space of time.

Bright yellow paint, Rather's restored crib complete with Bob Marley's silhouette and a variety of accessories and artwork from dear friends, family and car-boot sales all made their way into the room in the space of two days. The result was a complete transformation from a dull and rather lifeless room to one brimming with colour, warmth and cosiness. Barbara and I are also immensely grateful to her stepmother and brother for their hours of patience and skill over Christmas with a needle and iron, resulting in a pair of the most delightful curtains that go a long way to keeping the light out and the warmth in.

We are pleased with the result, hope Rather is too and will leave decisions about any further decorating to him one day in the future. We shall also refrain from waxing lyrical about any apparent comfort, deep sleep or undisturbed nights his nursery may promote, lest we instantly be proven wrong. Instead we shall be happy with going to bed and actually seeing it as opposed to stubbing our bare feet against it and not being able to swear.

Despite the obvious limitations, attempting to create a silk purse from a sow's ear can be quite a carefree exercise, as it requires no conventional methods or tools. Better still, failure is impossible as there are no benchmarks to measure the results against, unlike the messy drawer in the kitchen.

Force Majeure (20th January)

For almost a week now, the weather has been the news and the news has been the weather. Warning has been heaped upon advisory, and a seemingly endless queue of portentous weather presenters have been promoted from interpreting the weather chart to being interviewed about it by equally solemn news anchors. Having salivated over words like extraordinary, unprecedented and severe with metronomic persistence for long enough, they have almost certainly guaranteed that reality will fall short of expectation, and a seat on the board of Tesco, Sainsbury's or Morrisons might well be on the cards too.

Joking aside, I was thankful to finish working onsite on Wednesday evening, and managed to drive back from the other side of the country in safety before the snow came the next day. For the rest of the week, we have sat on the fringes of the much-reported 'red zone', and watched snow drifting from one side of the garden to the other in the strong winds. I have seen snow before and, when in Continental Europe, Sweden or North America, quite a bit more of it than is usual in the United Kingdom. However I have not had the joy of being in such an exposed location and seeing what the wind can do with it, and I am intrigued to notice that blizzards and sandstorms have more in common than I had previously imagined.

Venturing out with my camera on Friday lunchtime, I found that the wind was too strong to let any snow stay on top of the house, garage or cider barn; preferring to produce ground-level sculptures in the lee of each building's footprint.

Some drifts were two, sometimes three feet deep and any tracks I left were erased by new snow in less than half an hour.

I was fascinated to see outside my office window that a snowdrift had left the two-foot drop from the edge of the front lawn and the sloping path that borders it virtually undetectable. My imagination drew fanciful parallels between it and the treacherous mountain crevasses faced by Joe Simpson and Simon Yates in the Peruvian Andes, and I wondered which nocturnal animals might suffer a similar fate.

The chickens had left the safety of their house first thing in the morning, and headed straight for the feeding station where the blizzard kept them marooned for the better part of the day. I initially felt sorry for them, but then realised that they were fine, having been effectively subjected to a lock-in at the pub. Nevertheless, I cleared a path for them and used fruit scraps to tempt them back to the relative safety of their cage. Quite why I expected them to do as I wanted is utterly beyond me, and whilst I battled to attach a wind-break to the cage to prevent snow from filling their coop, they wandered off line astern to the other end of the run, looking for all the world like a polar expedition with a lazily malfunctioning compass.

All that remained for me to do outside before darkness fell was to bring another load of firewood from the animal shelter down to the house, and much to my annoyance I found that the wind had penetrated the shelter and covered the wood pile in a blanket of snow. I cleared most of it with a clever combination of shouting, swearing and kicking before loading up the wheelbarrow with as many logs as it would carry.

The stream of expletives emanating from mouth continued as I then struggled to push a heavily laden wheelbarrow through snowdrifts, but it dried up instantly when I spied nature's artwork on the patio in-front of the cider barn. A paved flat area, it had been stripped of snow almost completely where the wind could reach. The exception had been a beautifully sculpted aerodynamic fairing about a foot in length, created by an opportunistic clump of grass.

The temperature has now not risen above freezing for over a week, and the snow remains deep and crisp. The roads in the surrounding areas have remained passable since the snow arrived, with all types of vehicle able to make it up hill and down dale if driven with care. So far on this occasion we have been extremely lucky, but living in this location we know that it's only a matter of time before we experience the challenges of being cut off in terms of access or power.

Today it has been snowing again since mid-morning, although with less insistence, and this evening I sit safe and warm at my desk keeping a wary eye on the forecast for the coming week. I know that an Act of God may yet prevent me from getting to my first job of the week in Scotland, and writing this may well be tempting fate as the current cold snap seems far from over. Whether egg lands on my plate or my face, it somehow feels as though the dice are already cast, and all I can do is wait to find out what the Weather Gods bring.

Feckless Mr Fox (3rd February)

Roald Dahl's characters and their many adventures made an indelible mark on my imagination as a child. Charlie Bucket, James Trotter and the quite brilliant Danny were amongst my favourites, and they repeatedly had me on the edge of my seat as they pitted their wits against the beautifully flawed and occasionally grotesque adults who sought to control their world. Equally gripping to me were the exploits of Mr Fox who so infuriated Farmers Boggis, Bunce and Bean, and whose cunning caused their relationship with cider to grow ever stronger as a result.

Living amongst a fair number of organised hunts, it was probably only a matter of time before Dahl's book detailing a protracted battle of wits and brute force between three farmers and a fox would resurface in my mind after thirty years or so, but what really surprises me is that we have yet to cross paths or swords with one on our land.

The recent snowfall allowed me an exciting half hour of amateur sleuthing in which I could finally investigate whether or not the fox's reputation of being wily, cunning and clever is accurate or somewhat overrated. Trudging through the snowdrifts to let the chickens out one morning, I spied a single set of tracks crossing the driveway onto the lawn and went to investigate. I immediately deduced that they were made by something with four legs and four pads on each paw, and it had spent some time under the dying Lady Emily apple tree where the marks appeared to show it had sat and done little more than perhaps scratch its ear before heading off again.

An inveterate fan of Inspector Morse, I fancied I could hear his theme music stirring in the back of my mind as I realised the tracks were unlikely to have been made by a soppy Labrador. I seized the chance to track what I felt sure must have been a lone fox in the hope of finding out anything I could about him.

Warming to my new role as a paunchy detective with a penchant for the bottle, I felt I first had to establish in which direction the tracks were heading. To do this, I carefully studied the imprint of the pads and concluded that, being set equally around the paw, the pad arrangement was reversible and clearly told me nothing. I then studied the angles at which the snow had been sculpted by each step and was again none the wiser. Deciding that the direction of travel was not essential to know, the only conclusion I felt happy to make was that his gait was as dainty as could be, and I now had an image of a fox crossing the lawn like a freshly trained Lippizaner from the Spanish Riding School in Vienna.

The next step was to see where his tracks led, and it was a straightforward process to map his journey. Assuming the direction of travel, he had arrived by crawling under the hedgerow in the field and made straight for the house. Once in the garden near the greenhouses, he carefully circled the vegetable patch before exploring the area near the Cider Barn. From there tracked back down towards the house, pausing to relieve himself against the wall of the utility room, and then squeezed under the side gate and made his way to the centre of the lawn. His final tracks led from there to the centre of the driveway, where I had first spotted them, and then showed that he had trotted off into the road and disappeared.

At this point, I resumed my original purpose and went to let the chickens out and carefully studied the ground in the chicken run, searching for evidence of Mr Fox's prowling. After all, what else could he be interested in around here? The ground was a carpet of virgin snow and showed no traces of any life. A brief mental recap of his travels showed that he had wandered all over the garden around the house, Cider Barn and garage and driveway. In fact, absolutely everywhere except the chicken run. Was he full? Did he have a cold? Was it in fact a soppy Labrador?

Were I Inspector Morse, I would now probably retire to a pub with Lewis for a pint of ale in order to think properly and review the evidence. As it was early morning, I judged it too early for beer and so coffee and a scratch of the head would have to do. The evidence I had found suggested that Mr Fox had simply arrived, taken a tour, had a pee, considered his lot in life and then disappeared without showing the slightest bit of interest in Jordan, Jodie or Jade.

As I pondered all this, a few facts began to rise to the surface of my mind. Firstly, however much we have become attached to our chickens, they are pretty skanky by anyone's standards, and that evidently includes those of a fox. Secondly, our neighbour collects out of date food from shops and feeds it to any wildlife that wants it. Thirdly, just over the hill opposite us, is a twenty-acre farm that houses six thousand well fed and carefully maintained free-range chickens.

Therefore it seems that to a fox, Stone House is a poorly stocked Spar located next door to a free soup kitchen, which is just around the corner from a well-stocked Waitrose. Feckless, fussy or just spoilt for choice?

Spring Cleaning (10th February)

Our lives have been shaped physically by what happened to Barbara's foot almost five years ago, as our presence in Herefordshire bears witness to. Although there may be the occasional day that passes when we do not discuss it openly, there is not one where we don't individually reflect on it and mourn all that was lost with it. And with a prognosis that has steadily grown in complexity whilst remaining frustratingly vague, the changes have been inescapably psychological as well.

In the face of failed surgeries and artful litigation, Barbara has spent the last three years continually revising her expectations of the future, and we have now come to accept that the current limitations we face are almost certain to remain and gradually increase. Today, we inhabit a space known as pain management, and shortly we will hear the recommendations of a specialist assessment on how we should adapt Stone House for the future. In addition to this, crucially, the next surgery is on hold until we can work out the logistics that another six-month period of Barbara's foot being non-weight bearing imply.

Recently we realised that one of the impacts of all this has been a sense of historical erosion, in that neither of us can clearly remember what our lives felt like before 2008. Of course, plenty of photos and videos exist and our memories are intact, but as the past really is another country, and one where we couldn't visit even if we wanted to, it was only a matter of time before our idealism would perish under the weight of pragmatism.

A few months ago, I came home from a trip and found that Barbara had spent a good few hours rummaging around the cupboards in the garage looking for all her shoes that she is no longer able to wear. Some were damaged, most had survived storage and some had never even been worn. She had laid them out in pairs all over the workshop, cleaned them and then just packed them away again. I wasn't exactly sure what she was up to, but it was the first flakes of snow in what was to become a cleansing avalanche of quite some power.

Ever the queen of detail, she spent weeks over the winter preparing for what seems a focussed and incredibly thorough psychological pruning exercise. While old clothes were washed, sorted and photographed, she researched the inner workings of eBay, the cheapest packing materials available and the bewildering array of postage costs. Every corner of the house was filled with piles of clothes and pairs of shoes, and at times I felt as though I were watching Dwight Eisenhower marshalling his forces on the eve of the D-Day landings.

I wasn't quite sure when the balloon went up, but sometime in the last few weeks the internet connection started glowing as she listed jacket after skirt after heels on eBay. Not long afterwards, our evenings on the sofa began to be peppered with delighted squeals as bids started tumbling in and items started selling; the same joy she experiences at car boot sales was now bearing little profits from the comfort of home. In another month or so everything no longer useful from the past will have been sold, leaving us only with what we need, want and actually use.

We don't yet know exactly how much longer we will have to give our time and attention to this case, and in some ways it doesn't really matter as we know that it must end simply because all the lawyers involved will want their money sooner or later, and no end means no fee for them. As Barbara can never have her painless freedom of movement back, we'll probably accept whatever the result is with little question, as a win is no substitute for us.

Once we have sold the shoes and clothes, stopped dealing with persistent emails requesting access to this set of records and that set of histories and let the dust start to settle, we will be left with the residue of the case; the values by which we now choose to live and to not compromise. And those we never knew existed until a number of people carelessly trod on them. New dust, new broom.

True Grit (17th February)

As you will either know or can easily imagine, one of the most exciting aspects of parenthood is watching a child grow, learn and develop. Gushing coos of "Oh my, he's got the biggest smile", "Isn't he just the cutest boy ever?" and "gosh, he's so strong!" are commonly heard from new parents, and Barbara and I are no different in this regard, smitten as we are with Rather. I do draw the line, however, at making any self-aggrandising statements of genetic inheritance, as all I would be able to claim is that he eats, burps and farts just like his father.

Putting to one side this urge to bask in the youthful glow of rejuvenated DNA, which seems a fairly ubiquitous by-product of procreation, I think I have chanced upon another great pleasure of parenthood: the opportunity to openly laugh at one's offspring with no fear of retribution. Clearly this can't last for long, as otherwise Rather's life may involve endless therapy and counselling sessions, but I do intend to capitalise on it while I can, especially as there seems to be precious little worth watching on television these days.

Whilst some of the other babies in the groups that Barbara attends are already crawling, have teeth and are well on their way to passing one or two GCSE's by all accounts, Rather seems more interested in the journey as opposed to the destination. He's been teething for what feels like years, but has absolutely nothing to show for it. Whilst he can support himself on his hands and his knees, he can't be bothered to do so on both at the same time. He therefore gets from A to B through a curious combination of Commando Crawling, sideways Zorbing and Polar Bear mooching, which I consider utterly comical and totally inefficient.

I don't really know if I should be encouraging him to crawl 'properly' or not, but I'm too busy laughing at his attempts instead, as he frequently reminds me of Rooster Cogburn in Henry Hathaway's film True Grit. Even though he never uttered the line; "Get off your horse and drink your milk, Pilgrim" in the film, I think it would be very fitting coming from Rather's grimacing mouth as he huffs and puffs his way across the floor, favouring his left shoulder over his right, just as John Wayne did.

Having spent months content to stay on his play-mat, he discovered a little while ago that he could use this new-found propulsion mechanism to get to the hard wooden floor, or the box where his toys live, or the radiator, with which he has a noticeably particular and enduring fascination. Handily, he can also make his way to our feet when we are sitting on the sofa. This suits us just fine as now, rather than having to stand up and walk across the room to get him, we just wait for him to arrive at our feet before scooping him up. Alternatively, if another repeat of Grand Designs is the best the television has to offer, we just spin him around, send him off in another direction and wait to see what happens next.

With the seemingly enormous levels of exertion required for him to get from A to B, it's a good job that his stamina is developing at the same rate as his curiosity. If Barbara and I are in the kitchen and he decides to join us, there will follow a good five minutes of groaning, grunting and moaning while he makes his way from the living room. During this long and arduous journey, he will carefully navigate the perilous obstacles that lie en-route; the sofa, his toys, the floor sill that joins the living room and kitchen floors together and any dust mice or food crumbs that need to be carefully checked for quality and taste.

I swear if he had any teeth, he would be gritting them all the way.

Ever Decreasing Circles (24th February)

It was with surprise and sadness that we learned recently of the death of Richard Briers, the actor who brought the character of Tom Good to life on television almost forty years ago, and gave us here at Stone House a frame, however tenuous and fanciful, through which we try to articulate a little of what we are trying to accomplish here. Being arguably the most recognisable representation of our vision, we feel he deserves this place in our book.

I heard the news at lunchtime last Monday, just as I was preparing to travel to a job in the most western point of Wales for the week. Waiting for me, I had over three hours of meandering roads complete, no doubt, with tractors and lorries to slow me down and give me time to think. Having discovered over the last six months the delights of the *Desert Island Discs Archive*, which provides a welcome and highly addictive alternative to the familiarity and predictability of my music collection, I set off to the familiar and comforting sound of *The Sleepy Lagoon*. And no, I didn't know that's the title of the theme tune either.

Pausing briefly in town to brim the fuel tank with diesel, I headed into the bright sun and starting listening to Briers' account of his life to date from the episode he recorded in 2000. I know little about the man, but leaned forward a little in my seat and turned the volume up to hear what comparisons there might possibly be between an actor who years ago played a pretend smallholder, and a pretend smallholder who once played at being an actor.

As I crossed the Welsh border, I realised that there was virtually nothing that we had in common of course, and I was content to sit back, listen to and enjoy the commentary of his life as the miles fell behind me. Inevitably there were questions about The Good Life, which was undeniably the springboard to his international fame. He acknowledged the significant part that it had played in his career, but stated that he had little time for the character of Tom as in his view he was "an obsessive and rather irritating git".

Grinning broadly but somewhat uneasily, I considered taking umbrage at such a description, but remembered that Tom is only a fictitious character. I then realised that, fictitious or not, Barbara would probably see more than a passing similarity between us on the basis of this description. I judged it best to simply drive, enjoy his musical choices and raise my metaphoric glass to him for a life well lived. As the sun sank lower in front of me and the landscape got more remote, I briefly revisited my past and remembered that he and I actually did have some things in common, although they were only the time and place of an occasion.

In 1999, when I was trying to make a living from producing voiceover recordings in my home studio in West London, I received a booking from a fringe theatre company, as mine was one of the closest studios to where Richard Briers lived. He turned up at my ground floor flat on the following Sunday morning, a number of newpapers tucked under his arm, as he had agreed to record a short excerpt from the part of The Ghost in Hamlet as a favour to the production's director.

"You really do find studios in the strangest of places these days", he observed while gently easing his elderly frame backwards down the steep steps into my basement. There, surrounded by two layers of thick, damp curtains that were nailed to the joists of the floor above, and seated on a wooden stool, he recorded three lines from Act l Scene V in one take. I asked him to do a second take and then a third, because I felt the recording session should last at least ten minutes for the sake of appearing conscientious, but it was a pretence.

Emerging shortly afterwards from the basement, he politely declined the offer of a cup of tea, put his coat on and slowly wandered off in the direction of Chiswick High Road. He had asserted in the episode I had been listening to that he believed it was actors, and not just the state, who subsidised the theatre, and I had been lucky enough to witness him prove it.

The Sounds of Silence (3rd March)

As many will know, subtlety is not one of my strongest suits and, when combined with a propensity to speak either before or without thinking, it can often make problems bigger and more complicated than need be. Having an awareness of this, though perhaps not the strongest of desires to temper it, I am well placed to appreciate it in others. Eavesdropping on one of Barbara's telephone calls yesterday afternoon confirmed just how much can be achieved by it.

Every year at the start of winter, farmers everywhere start trimming the hedges that criss-cross a huge percentage of this country. As they provide a home for a surprisingly large amount of wildlife, the work cannot start until the residents have either flown south for the winter or gone into hibernation. By the same token, the work must be done before they come back in spring, and Defra guidelines state that any hedges not cut by March 1st can only be trimmed by hand. Farmer Harris looks after our hedges for us, normally completing the task around Christmas time with a heavy-duty hedge cutter attached to his tractor. As a farmer who owns a good deal of land himself, and tends a myriad of other fields like ours in exchange for the hay it provides his flocks, it is a job that takes a fair amount of time and planning. This year, the rain has caused delay after delay and so as the first day of spring approached, we crossed our fingers that our hedges would be done in time.

Our hopes were dashed as yesterday afternoon, when returning from a delightful afternoon drink at a local pub, it was clear that our hedges were still thick, bushy and, most worryingly, razor sharp. What was also clear was that all the other hedges along the B4220, including the many on Farmer Harris' land, were neatly trimmed and ready for spring. Whilst I mentally appraised the ramifications of this oversight and started simmering, Barbara calmly picked up her phone and placed a call to him. Their conversation was, it turned out, a bit like a good game of chess. After the rituals and clichés of a phone conversation were dispensed with, she carefully advanced a pawn by asking if she was correct in her assumption that, the first of March having passed, they were not planning on completing the work. John quickly sent his pawn first out and said that they weren't. By a clever mixture of innocence and silence, Barbara teased out all his remaining pawns which were a variety of teeth sucking, lambing season, tutting and moaning about the weather. Playing her first knight, she said, "Oh, but the little triangular field next door was cut recently, and I can't remember if it's you who takes care of that too?"

There followed a long pause during which his Bishops and Rooks nervously twitched and cleared their throats. This was eventually followed by an admission that it was indeed one of the fields they look after. Then there was a mumbled explanation of how the owner of that land had vociferously complained that his hedges hadn't been cut. Filing away this admission as a blueprint for all future dealings with him, Barbara continued with her skillful use of pausing. Presumably growing tired of the conversation, John's next tack was to state that he had already taken the hedge cutter off the tractor and didn't really want to put it back on. And in any event, he didn't think the hedges looked all that bad anyway. Barbara swiftly assured him that the look didn't really matter to us, going on to point out that it was more a case that I wouldn't be able to mow the grass around the field without lacerating myself on the hedge for the next six months. I thought I then saw an enormous tumbleweed roll right past the window in slow motion.

What felt like an hour passed, and while Barbara held her nerve I swear I could hear drops of sweat forming on John's brow over the phone. "Well", he nervously whispered as he gently tipped over his King, "I suppose I could send Jacko up there with the brush cutter to do the insides of the hedges for you..."

With neither the inclination nor the time to play at being squeaky wheels in search of grease, Barbara and I have already discussed plans to make a new and more structured arrangement for the end of this year. Farmer Harris will have first refusal of our hay and hedge, but he won't be able to hear us without having to listen to us. Pecking orders can be found everywhere it seems and our choice will always be to resist accommodating them, insisting instead on our equal place thanks to Barbara's irresistible and effective negotiation technique.

Pea Souper (10th March)

Returning from a job late last Thursday evening, I drove home from the airport with my spirits lifting at the thought of three days at home. The last leg of my journey takes me on the main trunk road from Worcester towards Hereford, which to me has become very much like a sort of reversible reality shift tunnel where, on this occasion, I entered in work mode and exited in home mode.

More or less exactly halfway along this road lies the intersection with the B4220, which starts with a very steep hill that is usually impassable in freezing or snowy conditions, and runs along the crest of all the hills that lie between Cradley and Bromyard. In total, it is roughly six miles long, originally built as a single-track road and Stone House sits alongside it.

At some point in the past, the council decided to upgrade the local infrastructure (in name at least), and presumably using some law buried deep in a drawer in Brussels, decreed that in some parts it was already wide enough to be considered a two-lane road. As a result, a white line was added to the wider parts, which often causes some confusion for drivers who aren't expecting it to suddenly vanish, as it frequently does. Quite what the traffic planners envisaged happening along this road might make for interesting reading, I often feel.

It was just after midnight when I turned up the hill and drove into what was the thickest fog I have ever experienced from the driving seat of a car. There had been no hint of any fog earlier on my journey, and within seconds I could barely distinguish between the road and the grass verge. As I discovered very quickly, there's fog and there's fog, and altitude probably has a lot to do with it.

Normally used to fog that thickens gradually, I was taken aback by its immediate viscosity, and my speed slowed to just above walking pace. Such was the reduction of visibility, all I could do was steer the car over the central white line, relying on the headlights to pick out the trail of cat's eyes.

I know the places where the road narrows and the white line disappears, but I was still caught off guard when it happened. All of a sudden, with no reference points, I had a very real sense of being blind and had to slow the car even more to a snail's pace, at one point only knowing the edge of the road by my wing mirror being gently folded in by a branch.

Progress was slow and only once in the twenty minutes it took me to crawl four miles did I pass an oncoming vehicle. All I know was that it was much larger than my Volkswagen and we were lucky to meet each other in a section of the road where it is wide enough to pass.

Once past the Pink Pub, and again grateful for its colour, I knew I was close to home but was unsure that I was going to be able to see our driveway entrance in all the murky gloom. Thankfully Barbara had left the streetlamp on, as she always does when I come home after she has gone to bed, and I was a little more relieved than usual to have made it home.

Blessings in Disguise (17th March)

Being middle aged with a small child, it is perhaps predictable and understandable that the freedom to indulge in some of life's more extreme pleasures is somewhat restricted at present. If you then include our current circumstances and future prognoses, everything hints at further limitations that will need to be accommodated.

Thankfully quite a number of my pleasures are relatively simple, and it has been a great delight recently to take on one particular job at Stone House that cleverly blends two of the most sublime activities that I could ever consider engaging in; messing about with noisy power tools in an attempt to perfect my macho posture, and sitting on my behind with a large glass of red wine staring at a beautiful view.

Since 2001 I have had in my possession a rather old and very solid teak bench which, along with my of vintage cast iron traffic lights, is the only proof that I have ever handled stolen goods. The bench originally lived in the outdoor smoking area of a certain drama school in West London, from where it was liberated by persons who shall remain anonymous. At the time, it was firmly decided that the principled and artistic purpose behind its theft was fully justified, as it was to furnish the nearby production of a seldom performed and truly delightful two-handed play called *A Walk In The Woods* by Lee Blessing.

It turned out to be very much more than just the icing on the cake, as it not only brought to life the calm serenity of a Geneva hillside in a suburban London theatre, but also managed on most evenings to be significantly less wooden than the two actors that sat on it. Over the two hours that each performance lasted, it was the constant feature through all four seasons of a single year, and provided the foundation on which East met West through a series of engaging, hopeful but ultimately doomed nuclear disarmament negotiations. I remember the production as being hugely enjoyable, desperately hot, well received and the only time I experienced a degree of satisfaction and pride as an actor. Afterwards, being the only member of the company with a garden, I offered to store the bench on a temporary basis. Very much in line with my ulterior motive at the time, this arrangement has continued ever since, and during the last twelve years it has become a good friend. To me, it represents reliability, simplicity and a comfortable place from which to enjoy a good view or an engaging conversation, whether in real or scripted life.

Putting to one side that it must already be quite an aged piece of furniture, it has withstood the hottest temperatures in London during 2003, the long deep freeze of 2010 in Gloucestershire and has just survived the wettest year on record in Herefordshire, all of which only serving to worsen its condition. Last October during a walk around the field, I noticed that it had begun to look very sorry for itself indeed. The wood, where it wasn't covered by bird poop, was turning green with an algae-like substance, and the repeated freezing of water in its joints was rotting it slowly but surely. There and then, I opted to haul it into the Cider Barn for the winter, whilst I decided upon the best course of action.

With the first rays of sunshine appearing in late February, it was high time I spent some time on this project, and I began by manhandling it on to the patio outside the Cider Barn. There I paused for thought, as clearly, if the bench was to survive, what was needed was some careful treatment that would involve sanding, preparing and sealing. This was obviously right out of the question, as it required know-how, patience and precision; none of which are in my skillset. I therefore disappeared into the workshop and returned with my Black & Decker kill-o-matic super destroy-tastic belted sanding machine. Sporting a large grin, I then set about skinning the bench alive, sending huge plumes of sawdust up in the air and all over me. Such was my level of enjoyment and so loud was the noise I made, that the chickens (who had hitherto been lined up alongside their fence nearby and watching me with a mixture of love, pride and unabashed admiration) shot off to the other end of their run clucking indignantly.

When I considered that I had finished the job, which should never be confused with the job actually being finished, I dragged the bench into the back of the garage and placed it on a drop cloth. Then it was a matter of drenching it in a dark wood stain in the hope that the blotches left behind by my haphazard sanding would be masked effectively. This was achieved over a period of several weeks, and by the end of it, I considered the job complete but for a couple of coats of durable varnish that would keep it in tip-top condition for years to come.

Yesterday, on the eastern edge of the field, I laid some flush stone foundations that should prevent its feet drawing moisture from the grass whilst allowing the lawn tractor to mow safely over them. This afternoon, all three of us transported the bench back to its improved resting spot, checked that it still afforded the best view possible towards the West, and considered that all the noise, sweat and posturing that had gone into its maintenance had been energy well spent.

All that remains to complete my joy is to wait for the warmth of Spring and for Barbara, Rather and I to take an evening walk in the sunshine with a glass of red wine, so I can quote from a short conversation between Blessing's characters when we get halfway around the field.

"Shall we sit a while?"
"Yes, what do you want to talk about?"
(A pause)
"Nothing."

Almost un Oeuf (1st April)

It has been an eventful and long holiday weekend with Barbara's mother making the trip over from Sweden to join us. We have eaten our fill, played with Rather, taken day trips and made outings to Leominster, Malvern and Worcester and enjoyed some wonderful warm fireside evenings. As expected, the Easter bank holiday weather has been little more than an extension of winter, but the lingering snow and bitter cold hasn't dampened our spirits one bit.

Not everyone on a smallholding takes Easter off, and so there have been a few odd jobs to take care of like cleaning out the chicken house, which we did on Friday afternoon. The closest I got to thinking about religion that evening was collecting eggs, and I was tickled pink that one of the chickens had laid a mini egg, but disappointed to find that it was neither wrapped in foil nor made of chocolate.

Normally I can tell who has laid what, as there is usually a high degree of consistency in the size and shape of the eggs produced, but this time I hadn't a clue. It was a pretty pathetic offering by anyone's standards, and one for which none of them were prepared to admit responsibility. Although its shell was perfect, it was about a quarter of the size it ought to be. Barbara and I were unsure about using it, and in the end both my curiosity and gravity drove it into the stone path outside. Inside I found a miniature yolk and white of perfect shape, colour and consistency. "Nice effort, chooks", I called out to them encouragingly on my way back inside as, although an egg, it was just not enough.

Perhaps it is becoming harder to ignore that our lovely chickens, who continue to form the most energetic and vocal welcoming committee for anyone arriving at Stone House, are all now well into the autumn of their egg-laying days. Approaching three years of age, they still provide more eggs than we can eat in a week, but Good Friday's effort may signal that a change is in the air. Whilst they may continue to lay now and then, we mostly plan for them to enjoy a long and leisurely retirement with us; an end which we hope will be more fun for them than a quick dispatch shortly followed by a gelatinous resurrection as a tin of Whiskas. Happy Easter!

Jeux Sans Frontières (14th April)

Barbara manages our household budget with great care in order to clothe, feed and provide entertainment for Rather as economically as possible. Much of this is done by creative recycling, a good deal through thrifty and opportunistic shopping and all of it is underpinned by neither of us needing him to be a dedicated follower of fashion. Come to think of it, we're not really too bothered by the gender bias of his clothes, although we are prepared should he one day develop a preference in this regard.

Car boot sales are a favourite destination and, with warmth and sunshine recently making an appearance, the season for them has at last begun. Unleashed like a coiled spring from the shopping wasteland of winter, Barbara visited the first one just in time to make sure Rather doesn't outgrow everything in his wardrobe, and has already been again this morning. My excitement is reserved for the surprise of seeing exactly how full the back of a Skoda can be for ten quid. Shortly afterwards, I am usually confronted by eyes faintly reminiscent of Puss in Boots' from Shrek and a gently imploring "Do you have any batteries in the office, darling?"

Frugality clearly runs in the family, as last Christmas Barbara's mother arrived with all manner of goodies gathered from second hand shops near where she lives, one of which I judged to be the most appropriate toy for our Herefordshire-bred boy: an electronic box called "Fridge Farm". We didn't need to waste any time trying to figure it out, as it was obvious; it's a colourful box that looks like a farm building of some kind, and the parts needed to make it work are magnetised halves of animals. The learning point is elegant and simple: find two halves of the same animal, attach them in the correct position, push them and Hey Presto! You get the appropriate noise and a song. Well, usually.

It's quite enchanting, Rather loved it and curiously for a bargain bought in Stockholm, it's a toy that speaks and sings in French. Before long, he was merrily eating the toy while listening to the exploits of La Vache Violette as recounted by the banjo playing Monsieur Le Fermier. As a second hand toy with a few miles on the clock, it's not the most reliable there is, and I have since discovered once in a while for no discernible reason it will bleat, whinny, oink, moo or quack from the depths of the toy chest. Although amusing, it's also somewhat unnerving when you're tiptoeing out of the house for work at 4am, I can tell you.

As soon as Rather's attention had wandered from this toy to another, it was my turn to examine it, and I did exactly what you'd expect me to. I thought I would see what would happen if I combined bits of different animals. I first tried to make a Porse and then a Shig, but sadly the game was having none of it and remained silent, presumably as such programming would undermine its educational credentials.

The toy, like so many others now, gets frequently moved between the box in the living room and the 'not being used for a few weeks' box under the stairs, and has been part of the landscape for several months. Its most recent outing was the other day. Barbara had a dentist appointment and so Rather and I settled down to an afternoon's entertainment while she went off to have her molars molested. Having tired of one particular toy, I fished around inside the box and chanced upon it. I first tested to see if it still worked, and found that it didn't. By employing the standard repair method for faulty toys (bashing it over the back of the sofa a few times), I tried it again and, for good measure, made a Shuck and pushed the button. It worked, and not only did it work, but it accepted my half sheep, half duck creation - and had a particular song for it to boot!

Rather may or may not have been interested in the toy by this point, but I'm afraid I didn't notice. In any event, all the king's horses, not to mention his porses, dorses and corses, couldn't have prised it away from me. I loved it and played it over and over again, and used what remains of my French vocabulary from school to figure out what the song was about.

By the time I had stopped giggling, I noticed my son looking at me with a look of despair far deeper than his ten months should allow. It's probably the same look that his teachers one day will give me, but by then I will hopefully have come up with a plausible excuse. Reproduced below is a rough translation of what I think the toy sings with this particular genetically modified animal inserted.

A sheep's face, a duck's arse
It's totally ace, what a laugh!

When Barbara came home with shiny teeth, I couldn't wait to show her. I can safely say that if little things please little minds, then we are very well matched. As for Rather, he's clearly got the most mature sense of humour in the house.

Hyperopia (21ˢᵗ April)

Maintaining everything at Stone House, like many older properties, is similar to keeping a slowly sinking ship afloat. As a leaking pipe is repaired here, a bit of render falls off there, and it's quite easy to feel as though it takes most of our effort just to stand still. Although we have been pleased to add the office to the house, most of the work we have been able to do has been the groundwork of removing sheds, fences and various other bits of general landscaping clutter that Ted and Jan had amassed over their forty years' residence here.

Some of these jobs have been the kind you take care of on a Saturday afternoon in a few hours, and others require weeks and weeks of planning. The easterly view from the house has always been restricted by a twenty-metre section of hawthorn hedge, the sole purpose of which is to lacerate my midriff as I pass by it on the tractor. As a plant that enjoys legal protection, we had to seek advice about its removal from our local planning office. Thankfully, it turns out that hedgerow that doesn't form the border between separately owned pieces of land is not protected, but you need to pay them £60 to tell you that, as it's neither common nor published knowledge. Not only was it now fair game, but as both Barbara and I yearn for a long hot summer of views and barbecues, its future suddenly looked very bleak.

I set about devising its death, and having previously waged war on the Leylandii hedge in an effort to reduce its towering impact, I knew enough to approach hedgerow removal with caution and sober expectations. It is with good reason that an enormous amount of wildlife makes their home in and under hawthorn; it affords incredible protection with its thorns and thick thatched woodwork. As well as doing it's best to keep intruders out, it will also leave its mark on those who try in the form of Thorn Synovitis; a form of temporary arthritis. Ask me how I know.

On close inspection, the hedge comprises of hundreds of individual stems stretching between about fifteen trunks and about as many dead stumps. It was thick, unyielding and, thanks to Farmer Harris' oversight, about twice as high and thick as it should have been. I headed back to the house with the phrase 'never send a boy to do a man's job' echoing around my head. Being far beyond my capability, I turned to Google, we arranged for some quotes and before long we found our man.

Rupert and Bob turned up on a Tuesday afternoon; a pair of likeable young men with quick wits, strong arms and some equipment that immediately turned me as green as the grass on which I was standing. It seems that my love affair with petrol-powered machinery will always mark me out as an amateur, as the real toys are diesel-powered. Although offering far better fuel economy, it is for another and even better reason that diesel is the professionals' choice: if you are going to cut down and chip a hawthorn hedge, you really need less talk and more torque.

Then began a sort of slow-motion ballet in which section after section of hedge was cut down, dragged aside and fed into the chipper. From its spout streamed chippings which would be sold as mulch or fuel for low-carbon boilers, depending on the chip size and quality. As each section was cut down, the curtain drew aside on our new view and even Rather, who came to inspect the changing landscape, gurgled with delight.

By lunchtime on Wednesday the hedge was gone and the scene was set for the stump grinder. Looking like it had just driven from the set of the latest James Bond movie, the remote controlled machine (apparently a close cousin to those used by the bomb squad to remotely detonate explosive devices) converted twenty metres of roots and undergrowth into mulch and earth in less than half an hour. Along this strip we will soon erect a post and rail fence to keep any animals out of the garden whilst allowing the eastern horizon in.

While Rupert and Bob worked, I figured we might as well clear everything from this part of the garden that we had decided was to go, and so I prepared to remove the two dead tree trunks that stand by the vegetable plot. It couldn't have been easier as I had to do nothing more than lean on them, and they gently collapsed to the ground. Their final role in life will be as a slowly decomposing adventure playground in the chicken enclosure.

Having finally found a local tradesman who's description of leaving a worksite 'clean and tidy' matches mine, I thanked and paid Rupert happily before he hitched his machinery behind his lorry and rumbled off into the distance, leaving behind a wonderful view and a garden finally clear of clutter.

Now we look forward to building a concrete base for the breeze house, which has patiently waited since we dismantled it in 2010, and which will be sited for the best possible sunset views. As our intention is to build raised vegetable beds in the orchard field one day, the existing patch will be returned to grass and incorporated into the garden. I've got a feeling that it's nearly Pimm's o'clock!

Perls of Wisdom (5th May)

In Peter Ustinov's autobiography 'Dear Me', he describes his collaboration with Charles Laughton during the filming of Spartacus in the late 1950's as "working with an aggressively vulnerable man who sat around on the set waiting for his feelings to be hurt." Such persistent petulance seems to characterise very well one of our neighbours, who tends his land with absolute precision whilst holding everyone else in utter contempt for choosing to not follow his example. He is a most fascinating and contradictory mix of recluse and busybody, and lives by an incredibly rigid set of rules about which he appears both unable and unwilling to compromise. For the most part his various eccentric behaviours are slightly amusing, but on occasion they become rather irritating. We seldom see and rarely speak with him except for those times when he feels compelled to make our business his business, and appears on our doorstep in order to complain in great detail about something that offends his sensibilities. Science tells me that we live as far from him as he does from us, and as I would need binoculars if I wanted to know what he was doing, it wouldn't surprise me if that's what he uses to spy on whatever it is we do that fuels his mercifully rare indignation.

In the twenty-one months that we have lived here, I have been reprimanded for driving past an animal that had been flattened on the road about a mile from our house, trimming our garden hedge to an unacceptably poor standard, hiring the wrong sort of company to install our soak-away, having our septic tank emptied in winter, poisoning rats in a manner not to his liking and doing some hedge work at the wrong time of year.

On one occasion he disparagingly called me "a bit of an idiot" for not putting enough manure onto our vegetable garden, and then fixed me with an accusing stare as he waited for my response. Rather than telling him to bugger off or asking him if he had nothing better to do with his time, I gave him a watery smile and agreed with a helpless sigh. I fear it rather killed our conversation that day.

Barbara and I now think that after almost two years of relentlessly disappointing him, it's a pretty safe bet that, as Fritz Perls articulated in his Gestalt Prayer: there is little chance that we will find each other, and it can't be helped. Local gossip likes to allege that he is "trouble with a capital T" and by his own admission he is no stranger to an argument, but our amateur diagnosis is that he is probably a bit further along the autistic scale than most. His belligerent manner during our most recent transgression of his code of conduct left me thinking that all he can ever have known is conflict and fisticuffs in the face of his rigidity, as those are what he seems to expect and almost seek; attack being considered by many as the best form of defence.

Fortunately, agreeing with him and respecting his point of view takes the wind out of his sails and leaves him helplessly clutching at straws. With his indignation unable to gain any kind of foothold, his reprimand quickly grinds to a standstill with him shaking his head forlornly and repeatedly muttering our offence to no one in particular in a sort of De Niro-esque "You talkin' to me?" kind of way as he leaves.

As we enjoy a peaceful life and know that living up to other people's expectations of it is not our strongest suit, our wish to ignore him is evenly matched by our desire to not fall out with him. It may therefore be that we continue to disappoint him for quite some time to come.

Birds of a Feather (12th May)

A few weeks ago I had a telephone call from Barbara at an uncharacteristically late hour to tell me that Jordan, one of our ex-battery hybrids, had died in the coop. The others were outside and, understandably, refused to bed down for the night until her body had been removed. From my hotel in Manchester, the best I could do was offer moral support on the phone while Barbara unceremoniously dragged the corpse out by its feet and shooed Jodie and Jade in for the night.

Strange as it may seem, we have become rather attached to our birds, and the loss of one was keenly felt. She had been the ringleader; the one who ruled the roost and told the others what to do. She had also been the social and energetic one, and the one which Barbara spent a good deal of time cuddling and eagerly trying to persuade others to do the same. Life in the chicken enclosure was sure to be a bit quieter from now on. When I returned that weekend, the welcoming committee that met me was half-hearted, poorly organised and thoroughly lacklustre. Something had to be done.

Thanks to Google, we found out that two was really not enough birds to keep given their gregarious nature and the often complex social structure in which they thrive. The remaining two had become inseparable; like an avian Hinge and Bracket that clucked and fussed over each other in their rapidly shrinking world, whilst completely ignoring any outside influences. Until, that is, three new birds arrived that Saturday, whereupon Jodie in particular became a picture of total outrage and indignation.

We felt that it was too much to once again drive to Coventry for the sake of buying ex-bats, so this time we turned to a local breeder near Leominster called Busy Bantams. Barbara, in one of those delightful moments when a failing memory combines with a non-native tongue to form a Freudian slip, excitedly proclaimed to Rather in the car that we were off to *Bitchy* Bantams to get some new friends for our chickens. The farm is run by a husband and wife team as a hobby, and consists of a few acres of land on which are housed hundreds of hybrids of all descriptions at point of lay, which is usually around twenty weeks old. Young, colourful and vigorous in ways that Jodie and Jade aren't, they peck, scratch and cluck in pens just waiting for someone to point at them and say "that one, please". The chap selling them seemed knowledgeable and pleasant, answering all the questions we had about age, eggs and the best way of introducing new birds to old. After making her selection, Barbara gestured towards Rather and said, "It's really important that any birds we have are happy to be handled and touched by young children." As he assured her that all would be well with the three that she had identified, I giggled and muttered under my breath "You're not fooling me." Barbara sent me a withering look. All chickens fight dirty when it comes to establishing their pecking order, but ex-battery hens come from the school of hard knocks where they grow up fighting tooth and nail for each and every square inch of perch that they have. Although they can give a good impression of being bad apples, they are in fact simply the product of the bad barrels into which they were born. Those that get a chance for a peaceful retirement like ours do enjoy it, but when threatened it seems very clear that whilst you can take the hen out of the battery, you can't take the battery out of the hen. Introducing them to hens from a different walk of life has been an interesting experiment to say the least.

When we got home, we followed the instructions by bundling the new hens straight into the coop and shutting them in with food and water for the rest of the day. Whilst they got used to the new smells of home, Jodie and Jade kept busy outside with a keen awareness that something somehow was different, and not necessarily in a good way. Then, at dusk, we did as we had been told by letting the darkness bring the old hens to the door, then opening it quickly and shoving them in before they had a chance to think. Pitch black inside, there was little more than a few shuffles and clucks followed by silence.

The next morning, however, all was quite different. As I approached the coop to let them out, there was an enormous fight going on inside, and when I opened the door the three new chickens were ejected sideways in a manner rather reminiscent of Wile E. Coyote when bested by the Roadrunner. The three new girls ran out of the cage and in circles looking for help in any shape or form, whilst Jodie and Jade sedately walked down the ramp dusting themselves off, swinging their handbags and muttering about "the youth of today" and asking "can you believe it?" of each other.

Since then, warfare has continued more or less constantly and it is Jodie, herself once the poor put-upon victim, who is the more vile of the two. As before, I find it both shocking and fascinating to see the similarity between humans and chickens when it comes to the nastiness of bullies and their cowardly ways. We expect this ritual to last another week or so, and if they are not able to resolve their differences through violence, they may need to try and talk things through, so it's just as well that our new birds are called Oprah, Trisha and Ricki.

Quartet (14th May)

There are four elements, four seasons and four corners of the Earth; in fact Wikipedia tells us that the number four is many things to a great many people. It is the points scored by a try in Rugby, the noble truths to a Buddhist and the atomic number of Beryllium to a Chemist. Whether these and other similar pieces of information will add a very great deal to our lives here at Stone House is both unclear and something about which we are not overly concerned.

Far more relevant, immediate and important to us now though, is that four is also the number our family will grow to in the run-up to Christmas this year. Ever since finding out that Barbara was pregnant with Rather just over a year and a half ago, we also began to feel that four is the number that is somehow right for us, and the one which would complete our family. With me reaching forty-five by the summer's end and Barbara's foot certain only to continue deteriorating, we felt that 2013 was probably the very latest that we would want to leave it, and so we have been propping up the bar in the Last Chance Saloon for a while now.

Following a three-month scan this morning at Worcester Royal Hospital, we can confirm that it is Very Happy Hour, and so this round is on us.

Them Apples (19th May)

Harvest time for apple trees is quite late in the year, usually around November. In my book, that's a time of year to be settling down by a warm fire with a good book and a glass of red wine. It is not, repeat absolutely not, a time of year to be faffing about in a muddy field collecting thousands of apples while the rain finds it way through each and every nook and cranny of your supposedly waterproof waterproofs.

If that weren't enough to put you off the idea of having an apple orchard, just imagine that the trees in it were of the Vilberie variety, which means it's almost impossible to distinguish between eating one of its fruit and chewing a wasp, as they're cider apples with a taste more sour than the look on Maggie Smith's face in Downton Abbey. Still keen on the notion? OK, we've got fifteen trees, each one producing apples by the hundreds. I rest my case.

With the memory of collecting last winter's harvest still very much in my mind and the muscles in my back, not to mention the energy and time spent on my first attempt at forestry, I was determined that the orchard should go before Spring took hold and leaves began to appear on the trees. No matter how vivid my daydream of being a true smallholder may be, the fact is that when the amount of effort required to convert a dream into reality reaches a certain level, the dream can not so much fade as shatter and that level, I freely admit, is what is probably considered by many as hard work. And so it was with great relief that I secured the services of Rupert to also remove the orchard after he had dispensed with the hawthorn hedge with enviable ease. Even if I wanted to explain away the ease with which he executed this task by the sheer amount of diesel-powered machinery he employed to do it, I would have to also allow his considerable skill and artistry as an arborist, as there is no way I could have done it. On average it took him in the region of twenty minutes to take one tree from it's original state and reduce it to a large pile of logs. Each tree was approached individually, taking into account shape, angle and geography and his meticulous planning resulted in the exertion of minimal effort. It was very impressive.

In the same amount of time that it took me last year to sever four branches from the large willow by the Cider Barn and convert them into fire logs, Rupert had removed all trace of fifteen entire trees. Anything less than three inches in diameter was fed through the chipper, and the rest was cut into foot long lengths which I transported to the animal shelter to await splitting and seasoning. For the present the bare field will be left to grow grass, and the maintenance required will be nothing more than mowing its borders. In time, once we have chosen what fruit trees we want to plant, a new, more useful and altogether more tasty orchard will grow in its place.

Shopping Spree (2nd June)

All of the garden tools and machinery that arrived with us at Stone House were originally bought when we lived in London, and although many have served us well since arriving here, they have been asked to punch well above their weight for almost two years. The change from a Hanwell garden to a Herefordshire smallholding has been too much of a shock for them, resulting a noticeable rate of attrition.

The tree loppers threw in the towel after attempting some minor mistletoe surgery, the hedge trimmer took one look at the hawthorn stretching around the field before committing suicide and every hand spade or trowel we have ever owned has snapped, split or shattered. Tines on the garden fork have disappeared in pairs, wheelbarrow tyres can't hold air for longer than an hour and our old lawn mower died in action last September whilst halfway through mowing the grass verge along the B4220; a sort of proving ground on which a mower's ability to deal with metal, concrete and all manner of detritus ejected from passing cars is thoroughly tested.

In fact, the only gardening implement that has withstood the harsh reality of the Herefordshire countryside is Barbara's favourite potting tool. She uses it for anything from seeding tomatoes to weeding the vegetable garden, and from harvesting potatoes to prising out rusty nails. I remember a time when it graced our kitchen drawer and looked very much like a stainless steel soup ladle, but it was called to serve long ago. Effective in its newer role it still may be, but when considering everything else that needs to be done around here, I must borrow a line from the film Jaws; "We're going to need a bigger boat."

There are few times in life when what you want to do is the same as what needs to be done, and in the first few months of this year I had the chance to properly scratch my petrol-powered itch. Feeling like a ten-year-old let loose in Hamley's, I scoured every inch of the internet looking for lawnmowers, hedge trimmers, strimmers and anything else I could think of. The main concern is the grass which, if left to its own devices, becomes unmanageable within a fortnight. Coming a close second is the hedge, but until I manage to secure some EU funding for several tons of Massey Ferguson, it will remain a job that must be outsourced.

Not knowing where to start on Google, I turned to Chris, the knowledgeable and polite mechanic who had serviced the tractor last year, and asked him about strimmers. He guffawed before pointing out that with over three acres, what I really needed was a brush cutter. My blank stare confirmed everything he had already suspected about my competence and knowledge, and intuitively zeroing in on my weak-spot, he showed me a reconditioned top of the range Stihl. It looked like an enormous strimmer with big chrome handlebars stolen from a Harley Davidson, which I immediately judged to be an essential feature and so I bought it on the spot. The force with which it now pulverises undergrowth is staggering, and I now have no choice but to wander about at weekends in a hard hat and mesh guard whilst endlessly revving the throttle like Henry Fonda in Easy Rider.

With one purchase made I moved on, and thanks to advice found on numerous smallholding fora, I then ordered an overweight self-propelled lawnmower with the widest possible cut, biggest grass-box, mulching plug and most reliable engine. I was quite beside myself in anticipation and felt that the 12 hours between ordering it and its delivery was far too long. It was out of its box, assembled and fired up in under half an hour, and it has already significantly reduced the ache I feel in my back after three hours of mowing. It's exactly like graduating to a moped from a bicycle. The best bit? It has alloy-effect wheels and sounds like an American muscle car idling at a traffic light; I can almost hear Jeremy Clarkson describing its torque as 'biblical'. Really, these things matter.

Having invested in all this machinery, I also had to think of the maintenance, longevity and overall economy of them. Most of the land at Stone House is flat and open, but there are a few areas which present more of a challenge. The aforementioned grass verge on the road which falls to us to maintain and other nooks and crannies of grass where it's hard to get to also need to be looked after, and rather than damage the big mower, I decided to pop in to B&Q and buy the smallest and cheapest petrol mower they had. Considering it as 'disposable', I have used it three times and already it is heavily battle scarred and in need of repairs. If it lasts the summer I'll be surprised, and if it doesn't I still have the receipt.

As I continue to discover, maintaining a smallholding is to tending a suburban garden what Formula One is to Dodgems at a funfair. My current strategy is a twin approach of removing anything that doesn't produce something useful or edible and employing petrol powered machinery to help me do it. It is a policy that may prove our somewhat selective approach to The Good Life, but if I get to play with toys like these I'll happily stand accused of anything you like.

Buttercup and Foxtail (9th June)

The most monotonous, moist and miserable spring that I can remember has apparently seeped its way into the recent record books, and our hopes for sunshine and warmth were starting to show signs of rising damp. Until, that is, we reached the end of May when an unfamiliar bright yellow orb appeared in the sky against a backdrop which was, we were reliably informed, a colour known as blue.

It seems clear that such a change at this particular time of year creates the catalyst for incredible growth, resulting in the fields transforming over a very short period of time from quagmires into hay meadows straight out of an Enid Blyton story. Lashings of ginger beer aside, it also confirms the interdependence between my mood and the weather.

The most notable event in recent weeks for us has been Rather's first birthday, and there being only so many similar functions one can go to in a single weekend, we celebrated it privately on the day, having arranged to hold a party for him the following weekend.

This gave us an extra week to prepare, which mostly involved the purchase, delivery and erection of a play area that includes swings, slide and seesaw. Utterly flummoxed by the picture that purported to be the instructions, its construction required a mere six or seven hours' swearing and hammered thumbs while occasionally singing Bob the Builder and wondering if Rather wouldn't be satisfied with a toy instead. Barbara and I feel that the farsightedness we employed in buying a "3-8 years" version more than outweighs the slight oversight that he can't use it in its current format until 2015.

The day dawned bright and sunny, and whilst Barbara whipped up a delicious birthday cake and assorted savouries, I concerned myself with putting up decorations and setting out blankets, chairs, toys and other such items required when you are expecting upwards of ten toddlers and their parents. We had planned it as a drop-in day; we were going to position ourselves on deck chairs with a view while Rather crawled, reggae played and people came and went. Ice buckets of beer and juice, along with a mouth-watering selection of nibbles meant that no mouth would pass by unfilled, and the only unanswered question in our minds would be where the last year had gone.

As it turned out, everyone more or less came at lunchtime, so to avoid recreating an everyday scene from the NCP in Ealing Broadway on a Saturday afternoon, we opened the gate to the small field and created a makeshift car park there. "We moved here from Twickenham two years ago", called out one friend as she approached with her family, "so we're not used to parking in a field of buttercups!" Me neither, I thought.

The next few hours were spent chatting, watching the older children running and jumping through the big field, comparing the mundane minutiae of recent parenthood and discovering that rocket balloons can surprisingly reach distances of up to thirty or forty metres if launched in favourable conditions. And that chickens will try to eat them unless you recover them first.

It was, we reflected later that evening, the first day in the nearly two years that we have been here, where we did no work whatsoever; we just played. Living as far away from our friends and families as we do, it is inevitable that we will see less of them, and so spending this day with our new friends from the area seemed the most appropriate way to celebrate Rather's big day. From dawn till dusk he was his usual contented and relaxed self, pausing only for a brief ninety-second mini-tantrum when we prevented him from burying his fists in his birthday cake. Well, it was his party after all, and the fact that it was framed by watching the sunrise, pass and set over fields of buttercup and foxtail only made it better.

Ten Pin Mauling (23rd June)

If the indescribable joy that comes from looking forward to a November which will not involve breaking my back through harvesting apples weren't enough, another happy consequence that comes from the removal of the orchard is the sigh of relief from my wallet as we have gained a rather large amount of firewood. Apple wood burns hotter, slower and is less smoky than the usual ash or beech sold for firewood, and as it's even more dense than oak, it's very rare to have a large amount of it to burn.

As Rupert felled and chopped each tree, I collected it in my Tonka Toy trailer hitched to the back of the lawn tractor, and drove it to the animal shelter. There it was tipped and I prepared to forget about it for a while. My unconcerned attitude was noted, and I was cautioned that I should begin splitting it very soon, lest it start to season and become harder than a splitter could handle. "Er, like, so how should I best do that?", I asked with the annoying habit that people have when they hire a tradesman and assume all their knowledge is paid for. Thankfully my request fell on receptive ears, and the retort "well, with one of these" came with a whistling thud as Rupert's splitting maul deftly halved a juicy log before my eyes.

A splitting maul is, as I found out, like an axe with a few important differences. The blade is shorter and, importantly, the body is much wider than a traditional axe. The difference seems to be that whereas the axe is designed to penetrate deeply, the maul sacrifices a degree of finesse in order to first wedge, then split wide its target. In short, if you are clambering ashore from a long ship and hope to decimate the cavalry's defences that face you, best leave the maul at home and bring an axe.

Having hauled the felled orchard into the animal shelter and ordered a splitting maul from Amazon, I then set about forming a strategy that would allow me to split around five tonnes of wood without the need to go to hospital. Rupert had warned me that the hardest part of log splitting came not from swinging the maul, but from repeatedly bending over to handle the wood. I had a few practises while I considered my options, and discovered that it seemed relatively straightforward.

I then devised the following plan: I would minimise the repetitive bending over part of the job by placing as many logs as I could side by side, and then attack each one in quick succession. Eager to test my idea, I searched for the largest and most stable logs to use as bases on which to balance the logs I would split, which had the twin bonuses of raising the target and lessening the likelihood of chopping through the floor. Oh, how I needn't have bothered.

I arranged my theatre of operations and was ready to start. My scientific approach was based on the premise that my arms are of a fixed length, and by standing both still and in the right place, I would be able to swing the maul and know it would land squarely on its target. However, I had not factored into my plan that my arms can move in a surprisingly large number of directions, and the result of my first swing was a large gash in the wooden floor of the animal shelter. Recalibrating my swing, the next one shaved about half a centimetre of the left side of the log which was standing to the right of the one I had been aiming at.

After a little while and a lot of destruction, I got the hang of it and actually managed to split a few logs. With time, a sense of confidence developed, and I began to swing the maul harder and harder. I then found my rhythm and the pile of split logs was growing slowly, but inevitably I became careless. I tackled the middle log of five with a huge blow that landed near the edge, and this sent the target log crashing to the left and its base spinning to the right. The result was a full strike with all ten logs spread across the width of the shelter on their sides; something which I have never achieved in a bowling alley. Go me.

There was far too much wood to consider splitting in one session, and so I continued to attack the job over a number of weeks with short bursts of ten or twenty logs at a time. This approach has paid off in that all the splitting is finally done, but it was evident that even after the first week the logs were beginning to harden. On numerous occasions, I swung the maul with all the force I could muster, and it simply bounced off the top of the log. Never again will I consider a wooden structure as a weaker cousin to concrete or stone. Quite the reverse, in fact.

As I worked my way through the pile, my thoughts turned to how best to season it, and I will never cease to be amazed by the information you can find on the Internet. Google and YouTube are firm favourites, but I am learning that they are quite generalist. For the more esoteric topics, of which I consider log seasoning to be an excellent example, you need to dig deeper into the mysteries of the World Wide Web until you come across the specialist interest forum.

In search of an answer to my question, I chanced upon the Green Living Forum, where I read of a great many ways to season wood. With so many options available, inertia-by-opportunity was a very real danger, but in the end I picked one method as it suited my prime purpose of doing as little as possible. A user had posted that I should "treat wood just like you treat your washing. Plenty of draught means your underpants dry that much quicker". I interpreted that to mean that I should just throw all the wood into the corner in a big messy pile, which is exactly what I have done. The logs that are already too hard to split will be seasoned whole and used as logs for Christmas Day and other special occasions when we plan to spend most of the day by the fire.

I am thrilled that the cost of removing the orchard and hedgerow turned out to be less than we would have had to pay for this much wood of similar quality, so I shall look forward to months of apple-scented winter evenings in the winter of 2014, when I shall raise my glass to central heating that although carbon intensive, is for once better than finance neutral.

George Smith Patton Jr. (30th June)

Often quoted for saying things like "A good idea today is better than a great idea tomorrow", General George S. Patton's speeches during the second world war were frequently laced with profanity. Whilst he and I share the laziness of using vulgar vocabulary, we differ significantly in our ability to plan. Or rather, to plan well. In fact, one of my recent projects makes me wonder whether there is room for the following adage to be coined; "No matter how bad an idea is today, it's still going to be worse tomorrow."

For a number of reasons, we have decided to decommission the existing vegetable patch with a view to creating a larger and more user-friendly one in the orchard field one day. Our plan is that the whole area will be returned to grass, with the exception of a new concrete base on which we will soon rebuild the breeze house. The only original part that will remain will be the raspberry patch, which will in time become a lawn feature; a place where you can lie down in the summer sun and occasionally pluck a snack when the urge surfaces.

Originally conceived by Ted a number of years ago, the patch was dug out so that drainage could be installed before a generous helping of topsoil was added. The result was a trapezoid shaped area of roughly four hundred square metres that produced food for a number of years. In an ideal world, I would simply clear it, sow grass and leave it, but unfortunately it is some four or five inches lower than the surrounding area. A combination of Barbara's foot and my sense of aesthetics mean that somehow it has to be made level with its surroundings before it can be seeded.

My brilliant plan was to ask Rupert the tree surgeon if he would like to dump his green waste mixed with wood chips for free rather than pay to dispose of it elsewhere. Common sense, experience and Google all tell me that wood chip decomposes over time, so all I would need to do it spread it around evenly until the ground was level with the surrounding grass, wait a bit and voila! A brilliant and nutritiously rich reclaimed lawn that I could bore guests about for years to come, and I can already visualise Barbara yawning and rolling her eyes.

Well, as it turns out, there were a number of variables in this equation which I failed to pin down. Things like exactly how long is "time" and how much is a "pile". Worse than that, once I knew that the answer was "very long" and "really big" I still went ahead with my plan and had a rather sizeable pile of woodchip on my hands that needed dispersing. And not just one of them, but two.

Spreading the chips was fairly hard going, requiring an awful lot of spadework to transport them to the edge of the patch in just the right quantity to ensure a level finish was achieved. As with all repetitive strenuous tasks, what little patience I normally have soon evaporated, and in a rare moment of inspiration-by-misfortune, I created a new dispersal method by standing on top of the pile, having a hissy fit and kicking the chips in all directions.

As the chips flew and my rage subsided, I discovered a beautiful example of nature in action. The chips, having been piled for something like seventy-two hours, had already started to decompose, and as the heap subsided, the heat it gave off was deliciously scented. When I thrust an arm deep into its middle, it was just like a hot Badedas bath. Wondering whether "things happened" after a hot wood chip and green waste bath too, I continued working long into the afternoon.

Beer o'clock had long passed by the time I had managed to spread what turned out to be several tons of wood chip across the patch, but I caught up with it while surveying my handiwork in the evening. It is by no means the smoothest finish you will ever find, but at least all the edges are level and the concrete pad blends in to its surroundings quite happily. For the rest of this year I will tip lawn cuttings over the top of it, having discovered that the nitrogen in grass is ideal for speeding up the process of decomposition. I have absolutely no idea when it may be ready for seeding, but when the weeds start appearing at least they will be green and can be mowed. One day it will be a low maintenance and hazard-free lawn, and no matter how daft a plan it may have been, it will be worth it in the end.

Replacing the drainage system in August 2012

Homemade produce in August 2013

Breaking up concrete in May 2013

Our beloved Breeze House finally rebuilt in June 2013

Removing the wall between the living and dining rooms in August 2014

Opening up the view on it across the garden in May 2014

The roadside fence and electric gates erected in May 2014

Installing the new wood burner in December 2014

Cropped Circle (7th July)

Modern crop circles are a phenomenon that started in the late 1970's when Doug Bower and Dave Chorley were inspired by the Tully Saucer Nest in Australia to flatten crops in a circular fashion. Their efforts in the Southwest of England became as famous for their designs as for their unexplained origins, and they finally admitted to the ruse in 1991. The practise has since become a global phenomenon with farmers everywhere fearing the destruction of their crops at the hands of 'Cereologists'; those who believe the circles are paranormal and seek spiritual enlightenment from visiting them.

Given that it all started with a prank, the purpose of a crop circle would seem to be fun, and so it was with this in mind that I decided to take advantage of having a two-acre hay meadow by making my very own. I felt that some clear differences between the nature and purpose of mine when compared with those that Wikipedia describes were in order, and ideally these should match my preferred DIY style of improvisation and poor finish. Predictably therefore, if judged by the usual criteria of geometry, precision and symbolism, my effort would be well below par, but on the plus side there would be little risk of a co-ordinated VW camper van invasion at dawn.

The idea behind the circle was nothing more than to create a secluded spot, surrounded by buttercups in which to enjoy a glass of wine. Hardly the stuff of enlightenment I realise, but that can wait for a rainy day. The result of a cursory survey suggested that crossing into the middle of the field through waist high grass with a full glass of wine was unlikely to be achieved without spillage, so a path would have to be made for access. At Barbara's suggestion, the bottom corner of the field was chosen as the entry point. At first I thought her involvement in my plan was a sign of enthusiasm and active participation, but it later became evident that she merely wanted the mistake I was about to make to be out of sight.

I wasn't sure whether the lawn tractor could cope with metre tall grass, but I didn't let this stop me; I raised the cutting deck to it's highest setting and made sure the gear it was in was the lowest. Then I positioned it at the pre-determined entry point, set the steering for the middle of the field, released the clutch and closed my eyes. With blades whirring at full speed, the tractor inched forward and began squealing like a stuck pig as soon as it encountered the tall grass.

Unrepentant and flushed with mechanical sadism I carried on, opening first one eye and then the other. A big grin spread across my face as I slowly made my way up and towards the centre of the field. The cutting deck was working hard to spew the long cuttings through its vent, and although there was no smell of burning rubber or overheating engine parts, I made a mental note to call Chris the next day and order some spare belts in case the punishment I was meting out proved terminal.

When I felt that I had reached a spot that afforded the best position, I turned the wheel hard right and then started a series of left hand circles. It took about eight or nine laps to clear a small space large enough for two sprawling adults, a bottle of wine and a crawling baby. Smiling with satisfaction, I then drove back down the access path allowing the second pass to remove any clumps that I missed on the way up.

Now all I need is a warm day, an empty schedule and a reason to do nothing for a whole afternoon. Barbara has yet to fully explore my creation, but I feel sure that she will approve of its calm and peaceful setting. The bonus is, I feel, that the tall grass bordering the circle and path leading to it will act to safely and effectively contain Rather while we watch the clouds race across the sky overhead.

Clearly nowhere near as artistic as other crop circles, I take comfort from the belief that mine is one of the most practical ones yet made. However, by a twist of fate as cruel as there ever was, my joy was cut short when Farmer Harris turned up a week later to cut the field for hay. It would seem that enlightenment, spiritual or otherwise, comes in many forms. Killjoy.

To Love and eBay (14th July)

A few years ago, when Barbara was about to turn thirty, I asked her what she wanted for her birthday. She said simply "a party in the garden with our friends". We discussed it and agreed to get some kind of marquee in case the British summer lived up to its reputation, and while she made lists, planned food and decided upon music it was left to me to tidy up the garden and get a marquee.

We have always had expensive dreams that are incompatible with our thrifty genes, and so second hand is first nature. Turning to eBay and freecycle in search of anything that would provide weather cover for Barbara's party, it came up with all manner of things from tents to log cabins. I ranked the results in terms of distance from our house, and found someone selling something called a Breeze House just a few roads away.

We had never heard of anything like it, but from the photo it looked rather like a small Caribbean beach bar and so I presumed that it must have been designed with us in mind. I arranged to go and see it that afternoon, and it was one of those moments when something you never knew existed was exactly what you had always wanted. An outdoor living space that was comfortable, snug, dry and would always remind us of our honeymoon in St Lucia and our eternal dream of living in a tropical paradise.

We were lucky in our bid being the only one placed and so won the auction, brought it home and built it in time for her birthday. It is a terrific structure which we have furnished and decorated with lights, a small sound system and shells collected from various beaches around the world. It spent three years at our house in London as the focus of our social life for a good six months of each year; hosting countless hours of idle chat, magnificent dinners and late night parties. When dismantled and stored in Gloucestershire, it had to weather the winter uncovered outside, which wasn't kind to it.

Since its arrival here, it has been kept in the Cider Barn, where over the last two years I have been lazily checking each of its seventy odd pieces, and restoring, repairing and treating them in preparation for constructing it once more. This is almost certainly the last time I will build it, and having all but finished opening up the land by removing fences, hedges, sheds and vegetable gardens, the time had come to pick the best spot for it. After much consideration, a concrete base was installed a few weeks ago on the edge of the old vegetable plot; the perfect place from which to survey our surroundings, the horizon and see the sun rise, pass and set.

Building it from memory was a job as fraught with problems as it was filled with fun. Which piece was this? Where did that bit go? Was there really a bit that went there? How on earth did I get that bit up there last time? That broken bit doesn't matter; no one will notice. I don't remember that bit at all from the last time. You get the picture. Thankfully on the day I put it together, I had both sunshine and Barbara to encourage me in my efforts and lend the ladder a steadying hand. In the end it stood sturdily and there were no leftover pieces, so I was more than pleased with my work.

With the exception of electrics and lighting, it is complete. Having treated every piece of wood with either varnish or outdoor paint, it is as protected as it can be and will, I hope, last for a great many years. Once again it will host meals, parties, late night conversations and moments of absolute silence. As the focal point of our outdoor lives at home, anyone visiting us during warm and clement weather is sure to find us in it.

Impatient as ever on the day that I built it, I went out later that evening to put the chickens to bed and to enjoy the fruits of my labour. Rather and Barbara had already settled down for the night, but having waited for this moment for almost three years, there was no way I was going to miss the opportunity of a warm and dry evening in, what is for me, the best setting possible when there is no tropical beach within reach.

Admittedly odd to hold outdoor furniture in such high esteem, I nonetheless felt that another piece of the jigsaw had slotted into place as I switched on the outdoor speakers quietly and then made myself comfortable under the new thatched roof. With a view of the Linton Downs ahead of me, I contemplated my lot while my glass of red wine went down as slowly, surely and gently as the setting sun.

Code of Conduct (21st July)

It's quite common for groups of people who feel either isolated or in the minority to derive a sense of safety through openly acknowledging those in the same position with a heightened familiarity, even though they may be total strangers. For example, it is unthinkable that the crews of two yachts encountering each other on the high seas wouldn't wave at each other, and anyone driving a classic car is almost certain to flash their headlights at another on the open road. Personally, I can attest to having been treated like a long lost relative by numerous strangers at a ZZ Top concert simply for wandering around aimlessly and drinking beer whilst wearing a baseball hat, dark sunglasses and false beard.

As we mark the end of our second year at Stone House tomorrow, it has become clear that living in a solitary rural setting surrounded by fields on a long and quiet road means that most people who pass will acknowledge our presence as smallholders of some sort, but the manner in which they do so can vary wildly.

Drivers will almost always stare as they pass; it's the same instinct that we all have on motorways when we see an accident on the opposite carriageway. These are the most unrewarding, as anything from wild waving through to complete indifference nets the same response; they carry on regardless as they never really had the time to focus on anything specific. Cyclists, as we have noted before, have little spare energy for us, but passing walkers and horse-riders can be the most interesting as they enter into conversation quite happily. Without fail I will return the effort, but I have to admit that sometimes there is a part of me that wants to find out what would happen if I just fixed them with a blank stare and muttered "Mister, I sure love the way you wear that hat" while gently plucking a banjo.

However, I hold a special fondness for passing farmers in their tractors. Jealous of their machinery I certainly am, but the seemingly complex construct of their acknowledgement is also intriguing. To me, it shares some of the qualities of a politician's artifice on achieving office when they jog to the podium and point towards an imaginary childhood chum fifteen rows back, their face taking on an expression of "aww, shucks, me?"

By my reckoning, there are several factors that influence this idiosyncratic greeting. Firstly, the fact that they are sitting some ten feet higher up in the air than anyone else must give them a sense of superiority, and being at the wheel of several tons of metal powered by several thousands of horsepower does little to diminish this. Secondly, they must enjoy the same power enjoyed by the safety car in Formula One, as they lead a column of impatiently tutting motorists trapped behind them. And finally, it's Pavlovian; if you wave at them they absolutely must wave back. However it is unlike any other wave I have ever witnessed and so, after two years of extensive research, I have now developed this; the definitive methodology for achieving the perfect tractor wave.

1. Be dismissive. On no account should you make eye contact and, if it helps, imagine you are brushing the crumbs from your table to the needy poor below. Holding a mobile phone to your ear with your other hand will undoubtedly help.

2. Be distinctive: You should develop your own particular style to suit the ergonomics of the machine you are driving: extended sweeping motions through open windows are good, but anything derived from a salute looks amateur and could possibly trigger one of the many hydraulic levers in the cab.

3. Be vague: Your wave should be languid and effortless, lasting for just a bit longer than you are in view to show that you didn't really pay too much attention.

4. Be subtle: You should be able to conjure a clever mix of superiority and a whiff of conspiratorial mischief regarding the caravan of traffic that follows you.

5. Be unselfconscious: Thanks to agricultural suspension being designed primarily for slow speeds across uneven fields, you have to do all of this whilst not minding that a substantial proportion of your body mass is undulating far beyond your control.

I can appreciate that the image of a farmer might not be an advertiser's obvious first choice for selling a men's fragrance, but I think it should be seriously considered as in many ways they remind me of the strap-line from the TV advert for Denim in the 1980's that read "for the man who doesn't have to try... too hard."

On Our Doorstep (4ᵗʰ August)

Novelty always wears off, and already we have begun to take for granted the beauty of Herefordshire that surrounds us. In our schedule of work, nappies and household chores, we forget how seductive it can be to idly pass an afternoon doing little more than curiously noticing whatever happens to be right in front of us, so it's more than a little nice to be reminded of it sometimes.

When a dear friend of mine recently made plans with us to visit for a weekend, Barbara immediately began to research what sights we might show her. Thanks to leaflets, town chatter and Google, she discovered that a farm not five minutes up the road was hosting a "fun day", which appeared to consist of refreshments, petting animals, enjoying views and taking a tractor ride. Feeling that it was perhaps not too far up the scale of amazing things to do, we arrived not really knowing what to expect. The drive twisted and turned high over the Bromyard Downs, and we eventually arrived at an arable and dairy farm of over 250 acres, sufficiently isolated to allow the imagination to wander through time without the usual distractions of modern infrastructure.

Owned by a family who shared their farm and way of life with pride and open arms, we were invited by a young man to first explore the immediate surroundings which included some fields which were filled with hand-reared sheep and, surprisingly, a pair of ageing milk floats, some stone sheds containing chicks and ducklings that were barely a week old and a beautiful timber-framed barn just right for parties. The owner later assured us that very loud reggae wouldn't disturb the animals.

We discovered that a neighbour of ours helps out there at weekends, and she recommended that we take advantage of the next tractor ride which took passengers along the ridge of the hill that formed the border between the farm and some common land. As we refreshed ourselves with a delicious drink, we looked at Rather's sleepy eyes and concluded that he could withstand a half-hour's ride before his nap, and set off.

Sitting on straw bales strewn across a trailer, we lazily chugged along behind a tractor drinking in views as far as the Black Hills to the West and the Cotswolds to the East. Occasionally we stopped for a brief description of this crop or that geological feature from the owner, and we immediately warmed to his humour and farming philosophy of "If I don't like it, chances are I won't do it"

On our return, I stopped to thank the young man who had earlier shown us around the farm buildings. He turned out to be the owner's youngest son who is a year into his Land Management degree at Reading University, and a truly charismatic young man who can't wait to complete his studies and return to work on the farm full time. Equally at home explaining the workings of the farm to us as he was adept at entertaining young children with wheelbarrows and an obstacle course, I don't doubt that he also fits in very well at the student union bar. Barbara and I later reflected that we wouldn't mind one bit if Rather grew up to be a little like him.

The forecast heavy rain drenched the farm as we left, and the rest of the afternoon was spent exploring arts, crafts and local produce at the Hop Pocket, a favourite local haunt of ours, before an evening of food, wine and good conversation. It was a wonderful weekend reminder for us to stop and look at what's right under our nose.

Civil Service (18th August)

As far as I can tell, dealing with local government is as unavoidable as are death and taxes. Equally certain is that it will involve navigating through an inordinate amount of pointless red tape and baffling bureaucracy, as without either there might be precious little need for much of the civil service in the first place. Only when it's unprecedented in terms ease or difficulty, however, does it become memorable.

For me, an example of the former was when I briefly lived in Antigua and was told one day that as I was working there, I had to get a local driving licence. I remember turning up at the police station in English Harbour, waiting for five minutes, and then being called forward by the desk sergeant. He asked to see my US driving licence, demanded 35 EC Dollars, gave me the thumbs up and handed me a scrap of paper with a polite "Irie" while pocketing the money and gesturing towards the door. Our business concluded, I fired up my moped and headed straight back to the beach where I basked in the warm glow of the sun, a Red Stripe and legal compliance.

Recently Barbara and I have experienced the latter, and we are still reeling from the calibre of logic, process and consistency employed by our local planning service. When we bought Stone House, we did so in the full knowledge that it was compromised by being an old house in need of some maintenance, as well as being closer and more exposed to the road than we would like.

We have already undertaken a number of jobs from the insignificant to the structural to improve the house as well as the surrounding land. The road, however, we obviously cannot move and our wish has always been to build a long wall to border our plot for the purpose of protecting children from the passing traffic, and providing some security and privacy for the house too. It is this plan that has brought us into unpleasantly close contact with those that administer local planning laws.

The application process would be laughable if it weren't so painful; the requirements being to submit a location plan and a site plan. Oddly enough, the use of satellite photography is not accepted, being considered poor quality. The preference is for 50-year-old Ordnance Survey charts which are wildly inaccurate and can be bought at great expense from, you guessed it, the council. A beautiful nuance is that even if the location plan and site plan show exactly the same information to the same scale, you still need to provide both and the receipts for each are the only proof that they are, in fact, different. Ker-ching.

To these plans you must add an architect's drawing of the proposed works that conform to rules that can't actually be explained; only interpreted. Our vision is to install new solid wooden gates and build a 1.8 metre high featheredge fence on the inside of our roadside hedge along its full length. In the preceding sentence, I believe I have both accurately and fully described our proposal in less characters than a full tweet, but the effort to get the plans to the stage where they could be considered took three months and over twenty pages of detailed diagrams about prevailing winds, trees and local topography.

Finally, in June, Barbara came home to find a yellow piece of A4 nailed to the driveway gates that announced our intentions to anyone interested. For a whole month we left the paper in full view and wondered who might object and on what possible grounds.

No one did object, but towards the end of July we received a phone call from the planning officer who told us that not only were our proposals not going to be accepted, but that they never would as our plans to erect a fence adjacent to the road were tantamount to "urbanising the area". When I asked him why everyone else around here had been able to do exactly what we had proposed, he officiously intoned that he was merely outlining his intentions as directed by the law, but that my actions were up to me. Naive I may have been by applying in the first place, but I have no wish to build what one day I may have to remove.

My response was to become equally pedantic. I first pointed out that as the land either side of the proposed fence is ours, the fence couldn't technically, let alone grammatically, be described as adjacent to the road. He countered that it would be considered as such through its proximity, and so I asked for a legal definition of the term. Was it one metre? Two? Ten? He had cited the law in defence of his decision, but my asking him to clarify it irritated him to the point where he icily confirmed that adjacent was, for all intents and purposes, whatever he said it was.

I next challenged the landscaping officer on her inconsistency in calling our proposed fence an 'eyesore' and refusing us what her department had previously allowed elsewhere. She became equally slippery and, tiring of her politics, I requested that she perhaps stop telling me what I can't do and consider telling me what I can do. After some pointless verbal ping-pong lasting three or four volleys, she quite took my breath away by stating that I had obviously bought a house that was unsuitable for children. I repeated her statement slowly back to her as a question to see if she might flesh it out with any detail, but the edge in my voice was evident and she thankfully remained silent.

As I often do, when faced with adversity and a challenge, I ranted and whined. I whined quite a lot, in fact. To Barbara, to the chickens and to anyone and anything else that would listen. Whining yielded nothing, so I next tried wine to see what that offered, and before long life seemed better.

A few days later, Barbara took matters into her own hands and, while driving home one afternoon, stopped a few miles down the road just in front of two houses that were each shielded from the road by exactly what we wanted to build. After taking a few snaps on her phone and having a quick chat with the owners, she was on her way and later that evening sent a beautifully innocent email to the planning officer, complete with 'then and now' photos courtesy of Google Streetmap.

Last Tuesday we received from the council a brief note to the effect that if we resubmitted the application without the sections of wooden fence behind the hedgerow, our request would be looked upon favourably. Therefore later this year, I plan to install new gates and bordering fences as originally intended, and when viewed from the road I imagine it will be rather hard to tell whether or not there are additional panels behind the hedgerow.

However, when I view them from the comfort of the Breeze House with a glass of wine, I will probably reflect that it's the service and not just the weather that's more civilized in the Caribbean.

Neither Here Nor There (1st September)

Since we can remember, Barbara and I have longed for a life in the sun; something which both of us briefly enjoyed many years ago. After we were married, we did try to emigrate with a rigid set of criteria for destinations, which resulted in a limited but enticing choice. In the end it was immigration policies that put paid to that particular dream, and we then agreed that where we were was probably the best compromise for the time being.

When it came to selecting the nationality for Rather's passport, we felt that choosing from all of the options available through his parents was less important than for him to grow up without the potential for feeling like he doesn't belong in his peer group. He can make his own mind up in due course naturally, but for now this has resulted in our family having passports from three different countries. It's probably a good thing that the closest Barbara and I come to displaying any feelings of national pride is during the Eurovision Song Contest.

Having lived as an American in the United Kingdom for almost all of my life, and having had a job for the last eighteen years that requires a fair amount of foreign travel, I am no stranger to the UK Border Agency or its queues. I have long found irritating its employees' use of the overly dramatic pause whilst studiously avoiding eye contact, and find it hard not to reflect this behaviour back to them as a rule. The laboured question "how (pause) long will you be staying with us in the UK (longer pause) Sir?" is usually met with at least five seconds of silence before a barely audible "Indefinitely" escapes my lips whilst I carefully examine my fingernails. At least they no longer herd my ilk and me into a queue labelled 'aliens', and I am grateful for this.

It is experiences such as these and others that have led to nationality and heritage meaning very little to me, as I consider them geographical and biological anomalies often having far less to do with character and identity than they do self-aggrandisement and elitism. Only by accident did I discover ten years ago that I am also legally Italian, when I was arrested at customs in Forli by two epaulette-laden officers. Their computer told them that I had not carried out the compulsory year of military service that all Italian citizens were at the time required to do. Unaware that this meant me, I imagine that the expression on my face probably didn't need much translating, but nonetheless my metamorphosis from tourist into transgressor was instant. I remember it as an embarrassing and ridiculous scene during which my limited vocabulary, barely adequate for ordering a glass of wine or asking for directions to the train station, proved utterly hopeless when defending myself against accusations of being a draft-dodger.

Often, when I return from a trip abroad, the journey through airport customs can take longer than the flight on which I have arrived. This delay is not in itself wholly remarkable, but my recent decision to reconsider my nationality for reasons of expediency was further underlined when we returned from our recent holiday in France. On driving up to the UK customs border in Fréthun and handing over all three passports, I was greeted with "So.... who's the American, then?", which was followed by the obligatory five minutes' occasional throat clearing whilst my ILR stamp was forensically examined from a number of angles. I distinctly didn't like the feeling of an imaginary line being drawn between my family and me.

Having earned the right to UK citizenship back in 1978, I thought that now was as good a time as any to avail myself of the privilege, and so set about filling in the multitude of forms required. For me, the highlight of the process this summer was taking the Life in the UK test, which was a set of twenty-four multiple-choice questions from which I must correctly answer eighteen to pass. In the end, I made errors on two and from now on I shall never forget that the first coins made bearing an image were produced in the Iron Age, and Vindolanda was the name of a fort on Hadrian's Wall.

I was then given a short period of time to attend a Citizenship Ceremony, during which I was to pledge my allegiance to the Crown. Such ceremonies are only held once a month, and my work diary meant that I would have to pay for a private one if were to complete the process in time. Whilst I stood in reverence in front of several flags at the Town Hall and theatrically repeated several sentences, I held Rather in my arms to prevent him from fidgeting. Barbara stifled her giggles in the corner whilst taking photos of us under a picture of the Queen. At the end I was awarded a certificate of naturalisation and presented with, of all things, a wooden apple. I kept a straight face while I thanked the lady that had presided over the service, and desperately wanted to ask if they had run out of wooden spoons.

Later this year, when I take a break from work in time for the birth of our daughter, I will be able to send my current passport away in order to receive my first UK documentation. Then, not only will our family be able to travel through customs together as one, but also my passage through passport control on work trips should become significantly quicker.

But now, as a new citizen, I find myself with a new problem. Most people that I know refer to themselves principally by their home nation; in fact I have rarely heard anyone identify themselves solely as British, and almost never as from the UK. Given that my affirmation of allegiance was to the United Kingdom of Great Britain and Northern Ireland, and contained no specific references to England, Scotland or Wales for me to choose from, it may be that I have succeeded only in adding yet a further layer of complexity to my mongrel pedigree. As long as it speeds up my journey from here to there, that's fine by me.

Professional by Proxy (8ᵗʰ September)

Thanks to the numerous errors that I have committed in the name of amateur smallholding over the last two years, I have proved myself worthy of a place amongst the ranks of the Federation of Master Bodgers, and my badge is proudly stuck on with duct tape. However, my membership may soon be revoked in view of the fact that I seem not only to be developing the ability to accurately gauge the probable outcome of a given venture, but to exploit this new found finesse by actually putting in place a strategy to ensure success.

I now find myself subdividing tasks into the parts that I can reasonably expect to achieve and those that I can't. This diagnosis is made according to any number of variables such as the availability of appropriate machinery, whether I have the time to do it or indeed whether or not I feel strong enough to attempt the job in the first place. Actual competence, you'll be relieved to hear, has absolutely no place in this equation.

There is no better recent example of this new modus operandi than the job of erecting of a new post and rail fence between the field and garden to replace the hedgerow that was removed this spring. As one of the more desirable qualities of a fence is that it be vertical and capable of withstanding me leaning against it in a thoughtful pose at sunset, I sought the services of Stan, a local who has probably forgotten more about fence building that most of us will ever learn. He came to have a look at what needed doing, and we agreed a price for which he would supply all the wood needed, hang both gates and install the upright fence posts.

When he turned up with his son and some heavy machinery the following week, I turned a predictable shade of green as he unleashed a 250 kilo weight attached to his tractor, and hydraulically pummelled a wooden pole not less than a foot in diameter about five feet into the ground. To it he attached the new wooden gate that I had found on eBay last winter, and then winked at me as he said "that's not going anywhere in a hurry". After that he started working his way towards the Cider Barn, driving half-round posts neatly into the ground at regular intervals as his son checked each one with a spirit level to make sure it was absolutely straight and true. I knew I was in the presence of true professionals, as the only thing I've ever used a spirit level for is to look at the bubble in amazement after one too many drinks.

To me would fall the relatively simple jobs of attaching galvanised stock net and two runs of rails. The benefits of dividing the labour in this way were numerous; from costing less to being properly done and letting me feel as though I have built a fence properly, albeit only in part.

It was, I dare say, a relatively pain-free and easy job. Once I had bought a fifty-metre roll of stock net, I spent a few minutes enjoying the fact that, when still in a roll, it shares many of the properties of a slinky. Standing on the highest part of the new fence by the Cider Barn, I positioned the roll on the ground, aimed it towards the lower end and gave it a hefty kick before enjoying its spring-like recoil. Attaching it was a matter of banging galvanised staples across the netting and into each post. I estimate that this job could be rated PG given that there was only moderate swearing thanks to the reckless way in which I wield a hammer, and my thumb occasionally being in the way. However, it was a sign of growing professionalism that I managed to avoid getting a single splinter.

One of the beautiful design aspects of a typical stock fence is that the net is sandwiched between the posts and the rails. This means that the various miscalculations and errors on my part, which resulted in the net being somewhat ill fitting in places, would be mostly smoothed out at the end. The finishing touch was to spruce up the old metal gate, now properly hung, with Hammerite paint to keep the rust at bay for a few more years. It may be arguable whether I've finished the job well or not, but I can't quite remember the last time I derived such pleasure from looking at the fruits of my labour.

The fence now gives definition to the garden on one side and the field on the other, and is almost exactly as I had imagined; allowing views from the house right across to the bench on the eastern border of the field. Later this year, once the last of the Leylandii is removed, the sight-lines to all four corners of our plot will be the uninterrupted ones we envisaged back when we first viewed the house in 2011.

This new strategy may mark me out as an eternal amateur, but outsourcing the complicated aspects of a job to professionals means that a hard day's work can now be little more than pure pleasure whilst yielding just enough of a sore back to ensure sympathy from Barbara at sundown. It also means whatever the job, it's more likely to still be there in a year's time.

Three Bags Full (22nd September)

Barbara would admit that she is not the most patient person to have walked the earth, and to tell the truth it's only through comparison with her that I even have the slimmest appearance of it myself. When we first arrived at Stone House, the dreams came tumbling out of our heads; chickens here, sheep there, vegetables over there and ducks, pigs and alpacas to follow. And all of it to start appearing next week, if possible. As this book chronicles, progress has been both slow and laced with a great deal of learning along the way. One of the earliest big surprises has been the reality of the financial cost of The Good Life, whether it's concerning utilities, transport, or general maintenance and upkeep.

Household bills are the same, but a full tank of fuel bought locally costs roughly £7 more than it does in London, and we have no tube, bus or Boris Bike providing an alternative. Having said that, vegetables and fruit are far cheaper to grow than to buy, which thankfully is a great saving, but the same is not true of meat. The cost of buying livestock, feeding it and then filling your freezer with it makes it far far cheaper to visit local supermarkets, even though they are noticeably more expensive than the branches in big cities.

Even if we could afford the fancy of keeping and rearing our own animals for meat, we would not be able to dedicate the time needed to look after them; yet we still liked the idea of enjoying a lazy glass of wine in the Breeze House while a small flock of sheep nibbled the grass a few feet away. As a compromise we decided that the best course of action would be to look for a farmer who needed extra land, and strike a similar deal to the one with Farmer Harris that we had inherited from Ted. Barbara, through her village contacts, put the word out.

Just after we came back from our summer holiday, there was a knock on the front door, and we opened it to meet Lewis the Shepherd. He had heard of our search, and had popped by to see if a deal could be done. Barbara and I invited him to have a look at the field straightaway to see if it suited his purposes, and as we made our way up past the garage it was obvious that he had great difficulty walking. I asked if he was alright, thinking that perhaps another day might be easier for him. With a manner that reminded me very much of the Black Knight in Monty Python and The Holy Grail, he answered breezily "Oh it's nothing; I always walk like this. Ever since I blew my foot clean orf with a shotgun, you see?" To emphasise his point, he raised his left foot, gave it a mighty thwack with his crook and a loud metallic bang shattered the afternoon peace.

We wandered around the field's perimeter checking to see the condition of the stock net buried in the hedge, discussing terms as we went. He said he'd put about twenty sheep on the field, visit them every few days and keep the place clean after shearing and dagging. In exchange for this, he would arrange for all our hedges to be cut towards the end of October, and maintain the borders.

It will be some time before we are ready to start reorganising the small field by replanting an orchard, building raised vegetable beds and installing a new concrete base for the greenhouses, so we also asked if he wouldn't mind letting his sheep occasionally wander through the gate from the big field to keep the grass short in there too. Our deal concluded as a yearly rollover arrangement, he left and I set about the last jobs that needed to be completed to make the land safe for stock.

In late August, a shy and gentle flock of ten ewes of assorted breeds arrived in the back of his trailer. Once the ramp was lowered, they tumbled out and disappeared to all four corners of the field to examine their new surroundings.

They now criss-cross the field lazily, chewing and snorting in obvious delight at the long grass that has been growing steadily since it was last cut in May, and the ground beneath is doubtless grateful for the plentiful quantities of fertiliser that they give back. Lewis visits every few days to make sure all is well, and having studied his practise from afar, I now know that if I want the flock to madly dash from the other side of the field to encircle me impatient for a treat, all I need to do is rustle a plastic bag to replicate the sound made when their shepherd digs deep into his pockets for a packet of Old Holborn tobacco.

Finally seeing a flock of sheep grazing in the field is for us a lovely scene, and Rather now takes as much delight from seeing them as we do. Over the weeks that followed their arrival, the flock increased first to sixteen and then twenty-two; Lewis' trailer only allowing for a small number to be moved at a time. As we get to know them and watch them through the passing seasons, we will learn their habits, they will learn ours, and if Lewis' generous words translate to deeds, one or two may end up in our pot.

For now though, and after only a few hours' observation, all we can say with certainty is that they are in possession of a metabolic rate that has to be seen to be believed. So fast is it, that I would wager that whoever wrote the lyrics to Baa Baa Black Sheep wasn't really referring to wool when they wrote the line Three Bags Full.

La Poire (29th September)

The fruit harvest was all but ruined by the sheer volume of rain that persistently fell throughout 2012, but this year the cold and late spring followed by a dry and hot summer meant that a bumper fruit harvest across Herefordshire was on the cards. Seeing the plums, apples and pears starting to form after the blossom fell away in May gave me the idea to try once again to make an alcoholic fancy by growing a pear inside a bottle and then pickling it in vodka.

Unfortunately my work schedule meant that I wasn't as watchful as I should have been, and by the time I noticed that the pear tree was producing hundreds of small fruit, there was only one specimen I could find that would fit through the neck of a bottle. Carefully I removed all the leaves and twigs near it, so that I could slip the neck of the bottle over it and secure it to the branch for the summer. I hoped that I hadn't picked a dud, and was pleased to see that it remained healthy throughout the summer. From time to time, as I passed between the house and garage, I glanced up at it to see it getting bigger and fatter inside.

By the last weekend of August, the damsons were falling and the plums were just becoming juicy. The two remaining apple trees wouldn't be ready to give up their fruit until the late autumn, and pears are best picked early and left to ripen protected from the wasps and other insects that normally devour them. With the pears showing the first traces of springiness to their feel when squeezed, I felt it was time to harvest my one bottle. As I carefully cut it from it's stem, it was clear that the bottle had collected rainwater as well as bits of leaf and dead insect over the three months that it had been suspended there.

Clearly my technique needs some refining to keep foreign objects out, but rinsing the bottle out with water took care of most of it. However, it wasn't until I used the garden hose set to it's highest pressure that I was able to get the bottle properly clean, soaking myself in the process.

Then it was just a matter of pricking the pear with several holes, filling the bottle to the brim with vodka and screwing the cap on. I have no idea how long it will need to sit for, and it's anyone's guess whether it will produce pear flavoured or just rather odd tasting vodka. In fact, the only thing I can be certain of at the moment is that this is not a hobby for the impatient.

Regardless of the outcome of this particular experiment, I have at least proved that the fruit-in-bottle process works, and so I'll make sure to be on the ball next year. With luck the tree will spend the summer with as many bottles as I can find attached to it and clinking in the breeze.

Along with the jams, cordials and Damson gin that Barbara produces, some Pear vodka could well be given away as gifts if it's good enough, although I'm sure Grey Goose will have nothing to fear from the competition.

Farm Fashion (6th October)

Having grown up in a family that for the most part seemed to prefer being where other people weren't, I have many memories of summer holidays spent either meandering through deserted parts of the Inner Hebrides on a boat, or escaping from the Welsh rain under the awning of an orange tent that never lost its damp smell in all the years that I knew it. Unless there was wind forecast in excess of a Storm 10, harbours were strictly avoided in favour of secluded anchorages, and I don't think I ever once visited a designated campsite, choosing instead to head far off the beaten track where our car almost inevitably became mired in some bog. On one memorable occasion, we spent a few days in the middle of a Ministry of Defence firing range somewhere near the Brecon Beacons. The shell craters did rather give it away, but we took comfort from the fact that they were mostly grass-covered and there were no red flags flying that we could see.

These holidays were without doubt the foundation for my relationships with the Tilley Lamp and Wellington Boot, both of which last to this day; but for very different reasons. Whilst the former remains for me very much a romantic fancy, the latter is now an absolute necessity. Thanks to the volume of rain that falls in Herefordshire, the high clay content of the soil that it lands on and the amount of poop produced by chickens and sheep, it's safe to say that that I have a new-found appreciation for Billy Connolly's The Welly Boot Song.

Shortly after we arrived at Stone House, it became obvious that my old pair that had only ever had to deal with Richmond Park on Christmas Day weren't up to the job. Luckily, my work took me to the Lake District for a week soon after moving in, and I thought that the rambling capital of the UK might be one of the better places to kit myself out properly. I duly found a shop during a lunch break, encouraged the shop assistant to steer me towards the higher-quality end of the store, and let my plastic take the strain. I was soon the owner of a pair of racy, very comfortable and rather pricey boots, which I brought home the following week and put to work.

They have lasted slightly less than two years in my service. Now they are riddled with holes from thorns and nails, have separated from their soles and the insides resemble a gutted fish in a number of ways. As a result I judged them to be too much Range Rover and not enough Land Rover when I threw them out, and this from the part-time use that I mete out mostly at weekends.

Now with a little more experience under my belt to rely on, I recently went searching for a new pair of boots that could give a good account of themselves when measured against the following criteria; something that the last pair had noticeably failed to manage: Are they easy to put on at two in the morning when the water pipes burst? Can they be used as a sledgehammer or crowbar when I can't find one? Would I notice a car driving over my feet whilst wearing them? How easy is it to remove animal poop from the soles?

After searching online and in person, I came up with a pair of beauties looking like something Captain Haddock from Tintin might wear. They are lined with steel both above and below the foot, and are very soft rubber everywhere else. The only other notable feature is that they are fashioned in a shade of beige that makes them hard to distinguish from much of the hotel food that I eat, so I'm confident that Gok Wan doesn't own a pair.

Within days of getting them, the outsides have become covered in dribbles of black paint, the soles are caked in mud, thorns and poop, and the insides have developed a lived-in quality that would challenge even the biggest bottle of Febreze. Who knows how long they will last, but at less than thirty quid, at least they'll be cheaper to replace.

As we ease once more into autumn, it's a little slice of country life that I doubt you'll ever find among the pages of Country Life magazine, and it's no wonder that people around me would rather be somewhere else when I take them off.

Free-ranging (13th October)

Chickens cannot fly, have the memory of a goldfish and are completely stupid. That being said, they also have beautiful psychological flaws that create clear personalities, and it is these that make them so endearing to us. With such a strong attachment to them, we take pleasure in and closely follow the ups and downs that are their lives. Over the course of this summer, we lost one hen to old age and gained a further six at around the same time, meaning that we now have a colourful and noisy flock of ten to keep us amused and chock-full of cholesterol.

With caution maturing into confidence through experience, the flock has so far enjoyed eighteen months of predator-free living. At first we kept them in their cage, only letting them roam their pen when we were at home. Soon after, we abandoned them to their fate in the pen, and enlarged it to fill the entire space bordered by the garage, cider barn and orchard field. Lately, the large field has been given over to sheep, leaving the smaller field to somehow seem empty by comparison, and we hatched a plot to let the chickens roam freely in there as well by fashioning a miniature gate to allow them to pass freely through the fence.

Freedom of movement must clearly be in the air at Stone House of late, as it was towards the end of the summer that Rather found the confidence to stop clinging to walls and let his legs do the walking. Having first stood unaided during our holiday in France, it seems to have taken him the better part of a month to get his sea, or rather, land legs. He has used them to great effect to explore every corner of the house and, when allowed outside, to wander around after the chickens. Clearly a young man with an eye for opportunity, it didn't take him long to escape through the new gate after the hens. The opening being larger than a chicken yet smaller than a sheep, a part of me thinks he knew I couldn't follow him.

At first worried that they might peck him, we are glad that the birds have so far accepted him and his clumsy curiosity, and they all seem quite content to roam the field together. Thankfully he draws the line at sharing their diet of worms, slugs and other slimy critters, although that has probably got more to do with our watchfulness than any discerning qualities of his palate.

Often staggering like a little drunkard, he ambles first here and then there with his palms facing upward, and usually uses either his bottom or his face to bring a halt his progress. Thankfully he is slowly learning to cushion the blow with his hands, and seems to have gained an appreciation that his head is perhaps not best suited to being used as a hammer.

The chickens, now with almost an acre to themselves, are heady with excitement as they explore the orchard field. The grass, uncut since May, is almost as tall as they are, and if you squint at the right angle it can look like a school of sharks lazily meandering in circles as the just-visible tail feathers scoot first this way, then that. It took them almost a week to venture far enough from their pen and discover the compost pile in the far corner of the field. Being something in the region of ten tons of decomposing matter, it is teeming with worms and utterly irresistible to them, and is the very reason why we can't risk leaving Rather to his own devices when in the field.

Having been raised as a city dweller, I always thought it was the case that animals were penned in to preserve as much garden as possible for human pastimes, and these hard-wired beliefs have persisted until quite recently. Originally Barbara and I planned the land around the house to take account of a clearly defined area for this and another for that, but on lengthy reflection I have come to realise that the very point of free-ranging is that it is neither planned nor artificially restricted.

A simple lesson that has taken a few years for me to learn, the plan has now changed in that we will preserve a relatively small area of garden around the house in which children can play safely and without stepping in poop, and cars can come and go without letting animals escape. The rest of the plot is fair game for sheep, chickens, Gerald, Fantastic Mr Fox and anyone else that wants to bunk down with us.

Laziness never far from my mind, the bonus is that the more land we give over to nature, the less we have to look after. Oh look, is that a glass of wine?

Decade (20th October)

David Blaine is an American illusionist who is famous for turning an ordinary activity into an extraordinary feat through resilience. Yesterday, it was ten years to the very day since he emerged from a glass box that had been suspended beneath a crane just by Tower Bridge in London. As he ended forty-four days of very public imprisonment, I was a stone's throw away on the opposite bank of the river about to end solitude of a more private kind.

Having initially made contact and chatted via the internet some months earlier, Barbara and I had arranged to meet for the first time at Fenchurch Street Station, and by coincidence it was on the same Sunday evening that the dramatic ending of the illusionist's stunt had drawn people to the area in their thousands. I remember almost no detail of the publicity circus that took place that evening, filled as I was with a totally unrelated but equally consuming expectation.

To this day I can bring to mind almost every detail of that evening. I see her walking down the steps from the platform to meet a very nervous me in the entrance hall below; about a million things going through my mind. As we walked towards St. Katherine's Dock, she took my arm and I remember the faint surprise I felt that a Swedish girl living in Essex should speak with a slightly Australian accent without ever having been there. I can also recall feeling absolutely certain that I would ask her to marry me, and left her alone with a hand-written note that hinted as much, while I loitered in the gents' toilet for ten minutes to give her the chance to make good her escape. Cool I absolutely was not.

There was no lightning bolt, no parting of clouds and no orchestra string section playing behind me; there was just a quiet certainty. I managed to get the question out just after New Year's, and thankfully she said yes. It is the best decision that I have ever made, and the only one arrived at without the influence of geography, capability or circumstance. It stands therefore as an ace amongst precious few diamonds, and whilst this post may well be off topic as far as the day-to-day aspects of smallholding are concerned, when it comes to articulating The Good Life, it is fundamental.

Momentum Conservation (17ᵗʰ November)

With the exception of August, I have been fortunate enough to work more or less constantly this year. Barbara and I had decided that I would take six weeks' paternity leave starting in mid-November, and so it was a case of scheduling all the work I could find before then, in order to fill the larder ahead of what will be much leaner times. Of course, the remainder of the year won't be a rest, but it will be a most welcome and wonderful change.

At one of my last workshops of the year a few days ago, I was fascinated to learn a little bit about something called The Law of Conservation of Momentum. Demonstrated simply; if you drop a tennis ball sitting on top of a football to the ground, the energy of the one hitting the floor passes to the other on top, causing the tennis ball to bounce far further than if you had dropped it by itself. As Barbara would admit, it has to be seen to be believed, and it's clearly a clever way of getting a bigger bang for your buck. I plan on exploiting something like this at Stone House over the coming weeks, having returned to a smallholding suffering from a noticeable degree of neglect.

After a half hour's wander around in the half-light the other morning I could see that the chickens have wrought havoc on the compost pile, converting it from a neat heap in the corner of the orchard field into a much larger area which resembles

Worthy Farm after a characteristically wet Glastonbury Festival. Having failed to get the lawnmower out for a final cut before the rains came in October, every corner of the plot is covered in overly long grass which prevents the ground from drying even if the sun shines for a few days. On top of this, all the trees are busy shedding their leaves which create treacherous walking conditions beneath. Not only do I have my work cut out, but none of it can be done by machine.

In addition to clearing the debris of autumn, I also have the next six weeks to complete a number of other jobs that cannot wait until the spring. Quite a few bushes and fruit trees must be dramatically pruned, thirty feet of raspberry bushes that lie on the border of the old vegetable garden need to be transplanted to an as yet undecided location in the orchard field, and an assortment of leaking gutters, askew roof tiles and other weather-worn items need addressing too.

If all of this is to be done before I go back to work in the New Year, yet take it's rightful place after the imminent arrival of "number two", then I will need to find any number of footballs on which to bounce a tennis ball. Sadly, however, I am no longer able to fuel my productivity with either illicit chemicals or youthful vigour.

Instead, I shall fortify myself with a well-tested cocktail of loud music, red wine and some uncharacteristically careful time management. Who knows, if I'm feeling really daring, I might even throw caution to the wind and try a spot of multi-tasking.

Family Planning (24th November)

As part of her stand-up routine in the 1980's, Victoria Wood once observed that the only way to find the Bullring Centre in Birmingham was to drive until you caught sight of it in your rear-view mirror, and then reverse slowly towards it. Whilst possibly true, her observation calls to mind that some plans only reveal themselves in retrospect.

In no way is this more true for us than with the appearance of our daughter this last week. Eighteen months ago, Rather's arrival had been quite traumatic, and so Barbara had planned long ago that her second delivery would be a more controlled affair. November 18th had therefore been marked in our diaries for many months, and we had decided to make as much financial hay as we could before the day. As a colleague of mine with whom I worked with two weeks ago noted in a congratulatory message: "You were cutting it fine!"

Indeed we were, and as soon as we had we arrived at hospital on the day and been given the first slot in the operating theatre, Barbara's contractions started as if on cue. Scheduled as an elective caesarean delivery, we would take our place behind any emergencies that cropped up, and we waited while our 9am appointment was delayed hour after hour. Just after one o'clock in the afternoon, a kindly face popped through the curtain and said, "Off we go!"

Having been first diverted to a changing room from which I emerged in green overalls looking a lot like Benny Hill and not a lot like George Clooney, I found Barbara in the middle of a large operating theatre filled with an enormous amount of machines, people and lights. I had, it seemed, wandered onto the set of Casualty. Though dressed like everyone else, I stuck out like a sore thumb by having nothing useful to do, and was given a seat away from the business-end by her head.

With my only other experience of childbirth being something akin to a war zone, I couldn't help but giggle when a doctor asking calmly called the room to order; "Righto, so before we begin, does everyone know each other?" Grunts and mumbles of acknowledgement were followed by requests for any concerns to be aired and shared, and before long I could feel myself itching for a flip chart and marker pen with which to facilitate and record the session's output. Despite this urge, I remembered my role and stayed silent.

The machines hummed, instructions were murmured and an expectant air filled the room as drugs were administered and nerve responses measured. After a few moments, the doctor stationed near us looked down and asked Barbara if it was all right for them to begin. "Of course" she answered with a smile, and was told "D'you know, that's good because we already have." Having been warned by friends beforehand that it would feel a bit like someone doing the washing up in her stomach, Barbara settled down to wait and I offered what I hoped were sweet and appropriate reassurances. If I had ever thought that my part in our second child's creation was minimal, my place in the room of her birth served only to remind me of the fact.

Some five minutes later, I was encouraged to stand up to have a look and take some pictures. At 2.00pm on Monday 18th November in Worcester Royal Hospital, I saw our daughter's head being gently eased into the fresh air and my first thought was that she was almost exactly the colour of

Campbell's Cream of Tomato Soup. With a little more wiggling and twisting, there she was in all her glory looking completely fed up at being disturbed from her comfortable slumber. Well, late checkout at hotels can cost, she hadn't paid and what better time to start learning one of life's many lessons?

I was then invited over to the resuscitaire to trim the cord and take more photos while the assembled health professionals, now resembling a well trained formula one pit crew, set to work on Barbara's midriff. Apparently having neither fainted nor gotten underfoot, I was allowed to bring our swaddled daughter back to the chair, and we spent the next half an hour cooing and kissing amongst ourselves before it was time to head back to the post-natal ward. Security being what it is these days, an electronic tag was attached to her foot within seconds of arriving at reception, and before you could say "unexpected item in bagging area", she was rooting around Barbara's chest in search of her first feed. As we counted fingers, toes and other items, we noticed that she was born with a set of surprisingly long fingernails that had a distinctly purple hue to them. Like mother, like daughter indeed.

There followed almost exactly forty-eight hours of observation and tests for mother and daughter, while father and son commuted to and from the hospital and pined. On Tuesday when we first arrived for a visit, Rather first set eyes on his sister and promptly dissolved into tears for about five minutes. Then, presumably having weighed his options carefully, he started drenching her with his own special brand of watery kisses.

By lunchtime on Wednesday, we were finally ready and for the first time ever, our whole family piled into the car and headed home to find that our driveway had been decorated in our absence by utterly thoughtful and thoroughly dear friends. And so it is with the greatest of pleasure that we introduce to you our daughter, whose nom du plume echoes that of her brother, and reflects the fact that her arrival completes our family.

Now with the benefit of hindsight, we see clearly not only that having two children was an excellent plan, but that it also makes our lives really rather *Jolly Good*.

Mergers & Acquisitions (1st December)

In 1979 my father came home from work one evening, beckoned me to the front door and pointed down the path that led to the pavement. On the other side of the street I could just make out the silhouette of a black car lit by the orange streetlamp above it, and as he closed the door he whispered "We'll go for a drive this weekend." So began, at the age of eleven, my love affair with what is now referred to as the Saab 900 *Classic*; a model of car that has lasted 34 years, shows no sign of abating and doubtless earns me my stripes as an anorak. To this day I can recognise them from half a mile behind on a motorway, could pick their exhaust note out of the passing traffic at Piccadilly Circus while blindfolded and sometimes spend hours discussing them with similarly besotted enthusiasts. I find them a beautiful automotive expression of a form almost wholly influenced by function.

Since 1990 when I bought my first example, I have traded up numerous times, and I flatter myself that after many years' work, mine is one of the finest unmolested examples you will find in the country some twenty years after they went out of production. It is, like all consuming affairs, entirely irrational and has its own rules. However, the changes to our lives since 2008 have meant that function has increasingly overruled form in many decisions, latterly including those concerning my hobby. Whilst there once may have been room for three of us in this marriage, those days are now over and the something that had to give was always going to be the car. Having once claimed that it could only be prised from my cold dead hands, I advertised the car just after Barbara fell pregnant for the second time. My heart was never really in the sale from the start, and things weren't helped by the fact that she on more than one occasion tried to talk me out of it. The result was that I picked a price, forgot about the advert and refused to negotiate on the odd occasion I received a call about it. Hardly the most effective way to sell a car, but I felt that whomsoever bought it should be bitten by the same bug as I.

Living about a hundred miles east of us in Oxfordshire was a chap of similar age to me who was looking to realise his dream of owning one of these convertibles at last. For both of us 2013 has been a year of possibility; for me it was about mergers now that we had young children, whilst for him it was a case of acquisitions now that his were a little older. At the start of the year, he had drawn a picture of one and stuck it to his fridge as a reminder of his dream. When he came across my advert, I imagine it would have been hard not to make enquiries.

There can be few worse times to sell a car than around the time of childbirth, but that's pretty much what happened. With a patience that most buyers don't have, he and his wife entered into an intermittent dialogue with me about the car that was respectful and suggested more than a passing interest. With Barbara in the final weeks of her pregnancy, I expect my answers were vague and probably less clear than is ideal, but nevertheless they were accepted. Immediately after Jolly was born, we agreed that the following weekend would be a good time to see if a deal could be done. I felt reasonably sure that anyone willing to make a two hour train journey to see a car was pretty certain to buy it as long as it was as described, and both he and his wife seemed as smitten with the marque as I am. Two hours of examining and testing took place last Saturday before we shook and the car changed hands.

As he prepared to return home with his dream now a reality, I noticed that the loss of mine wasn't as much of a wrench as I had expected. I watched him disappearing down the B4220, and imagined the huge smile that was almost certainly spreading across his face; after all, these are cars that you wear rather than drive, and for a petrol-head that's a feeling worth having at least once.

In quite a number of ways, the last few years have taught Barbara and I a very great deal about the past being another country, and I wondered whether my contentment was a quiet indication that another difficult decision had been arrived at after a good deal of consideration. For us it seems clear that without function, form alone is of little value.

Build Inequality (8th December)

It may be that my purpose in life is to serve as a warning to others, and if so, it would probably be to highlight the gulf that lies between the correct way to build things and the other way. As if to reinforce this, a regular feature in the mental soundtrack of my life is Stinger from Top Gun wagging his finger at me and saying, "Son, your ego is writing cheques your body can't cash."

For the last two months or so, we have given the chickens free rein of the old orchard field. This, in addition to their own quite substantial enclosure, should be enough for most birds. However, it clearly isn't as a combination of falling leaves and the erosion of the compost pile revealed a chicken-sized hole in the undergrowth, and led by the ever-curious Oprah, our brood seized their opportunity and escaped through it.

Sitting at the most south-western corner of our land, the compost pile occupies a shady position against the road and the hedgerow that borders our neighbour's field. Over time is has been left largely to its own devices, and this includes the gradual falling into disrepair of the ubiquitous stock fence. It was this that needed replacing, and was a job I felt was well within my ability. Cometh the hour cometh the man, I hear you say.

Suitably dressed in muddy boots with an impressive thatch of bed-hair, I swaggered into our local Countrywide. I then tutted about chickens escaping with a dismissive air, and proceeded to buy the wrong sort of stock fence with the wrong sort of fence posts. Having reversed the Volkswagen up to the collection point, I nonchalantly loaded it up with the sort of equipment one normally needs to contain a herd of stampeding wildebeest, and felt sure that the shop assistant was regarding me with appropriate awe. Isn't it funny how awe and disbelief can look uncannily similar?

Back home I tooled up with a mallet for the posts, a hammer for the galvanised nails, some pliers for the stock fence and a sledgehammer because I just like hitting things, and set off for the corner of the orchard field. Having locked the chickens in their enclosure, they lined up against the fence and gossiped amongst themselves about what I might be up to.

The first job was to clear away the overhanging branches that were in my way, and this I attempted with my bare hands, as I was too lazy to go back to the garage and fetch a pair of gloves. Whilst I am unsure of which particular area of my brain is responsible for producing this laziness, I am absolutely certain that it is the same part that fails to make me go for a pee at 3am when I really need to.

Once I had the boundary clear of undergrowth and hedgerow, it was time to set the fence posts. Having reasoned that the ground was relatively soft thanks to the autumnal rain of previous weeks, I thought that it should be fairly straightforward to position the sharp end before slowly tapping the post in with a sledgehammer. For a really clear sense of what I was attempting to do, try standing up whilst holding a 9lb weight at arms length, and attempt to knock a piece of scaffolding through a bullet-proof vest with it. Remember, of course, that you can only hammer with one hand, as the other was busy holding the post upright. Bound to succeed, eh?

After a good half hour's swearing I had three posts buried in the ground by a centimetre or two, and had completely decimated the tops of the posts before my laziness gene kicked in again. I calculated that so long as they remained vaguely upright and wedged amongst the hawthorn, the fence could withstand the force exerted by a chicken trying to break loose. Further justifying my shoddy work, I also decided that the stock fence, once attached, would lend the structure a sturdiness that would make it seem positively over-engineered.

I eyed up the 50-metre roll of fence and estimated that I would need about six metres to attach to the three poles. In order to release the roll, it was a simple matter of cutting through the end wires that were looped back on themselves, and then I could measure and cut. Well, I could if I had bought the correct 2mm gauge stuff. In my manly haste, I had thrown a roll of 3.5mm gauge wire into the back of the car, and trying to cut through that with my budget B&Q wire cutters was like trying to perform major tree surgery with a penknife. I can tell you're impressed. Luckily, I found the leftover stock fence from my last bit of fence-building lurking in the animal shelter, and so I was able to use that whilst making a mental note to take the other roll back to the shop. The last stage was attaching the fence using galvanised nails, and once again I thought it should have been straightforward.

Holding six metres of stock fence up against a wobbly wooden stake and trying to bang a galvanised nail into it with only two hands at my disposal is a feat beyond anyone. You'd need four at least, preferably six to stand a chance. It was like trying to fix a leak by nailing clingfilm to jelly, and it went as well as my metaphor suggests. Nevertheless, after an hour's bruised fingers, swearing and shouting, the fence stood reasonably upright and didn't wobble too much.

No sooner had I finished the job and released the chickens from their enclosure than they headed straight back to the compost. I immediately heard indignant clucks of "Spoilsport" and "Hey, no fair!", as they found their escape route blocked. Feeling relieved that I had accomplished what I had set out to, I told them that if an acre wasn't enough land for ten birds, they had another thing coming. Little did I know how right I was. After putting the tools away and cleaning up, I returned to survey my handiwork with, if not pride, then at least a sense of achievement. I found on my return that they had immediately begun scraping away the earth at the bottom of the fence, and were slowly but surely opening up a gap through which it would only be a matter of time before they squeezed through. The best fix I could think of was to find a large piece of square post in the animal shelter and lay it along the ground like a form of draft excluder. It is probably the sturdiest bit of construction on the whole job.

Nature then conspired to remove the need for my work to withstand any more than the briefest test of time. A fox broke into the coop that night and slaughtered seven of our ten birds, leaving a scene of utter carnage for me to clear up the next morning. How's that for a moral?

Metamorphosis (15th December)

Meaning a marked change in appearance, character, condition, or function, the word metamorphosis aptly describes quite a lot of what takes place at Stone House. As I write, the sheep are busy transforming the big field from a grassy meadow to a poop-infested mud bath, the chickens continue to create rather fetching patterns in the small field by scratching through the leaves in search of food, and our children are busy converting food and milk into, well, you can imagine.

For me, it also describes the process by which old clothes, toys and other objects become new again when Barbara finds them at car boot sales. Her thrifty nature and tireless efforts have meant that, with the exception of generous gifts from friends and family, Rather and Jolly have full wardrobes and bursting toy boxes provided on a shoestring budget. The only problem with this is that Stone House has less storage than we would like, and so every now and then some items must either find a new purpose or a new home.

Yesterday evening as Barbara was around at a friend's house for a few well-deserved glasses of wine, I took the opportunity to creatively re-deploy a wooden shape sorter by combining laziness with my well-documented pyromaniacal tendencies and a keen awareness of our rising energy bills.

After an evening of bottles, nappies and tuneless singing, both Rather and Jolly were tucked up in their various beds and baskets, and I settled down with a glass of wine to examine the toy for all its possibilities. I felt it was shame that so many of its pieces were missing, as by being of solid pine construction it stood out sharply against the arsenal of plastic toys that littered the floor.

I could see no other practical use for any part of it, and so I felt the best way of helping it to the next stage of its life was to throw it in the fire, which at that point was in need of stoking. Little did I know that whilst child friendly paint might contain no harmful toxins that can be ingested, it certainly seems to contain some form of accelerant. Within a minute of being added, the fire was transformed into a mini blast furnace.

Suddenly remembering the chimney fire of two winters ago, I considered closing the doors and shutting the vents, but a wave of deliciously warm air rolled over me and instead I sat back and wiggled my toes in delight. After a few moments, the fire settled and I relaxed with my wine and watched as the toy turned slowly into glowing embers.

Something that had cost us 40 pence and which gave Rather pleasure for over a year had now briefly heated our home, for less cost than the same amount of wood when sold as kindling. As I was preparing to head upstairs to bed, I reflected that we had probably extracted about as much value and gain as we could from it, and then I remembered that I collect all the ash from the fireplace to be used as fertiliser in the spring. Waste not, want not, as Barbara likes to say.

Tipping Point (23rd December)

Lacking even a single straight line or right angle in its construction, this quirky, rather damp and somewhat tatty little cottage with a few outbuildings in a quiet corner of England is our home, has been our refuge and will now need to grow with us in the years ahead. It seems like it will be a never-ending project in which a stumbling step forward can sometimes be the prelude to a swift leap in quite a different direction.

Nevertheless, we feel we have been able to accomplish a great deal this year, and as 2013 draws to a close Barbara and I can reflect on and celebrate the many changes that have happened around the house over the last twelve months. We are almost sure that, after more than two years wholly devoted to destruction and removal, a new era of construction and creation has dawned and is quietly gaining momentum.

Now that the new weatherproof wood store sits against the house behind the office, last winter's constant and often miserable chore of trudging through mud to fetch logs from the animal shelter by wheelbarrow is a thing of the past. Across the summer and autumn we stacked it to the rafters with several tons of seasoned firewood, and now it takes the bare minimum of effort on our part to keep the house warm and snug every evening.

The stock fence that replaced the hawthorn hedge by the old vegetable patch now gives us panoramic views through the big field towards the Malvern Hills, whilst the foreground is often filled with curious sheep staring back at us as they huddle together idly chewing.

The chickens, back up to six in number with the recent arrival of Korma, Madras and Vindaloo, are once again filled with curiosity and roam bravely as far as they dare. Having installed a new electric door for their coop, we are grateful to stay in the warm while they are automatically released from it at dawn and secured back inside it at dusk.

Detailed and often complex negotiations with a number of contractors continue as we plan two big construction jobs for next year. On the outside we look forward to erecting a six foot high fence with automated gates to protect our roadside border, keep the children safe and make coming and going easier. Inside the house, we cannot wait to knock down the wall between the dining room and living room to increase the light and space where we spend most of our time when indoors.

With the exception of the new office, there is nothing inside the house that we don't dream of one day remodelling or replacing. It would not be an exaggeration to say that if we ever get the house the way we would like, it will be a monkey that was caught incredibly slowly.

Obviously the most significant event this year has been the arrival of Jolly, and so to help us celebrate our first family Christmas together, we welcomed the other day Barbara's mother and two of her sisters who have travelled from Sweden and Australia. With seven of us under the one roof, the house has been stretched to its limits with suitcases filling the utility room, clothes hanging from every available object and enough wine to make even Keith Floyd smile.

With so much to be grateful for, it is tempting to regard Barbara's court case as increasingly isolated and insignificant by comparison, but hard lessons have been well learned and so we will remain braced for surprises until the bitter end. Nonetheless we hope that 2014 is the tipping point for us, and that in the year ahead this large scar that blots our landscape finally sinks from view. Merry Christmas!

52° 3'11″N 2° 20'53″W (1st January 2014)

My early childhood memories are of Christmas being a wonderful day filled with the obvious delight of brightly wrapped presents. In addition, and far more memorable today, it also contained the scent of pine needles, pot roasts, counting Christmas trees along a deserted Chiswick Mall and conversations over the dinner table. Much of this magic faded in the face of age and circumstance during the eighties, but was replaced in the early nineties with equally notable alternatives involving close friends, port, stilton and some rather enormous cigars.

Celebrations for Christmas and the New Year were all but gone for me by the mid-nineties, thanks in part to a late dear friend of mine, not completely unlike *Ebenezer Scrooge*, who unwittingly encouraged me to re-evaluate my expectations. He light-heartedly referred to the annual fuss as a "numerical anomaly best experienced from some unsullied faraway beach under the sun." From that point on I followed his advice as often as I could.

In a recent re-awakening for obvious reasons, the celebration of Christmas at Stone House has started to take shape. For the most part it is an eclectic and fluid mishmash of European customs over a forty-eight hour period that have no consistency from year to year, which we hope will give our children an appropriate understanding of their lack of any particular nationality. However, Barbara and I are keen to create something for them that is original and that lasts as long as they wish, and it seems that we have might have begun to do that with our Christmas Day Walk. Some ten miles to the south of us are the Malvern Hills, which we have yet to fully explore for their natural beauty. Towards the southern end of them lie the impressive earthworks of the *British Camp*, an Iron Age hill-fort now surrounded by a multitude of paths that weave their way to and from various scenic spots. Nearby, running along the crest of the hills, is the Shire Ditch, an ancient hilltop boundary on which sits a small toposcope, and from here you can see what the 17th century diarist John Evelyn accurately described as "one of England's goodliest vistas."

It is to this place that we and those with whom we have so far shared Christmas have walked for the last two years. With the exception of a short initial climb, it is a leisurely stroll from the nearest car park just below the crest of one of the hills. Benches are placed at regular five-minute intervals along the route, which are both welcome and necessary given the restrictions of Barbara's foot. As her pain prohibits anything more than a short walk around the block, and we have had bitter experiences with selectively edited covert surveillance, we now feel the need to display a notice on her back so that nothing can be artfully misconstrued on this special occasion when she straps her foot into a cast, fills herself with painkillers and grits her teeth just to enjoy a short walk with her family.

By way of compensation, at almost every step there are breathtaking views. Over the British Camp Reservoir to the East you can see the distant Cotswolds, while Gloucestershire spreads out like a carpet down to the Severn Estuary and the Black Mountains provide a beautiful Westerly backdrop to both Herefordshire and the Welsh border. We have to date been unusually lucky with the weather, never having been there without brilliant sunshine and blue sky, but it is inevitable that one day our hardy resolve will be tested.

Once there we perch for an hour or so to rest, chat, admire the views in all directions and strike up conversations with passing ramblers and their dogs. It seems you get to meet all sorts up there as this year, while Jolly slept in the pram, Rather was lucky enough to meet an extremely erudite and somewhat pickled Santa Claus before we all tucked into slices of tasty Panettone, washed down with delicious Hot Chocolate.

The notion that Christmas has less to do with presents or indulgence and more to do with interaction and intimacy rather suits what Barbara and I hope to create for our family. If, in the years to come, we aren't lucky enough to spend Christmas on a beach somewhere, we'll try our best to make the walk whether Santa and the Sun want to join us or not. Happy New Year!

Mot Juste (12th January)

One of the many things you have to master when living in a rural setting such as ours is the wood-burning stove and all its associated maintenance. We are fortunate in having a rather sophisticated system, which works well and requires almost nothing other than the twice yearly sweeping of the chimney.

The chap we use for this is somewhat eccentric to say the least, and I shall probably never forget the first time we met when he tried to engage me with some polite chit-chat. "So, what d'you think of Enoch Powell, then?" was his opening line, quickly followed by "If you know anything about him, you would agree that he was really quite misunderstood." I declined to comment directly, but managed to refer once or twice to being an immigrant, which prompted a flicker of diplomacy in the form of the subject being dropped.

With a background in engineering he brings a wealth of experience to bear on maintaining our stove, but it comes with a rather surprising conversational style, not to mention an arresting choice of topics.

Last autumn I had asked him about an occasional problem we have with the chimney failing to draw air properly, and he made a house call to investigate the problem. Similar to when you take your car to the garage to investigate a strange noise, the chimney operated flawlessly throughout his visit, and he concluded that he had better come back and observe the chimney from the outside on a day when downdrafts were more likely.

One evening about a week before Christmas, Barbara and I were up in the spare room rearranging furniture so as to better accommodate a full house over the festive period. It was during one of the many storms that barrelled in from Wales, and the window gives a perfect view over the road of whatever weather approaches from that direction.

All of a sudden our attention was drawn to a car stopping in the road directly outside the house some forty feet from the driveway entrance, with its hazard lights flashing and we wondered who on earth it could be. Opening the window into a forty-mile an hour gale bearing horizontal rain, we shouted down to a dark figure with a flashlight running from his car. "Can we help you?" It being a rather dramatic scene, I presumed he was lost and it seemed the best thing to say under the circumstances. In any event I was pretty sure the wind would prevent my words from reaching him.

He stood waving in the road directly outside the window, and was clearly shouting up towards us. Hearing about one word in three, we think we heard "I've... check... cowl... coping... gale." Barbara quickly put two and two together and realised that only someone as eccentric as the man who sweeps our chimney would be happy to stand outside our house in the pitch black and pouring rain in order to gauge the wind's precise velocity and direction, and the resulting impact on our chimney's ability to draw air properly.

Suitably relieved that we knew him, we waved and then, not really knowing what else to do, we waved a bit more. In one of those moments when you can't think of what to say, but know an encouraging word or two would be appropriate, I shouted down the only words I could think of before slamming the window shut and leaving him to his calculations. "Well done. Carry on!"

Ruddy Kindling (26th January)

In his famous nineteenth century celebration of stoicism, Rudyard Kipling's poem suggests that, among many other things; "if you can meet with Triumph and Disaster and treat those two impostors just the same... you'll be a Man, my son!" Well pardon me, but I refuse to treat a roaring log fire and a pathetic five-second glowing ember with the same respect, so by his standards I fail completely and therefore I'm anything but a man.

Now I appreciate that I could be adult about this and hold myself to account, but as it's my party I won't, and I therefore lay the blame firmly at the feet of whoever is responsible for store-bought kindling being utterly rubbish and shockingly expensive in equal measure. In fact, if you have money to invest you should forget about gold, property and the stock market and buy as much woodland as you can. You'll make an absolute fortune from selling kindling to idiots like me, and I believe I can illustrate this in terms of cost efficiency and effectiveness.

Firstly, pound for pound, kindling costs probably three times as much as enriched uranium. The pedants among you might point out that I clearly haven't a clue how much enriched uranium costs, and you'd be right, but I'm pretty sure it's a lot. I am equally certain that it would be cheaper to buy half a dozen Billy Bookcases from Ikea, hire a stretch limo to transport them here from Birmingham and then hire Richard Branson to personally chop them up into small pieces using the Crown Jewels. The cheapest bulk supplier that we have found is through Amazon, but the stuff is still ridiculously expensive, which probably explains why the seller chooses to despatch it in packages that wouldn't look out of place strapped to the back of a mule in Putumayo.

Secondly, in terms of efficiency, it is woefully poor. In fact, all those films and books which talk about burning money to keep warm as a metaphor would be well advised to consider using the line "I burned kindling to keep warm." It lasts for no more than a couple of seconds and, crucially, fails to produce any embers of enough substance to ignite even the smallest log fire.

I've been hunting high and low for alternative ways to light log fires, my efforts so far being both unpredictable and unreliable. When it comes to the lowest level of Maslow's hierarchy of needs, close isn't good enough, and so an answer is required.

Through persistence alone I flatter myself that I have developed a certain proficiency in my firelighting ability after some three years of rural living. As the vast majority of our winter heating comes from log fires, it's not just an affectation and I'll need to continue to hone my skills. Being somewhat lazy, I suspect I will need help to keep going, and if stoicism is what's required, then Kipling was wrong, as I'll probably need to keep some red wine about me while all others have drunk theirs.

Frank and Ernest (2nd February)

On hearing about Jolly's expected arrival last year, a colleague of mine advised me with a wink that I was set to discover a mathematical anomaly known only to parents of more than one child. "Oh really?" I enquired over a glass of wine one evening. "Oh yes" he stated knowingly; "you'll discover that one plus one equals five." Far too oblique a statement for me to grasp with any clarity, this pearl of apparent wisdom disappeared from my radar within minutes.

One morning last December whilst I was in our local town, I was reminded of it when I wandered into the supermarket, pushing both children in the pram ahead of me. A total stranger, glancing down with a smile, enquired of me sweetly; "two under two?" I nodded proudly, preparing myself for an avalanche of clucking and gushing praise, but I was stopped in my tracks as she spat out "Oh shit!" with a grin and walked away. A tenuous link it may be, but I joined the dots with ease.

Vocabulary aside, they were both speaking with empathy and from experience. The difference between caring for one child and two has been wholly unprecedented in terms of energy, focus and time. Both of us now frequently find ourselves standing in rooms needing to ask the other why we entered them, we reminisce noticeably often about showers we once had, our clothes frequently walk to the washing machine by themselves and we approach the weeks when I am mostly away with a degree of trepidation on the one hand and guilt on the other.

Whilst the above may be a slight exaggeration for effect, neither of us can deny the deafening absence of the space in which we once used to think. Before Christmas, Barbara and I had not enjoyed a moment on our own as a couple for over eighteen months, and as we live without any family support within easy reach, we run the risk of drowning the couple that we are in the nappies, bottles and playgroups that form so much of the couple we are becoming. Whilst we in no way wish to turn the clock back or shirk our current responsibilities, we both know that one day Rather and Jolly will both leave home, and we are selfish enough to want to keep an eye on what happens after that.

It was therefore with the greatest of relief that over the Christmas period we exploited the arrival of Barbara's mother and two of her sisters, who came to spend a week of fireside conversations, wintry walks and good food. Included in that was a day and night of childcare and all that goes with it, while we escaped for a massage, meal and overnight stay at a nearby country house hotel & spa.

You'd be right in guessing that 9pm was about as late as we could manage before turning in for the night, but before then we indulged in full body massages that weren't interrupted, thrilled in the decadence of the outdoor heated whirlpool without rushing to get out, and the silence of our thoughts was pure gold. We've only just begun as parents, but it does feel as though we have already come a long way.

It also means that I am no longer able to return from a trip and regale Barbara as I once did with tales of how long and hard I have worked. Instead, every time I come home I am reminded of the Bob Thaves' comic strip scene set outside a film festival in which one of the characters says of the dancer Fred Astaire; "Sure, he was great, but don't forget that Ginger Rogers did everything he did, backwards... and in high heels."

Drink Up, Dreamers (16th February)

Like almost everyone in the country, we have been accommodating the weather since Christmas the best we can. At around 500 feet above sea level and on top of a hill, we are one of the lucky households not at immediate risk of flooding. For us, it's mostly a case of making sure the house and outbuildings stay dry and keeping an eye on travel reports to make sure I can avoid the many road closures in the area when on my way to and from work.

Today dawned bright and sunny, which was a welcome respite from what seems like months of persistent grey dullness. It was therefore time to start the clean up operation, with several items requiring my attention including a fallen tree, the buckled chicken cage, a damaged greenhouse, numerous broken branches littering the ground and a few loose fence panels.

Before starting, I took the opportunity to walk around the plot and inspect the various roof sections and tiles that have taken a hammering in case professional help was required. The Herefordshire mud made the going slow and occasionally comic, but I made reasonable progress. Stopping to check the animal shelter, I heard the faintest of noises at my feet. It sounded like a distant babbling brook, and glancing at my feet

I could clearly see that the saturated ground was awash with water heading in a downhill direction.

I trudged up to the highest part of our plot, which is also the high point of the surrounding area, and looked down to find a large puddle. In fact, wherever I looked, sitting water was waiting for the chance to flow downhill like so many planes circling Heathrow wearily before receiving clearance to land.

Some news reports have indicated that while the rain may have stopped for the moment, the river levels have not necessarily peaked yet, and I wondered if I was standing on the reason why; the ground is full to the brim. Everywhere I looked the earth simply couldn't absorb any more water; even our well is overflowing, and that sits only about twenty feet below the high point of the hill. All the water here must either evaporate or more likely find its way into the Severn Estuary.

My basic geography and map reading skills tell me that once it reaches the bottom of the hill, it will drop into the Linton Brook which will feed it through two smaller rivers (for those interested, first the Frome and then the Lugg) before joining forces with the Wye, which meets the sea just by the old Severn Bridge.

I have no idea how long this journey of something like a hundred miles will take to complete, but I suspect it isn't a matter of a few days, and the Environment Agency's live flood map tells me that the Wye is already flooded from Hereford to Ross. With thousands of similar hilltops waiting to feed just as many brooks that all need to get to the sea, I can imagine it will be some time before we run dry and the river levels can start to fall.

I know neither how long the current rains will last, nor when the next ones will come, but it's hard to imagine this won't happen again, and with greater frequency.

Newtonian Pruning (2nd March)

Everywhere you look at Stone House are trees, shrubs and bushes. For a smallholding in Herefordshire, this is exactly as you would expect, and we wouldn't want it any different. However, there are times when I curse each and every one of them to the deepest pits of hell and back, and these times are when I walk into them.

During my long break from travelling over Christmas and the New Year, I had planned a few maintenance jobs amongst the festivities, and pruning was one of them. After two years of steady growth, my arsenal of tools is now more than adequate to dispatch all manner of vegetation with ease, and so I devoted one day to the job of cutting and another to that of burning.

When I mentioned my plan to Barbara she wisely advised me to check on the Internet about what time of year pruning should be done. Worried that it might say I shouldn't attempt the job in December, I cleverly forgot about checking and went ahead with the job anyway. At my disposal I had secateurs, loppers, a telescopic tree pruner and my increasingly battered chainsaw. I also had an itch that only a petrol-powered tool could scratch.

In my sights were two of my biggest headaches, between them responsible for the vast majority of cuts and bruises that usually cover my head. The main reason for this is their location near the path that runs between the house and garage, but I also suspect they are highly skilled in the art of covert warfare.

I must admit that one of the schoolboy errors I made the previous time I pruned them was to overlook the fact that fruit weighs quite a lot when ripe. Branches that in April were well out of harm's way had descended to head-grazing height by July. By the end of August, they were perfectly placed to inflict maximum pain, and they did so on a regular basis. After the harvest, I promised myself they would never do so again.

Like a true professional arborist, I studied the trees from a number of angles. I squinted up into the wooden canopy of each whilst calculating which branches could be cut and in what order, so that I would be left with a smartly pruned pair of fruit trees and a pile of wood in search of a match. In the midst of my planning, Lewis the Shepherd wandered past on his way to check the sheep and asked what I was doing. "Pruning" I said. "With a chainsaw?" he asked, staring at all the tools lined up by the garage wall. He was still chuckling five minutes later.

It is said that the human brain can only hold seven pieces of information at one time, and although you may agree I'd bet that mine is only capable of two. After restarting my calculations for the fourth time, I seriously considered getting my bag of flipchart marker pens from the office and numbering the branches so that I stood a chance of remembering the order in which I would cut them. As this is just the sort of thing that Barbara would catch me doing, and then spend the next forty years teasing me about, I decided against it.

I decided that I had already wasted enough time and should simply get on with it, and so with a pair of hand loppers proceeded to cut any branch that I could reach from my position on the ground. Having chosen to carry out a cut rather than a trim, I estimated that four or five feet from the tree was about as far as I wanted any future fruit to drop. Before long, I could see progress was being made, and the scene looked more and more like a barbershop with cuttings littering the grass around the trunk.

Once everything that I could reach had been pruned, it was time to bring out the next piece of equipment. I had been waiting to play with the chainsaw, but I realised that at about half the length of the hand loppers, it really wasn't going to be of much use. Instead I could only use the telescopic pruner which, at over three metres in length, could reach as high as I needed.

There's a little trick with telescopic pruners that you really need to consider before using them, and that's the fact that they are hand operated. This is all very well if you happen to have remote arms or perhaps help from a friend you don't much care for, but if it's just you then I would advise some forethought of the kind that I consistently fail at.

Let me walk you through the problem step by step. You're using telescopic pruners because you want to cut branches you can't reach, right? They are therefore some distance above your head, and when you cut them they will fall. A simple understanding of gravity is all you need to realise that you shouldn't cut them from immediately below, but to the side. To do so, you need to find a clear route through the branches from where you are standing to the point on the branch you want to cut, so you can feed the pruners through and chop away.

The thing less obvious about this procedure is that whilst a falling branch obeys the laws of gravity, it also does so via the path of least resistance, which is likely to be along the same route as the pruners. If Isaac Newton formulated his Universal Law of Gravitation when an apple fell on his head, then perhaps he might have come up with something equally momentous if his chest had been on the receiving end of a two-metre branch of dense apple wood travelling at ten miles per hour. Being neither a physicist nor a mathematician, I only discovered that it hurts.

Planting the orchard in January 2015

Planting raspberries in February 2015

Putting in the kitchen garden foundations in May 2014

Building the first raised vegetable bed in March 2015

Rather helping with the Dumper in June 2015

Jolly getting to grips with the mini-digger in June 2015

Removing the old vegetable plot in June 2014

Building the wood store in March 2013

Many Hands (16th March)

It's not often that we have people staying with us for long enough to make asking them for help not seem blatantly opportunistic. Therefore when we do, it seems natural to take advantage of it as some jobs are beyond me, and Barbara is unable to join in when it comes to lifting and carrying.

Having her mother and sisters here over Christmas made for lively and entertaining evenings, busy days and gave me the chance to complete the last job in the old vegetable patch that had been nagging at the back of my mind for ages. The removal of the raspberry bushes was the final part of the long process to open up the garden all around the house.

If we were going to work well together as a team, some clearly defined roles needed to be assigned. I felt that primarily I was there to provide vision, leadership and encouragement, and this would be best provided by leaning thoughtfully on a shovel, stroking my chin at regular intervals and deciding as quickly as possible that the job would go far better if we managed to use the tractor somehow. If the truth be told, it's a role that I enjoy regardless of whether others are present, or anything needs to be done

Rather, who had come along to inspect the goings on, was in charge of collecting any worms uncovered by digging, and then keeping them in the bucket on the back of his tricycle for feeding to the chickens later. Barbara was in a supervisory health & safety role to prevent Rather from eating the worms himself, which is sometimes a risk. Everything was in place and the scene was set for the removal of the bushes to take place. Well, all except the actual digging part, and this phase was admirably taken care of by one of Barbara's sisters while I helpfully said "over here" and pointed out where the trailer was for her to put them in. Looking back on the job now, I think it's clear that my attention to detail was the one component that guaranteed the success of this operation.

Thanks to the volume of rain that had fallen, the ground gave up the plants with relative ease, and they were stacked haphazardly into the trailer. Although we know where we eventually want to replant them, I have yet to find the time to build the raised border essential for allowing the soil around them to drain. Needing somewhere to temporarily store them, I chose an area alongside the Cider Barn where they will be protected and fired up the tractor. Utterly failing to take into account the weight of the trailer, and the fact that this weight was not over the wheels, I engaged forward gear and gunned the engine.

The expectant smile of satisfaction on my face briefly wavered and then vanished as I glanced down to notice the rear wheels digging deep ruts beneath me. Whilst some might pause for thought at this point, I shouted to Barbara's sisters and invited them to sit on the wheel arches and bounce in order to help the tractor gain the grip it needed to move forwards. Still spinning its wheels in third gear, the tractor ponderously moved forward, leaving a twin track of muddy ruts behind us.

Come the spring, the rotavator will do the hard work of chewing up the earth one last time before the whole vegetable plot is levelled and graded using the earth that was excavated during the installation of the soak away two years ago. All evidence of the vegetable garden will then finally disappear under freshly sown grass, creating one large lawn around which sit the house, garage and cider barn and on which will play children and adults all summer long.

Breaking the Mould (23rd March)

A single event can be a fluke. If it happens for a second time, that could be coincidence. The third makes it a pattern as far as I am concerned, and as we approach the end of our third winter at Stone House it seems clear that the house is both cold and increasingly damp during the darker months. As cosy and warm as the fire makes it during the evenings, the windows are awash with condensation every morning. Once the central heating starts the house warms relatively quickly, but it is a matter of too little too late for the moisture that coats most windows. When we found mould growing around the bedroom windows, we knew something had to happen, as it was a matter of health rather than comfort.

As one of the more pressing matters that needed our attention, Barbara and I launched ourselves into Google with the usual vigour and quickly learned some rather surprising facts, all backed up by a level of common sense that even I can understand.

To some people Rising Damp is the name of an old television sitcom from the 1970's cast in the same mould (pun not so much intended as fallen over) as the one that frames our lives in this book. To other people it is a large problem that either attracts or repels significant quantities of money in equal measure, and we were shaping up to join the queue.

Thanks to an almost vitriolic article that Barbara found on a website that provides advice to those who care for older properties, we have learned that rising damp treatments are sometimes a cure in search of a problem. Of course we know that damp exists and we have plenty of it, but ours isn't rising from the ground so much as condensing from the air. Critically, it's also trying to get out rather than in.

The coldest part of the house at any time is usually the windows, and as the temperature drops at night and the dew-point is reached, moisture will form, or adsorb, on the glass in much the same way that it will form on the outside of a cold beer bottle on a summer's day. It is not a coincidence that each of the last three winters has witnessed more condensation than the preceding one, as the population of this house has been steadily growing in that time. With a far greater amount of cooking, washing, cleaning, bathing and breathing going on inside these four walls, the levels of humidity have skyrocketed.

Stone House was built at a time when the quality of roof, windows and doors would have meant that almost as much wind blew throughout it as around it. Thanks to the wonders of double glazed UPVC windows and loft insulation this no longer happens and is precisely the cause of our problem. It's a case of Catch 22; if we don't ventilate the house adequately, we'll have condensation and mould inside it. If we do, we'll either be freezing or forever in fuel poverty.

This led us to the discovery of Positive Input Ventilation, the science of which adds up, and the companies that provide it claim to have all but solved the problem. We felt that it was worth the investment, especially as they were confident enough to offer us a no quibble one year 100% refund if it didn't work to our satisfaction.

The unit is an almost silent and heavy-duty fan that sucks in fresh air through the loft and forces it down into the house in a continual trickle, which can be varied according to need. Taking about two weeks to gradually build up pressure inside the house, it then forces air to circulate from top to bottom before being expelled through any gaps, vents or other openings it can find. If there aren't any, one needs to be installed for it to work. The recycling of air inside the house means that humidity is continually removed before it has a chance to condense, and the unit we installed has the added benefit of being able to heat the air as it enters the house.

It was fitted during the recent spring-like weather, but with overnight temperatures now well below the dew point once more, we can say with cautious optimism that after less than one week, the system seems to work as intended. At a fraction of the cost of a retro-fitted damp-proof course that wouldn't affect levels of condensation anyway, it is a solution well worth considering.

I do apologise for the fact that consumer advice has seeped, rather like damp, into this book. You may rest assured that normal service will be resumed shortly, when I attempt to enhance the living accommodation of some of our livestock, safe in the knowledge that the Health and Safety at Work Act of 1974 does not apply to chickens. At least not specifically by name, and this is a loophole I intend to ruthlessly exploit.

Porcine Palisades (6ᵗʰ April)

The other weekend, as I was preparing to head outside for an afternoon's garden maintenance, there was a knock at the door and a stranger politely enquired of me, "Excuse me, but do you happen to own a large black pig?" I immediately adopted a casual yet thoughtful expression that I hoped was indicative of a mind sifting through an encyclopaedia of livestock, and eventually replied, "No, I don't believe I have one of those." I then began to enthuse about the breed, but quickly tiring of my ramble he said "Um, because there's one running around in your driveway." Covering my surprise I thanked him before crossing to the gate where I was greeted by the sight of Margot and Jerry zig-zagging back up the road, shooing one of their Kunekune's in front of them with a broom.

By coincidence, it was the same day that a local contractor had arrived to start the foundation work for our new roadside gates and fence. It was clearly not before time, given the escaped pig from up the road and our current state of mind here at Stone House, and so after a little research Wikipedia told me that a Palisade is perhaps a better way of describing it. This is defined as a fence or wall made from wooden stakes or tree trunks and used as a defensive structure. It goes on to say that the posts, or more typically trunks, were sharpened or pointed at the top and was an excellent protective option for small castles. Now we're talking my language.

Nothing quite as guaranteed to turn me into a simmering Victor Meldrew quicker than someone racing past the house in excess of the national motorway speed limit. The hedgerows up and down the length of this eight-mile road bear witness to the frequency with which people come spectacularly unstuck, and as you can see from the picture towards the beginning of this book, the house and land are completely exposed to it. This was fine in the days before satnavs in articulated lorries revealed it to be a useful shortcut, petrol-heads looking for thrills on two wheels or four came to pit their skills against its twists and turns and, let's face it, before I became quite so middle-aged and grumpy.

With Rather now faster on his feet than a speeding bullet and Jolly shaping up to follow by next summer, it had become more important than ever to put an effective barrier between the road and us. That is also offers us a higher degree of privacy and security is a welcome bonus, and after eighteen months of negotiations with the local council and a number of contractors, it was a joy to see the new gates being erected and the sides to our splayed driveway entrance being enclosed.

To make things easier with Barbara's foot and the children, we felt it best to have automatic gates installed so that they were only ever open when we are inside a moving car, but I can't help but smile when I have a 4am departure for work and no longer need to wander around in the dark opening and closing gates.

Remotely operated from house or car, the whole construction gives the garden a much more private feel, and it will take some time to get used to navigating the complex array of optics and safety measures that prevent objects like hands, feet or chickens from becoming trapped in the mechanism when the gates are in motion.

The lawn in front of the house finally feels like a garden, Rather can roam safe from passing traffic and should the pigs whether from up the road or further afield feel like a return visit, they'll have to ring us on the intercom if they want to come in. Just like everyone else.

Believe in Better (11th April)

Not everything that can be measured counts, and not everything that counts can be measured is an aphorism that describes perfectly why the law is a hopelessly inadequate tool with which to resolve personal injury disputes. People don't measure an injury by what it is, but by what they've lost as a result of it. However, the law will not let you prove that your pint glass is half-empty, only that it contains ten fluid ounces. Any loss you have experienced is therefore not fact but opinion, the description of which is at the mercy of interpretation, agenda and politics. It's a game of Chance for those who prosecute, Risk for those who defend and Patience for those caught up in it. And now for us, it's finally over.

It has been almost six years since Barbara had the accident that caused so much upheaval and change in our lives, and the legal action which followed has been casting a shadow over us ever since. As the claimant in a David vs. Goliath case, we were individuals prosecuting an injustice against a complex web of corporations mostly worried about their mistake setting a costly precedent, and this meant that it was more convenient for them to consider her a criminal than a victim. Everyone else mentioned in this book enjoys the privacy of a pseudonym, so it would not be fair for me to deny the defendants in this case, her former employers, the same courtesy. I'll therefore refer to them as Eye Screw You and Cocks, best described as Broadcorping Castrations and both controlled by the same multinational parent company, News Crap.

The accident was caused by a well-connected builder with a track record of profit-driven carelessness. He had the job of renovating several parts of a busy office space where some one hundred and fifty people worked. They were liberally equipped with floorboxes; those essential bits of office architecture that have made extension cords a thing of the past, and a number of these needed updating that were sited just inches from a busy walkway along which people constantly passed.

The builder needed access to the wiring that ran between each of the floorboxes, and so he removed them, thereby exposing a series of foot-deep cavities. As his main concern was maximising profit by making the job as simple as possible, he paid no attention to the fact that he had left deep holes in the floor right where a great number of people constantly walked. When later asked why he had not placed any barriers or warning signs around the holes, he stated that they would have hindered his progress. He was responsible for a total of five accidents in Barbara's office, hers being the second, and despite assurances that he would no longer be used; his continued presence was a sign of things to come.

It was only a matter of hours before someone had the accident that was waiting to happen, and at lunchtime on Wednesday October 15th 2008, it was Barbara who fulfilled this particular destiny. In a scene later described by a witness as something out of a Charlie Chaplin film, she was crossing the room, had turned to her left to answer a colleague who had called out as she passed, and stepped neatly into a hole. A second was all it took for her to collapse to the ground, the pain-free and mobile chapter of her life closing as she landed. What has followed since is a story of medical intrigue on the one hand, and some impossibly nasty legal footwork on the other.

The legal story is as simple to explain as it has been frustrating to witness: there was no health & safety policy in the building where the accident took place, let alone anyone to enforce it. They knew they had no leg to stand on, and admitted liability very quickly. What they have proceeded to do in the years since is comb through Barbara's medical history from the day she was born in an attempt to avoid responsibility by arguing that the condition her foot was left in is acceptable, and would have occurred naturally in any event. It's rather like mitigating the act of shooting someone by citing the inevitability of death.

Not content with their lawyers' artful sophistry in defining what the length of a piece of string isn't, Cocks also subjected Barbara to a generous amount of bullying during the time she remained trapped in their employ after the accident. Frequent impromptu meetings with the heads of Legal and Human Resources piled pressure upon veiled threat, the particularly vile cherry on the cake being to force her, against her will and despite her many protestations, to become responsible for health and safety for all one hundred and fifty employees. In this position she was directly and overtly undermined by none less than the Managing Director from the very first day, while the builder continued leaving a trail of destruction behind him. This was the coup de grace that led to her breakdown which drove us from our life and home in London.

It would seem that a corporate culture, if it is to be effective, must first successfully permeate it thoroughly. To then thrive it should either be virtuous or vicious; bland and inoffensive being too vague to appeal to any side of human nature that would give it lasting momentum. Since 2010 it has been publicly revealed that the corporate culture of News Crap has been completely rotten for quite some time; ethics taking their place far behind profits, and confidentiality applying only to their own underhand activities. Indeed, corporate culture can cause the blindness that allows people without power or influence to be regarded as nothing but pawns bearing little losses and net profits. Just ask Sally and Bob Dowler.

The medical story has been more complex simply due to the fact that Barbara has an unusual mixture of pre-existing conditions. She is hyper-mobile and also has flat feet. Up until the accident, these had been easily manageable conditions, but when combined with the damage caused by the fall, they have proved a devastating cocktail.

After their best efforts, the medical experts concluded that the damage is too great for her foot to return to anything approximating its previous condition. After the equally sterling efforts of the legal experts, there now exists a new interpretation of the Eggshell Skull principle, the legal precedent which states a victim must be taken as found, from which Barbara is strangely excluded. Despite numerous requests to explain this, we are still none the wiser. Talk about being caught between a rock and a hard place.

Barbara had her first operation in 2009, at which time her employer's insurance agreed to underwrite the cost of getting the doyenne of orthopaedic surgeons to carry out a procedure to rebuild her foot. Unfortunately the operation was not successful, but it took six month's of pestering and being accused of being a malinger to be granted the funds for the scan that would prove this. Arguing against one of the country's top experts is not an easy task, and it was during this time that the combination of physical pain, emotional stress and lack of consideration and support at work finally tipped Barbara over the edge.

Now no longer able to commute by public transport and in urgent need of further surgery, we took the decision to leave London, and her second operation was carried out in 2010 after we had moved to The Cotswolds. Unfortunately both her former employer and the health insurance company with whom she had a policy refused point blank to meet the cost of this surgery, and so they fell to us exhausting our life savings in the process. Luckily the operation this time was a success, but it revealed the growing extent of the arthritis that was caused by the accident and subsequent surgeries.

Barbara's third operation was carried out successfully by her new doctor at the end of July 2012. He removed some of the metalwork from previous operations, which means that once more she can use orthotics to reposition and support her feet inside shoes. He also removed a good deal of scar tissue that had been aggravating the pain, and he noticed first hand the growing extent of her arthritis. In his words, he and Barbara will become 'great friends' over the coming years as she hobbles inexorably towards a full foot fusion operation.

American author Upton Sinclair once noted; "It is difficult to get a man to understand something, when his salary depends upon his not understanding it." We have found this observation to be remarkably astute; having battled now for years with experts on all sides who have misrepresented us through a potent and cavalier mix of carelessness, closed ranks and expediency. We have been prevented from challenging these inaccuracies by our own legal team; professional egos and future relationships being considered a more valuable commodity than factual accuracy.

In the run-up to the summer of 2013, new statements from Barbara's former managers written four and a half years after the event materialised. Containing lies ranging from the vague and artful omission to the malicious and outrageous commission, we were once again faced with a series of unpleasant meetings. Due solely to Barbara's meticulous record keeping, we were able to submit paperwork that disproved many of them.

With all evidence submitted and exchanged, a Joint Settlement Meeting was held in October 2013. This is a legal ritual where both parties agree to go on a date, say they want a sure thing, and expect the other to bend over first. Predictably, it started out in a rather pedestrian manner in which the gulf between the two sides was clearly articulated, and we all waited for the music to start. It quickly took a turn towards the bizarre, as rather than stepping out to dance, ESY's legal team quickly made a final offer that was less than the total amount we had already spent. When it was refused, they sidestepped legal process and pressed a DVD into our barrister's hands. Neither Barbara nor I were surprised, as for years we had been aware of being followed and had seen on numerous occasions people standing on step ladders taking photos of us over our hedge with paparazzi-style lenses. We had pleaded for it to stop many times, but been told bluntly that we would have to prove it was covert surveillance and not earnest bird watchers. Some of those who work for G4S must be very keen ornithologists indeed.

We were ushered into a mini-cinema by a very worried looking legal team who were itching to capitulate, and Barbara and I had a very real sense of carpet being pulled from under our feet. The timing and delivery of the package had evidently been a dramatic bluff calculated to force us into submission before the video could be played, as the best of the footage they chose from all that was available provided nothing but proof that we had been telling the truth.

From the failure of this meeting, a court date was agreed for the following April, and both sides retired to prepare. In January 2014, ESY unexpectedly made an application to submit to the court the video evidence with which they had tried to persuade us to settle three months previously, but which they had oddly never sought permission to use formally in the fourteen months since it was filmed. As they had already shot their bolt at the Joint Settlement Meeting, a failure to submit it would have been an admission of its flimsiness, and the only way to get any value from it was to try to delay the court date. On March 17th the judge ruled that he could not deny the video evidence but would not let the trial date slip. No problem; see you next tuesday in court, or so we thought.

The stark truth is that the truth never has and never really will matter to anyone but us. From the start, this case was riddled with shoddy work, inaccuracy and the aroma of deals being done; something which we could neither fathom nor effectively challenge. A number of years ago, when Barbara and I realised how big a lie the phrase "my duty is to the court" is, we began to record and document our meetings, the submitted transcripts of which prove instances of false testimony. Despite this, our barrister changed his tune completely after the final meeting in what was a breath-taking display of duplicity. Concerns of ours about the accuracy of experts' statements from three years ago that were pooh-poohed at the time were suddenly repackaged as critical, and what he once considered strong and compelling evidence was now rebranded as weak and inconclusive. For whatever reason, his faith in our case had evaporated and his recommendation was that we should timidly submit an offer but ultimately accept whatever the defendants put on the table. With hindsight it seems clear that this had been his intention all along.

One of the conditions of no win no fee trials is that you must take out insurance against losing, which seems perfectly sensible. Less well known is that should your barrister either get cold feet or want to recommend an out-of-court settlement despite your wishes, your insurance immediately becomes invalid, and that is a loaded gun held to your head with a weak smile. With our hands tied we were left with no choice, and our long game of Patience was over. We folded on the afternoon of Tuesday, April 1st 2014, having been played like fools for years.

Barbara will need further treatment and operations for the rest of her life. She will never be free of pain and will never have more than rudimentary mobility, which itself in time will require aids of one kind or another. Gone are the long walks, nights of dancing and island hopping holidays of yesteryear. Instead she faces a life spent primarily at home whilst those responsible congratulate themselves behind the protective legal cloak of a morally bankrupt corporation. We feel and consider that we lost the case, and that the last five and a half years were a waste of time.

Barbara was awarded less than we had been told she might reasonably expect and was robbed of the chance to tell her story in court. Although we knew justice was not possible and a sense of vindication was unlikely, we had wanted to see the whites of their eyes and hold out for at least a degree of fairness. The practise of law, having absolutely nothing to do with truth or evidence, sadly makes no provision for any of that.

I shall probably forever rue the fact that I couldn't persuade all the experts concerned with this case to put their egos to one side, and realise that what they spent 1,995 days pushing around their desks was never actually a dispute, but some of the best years of Barbara's life. I'll also continue to relish the thought of five minutes in a quiet room with a few of her former work colleagues to personally thank them for inventing details that never happened whilst denying a few that did. And for the octogenarian who claws to preserve the reputation of his empire through hollow public contrition, corporate gerrymandering and all the sound and fury he can muster; I'd like to give him the right hook his ex-wife once used to protect him.

For each one, I wish the opportunity to measure for themselves the pain and limitation she lives with by enduring just one day of it. Then they'll know exactly how much mobility counts.

Our marriage and family relationships have been under immense strain for many years, and it's now time to stop feeding the wolf of anger, disgust and resentment so we can finally move on. We feel immense gratitude and love for those who have supported us through all the tears and pain, and will forever remember the kindness, consideration and sympathy we received. We appreciate that many will want to know how the case concluded and we hope that this letter adequately charts our journey from the start, leaving you with a picture of how our world now looks at the end. There is nothing more we can or want to say.

Wishing Well (20ᵗʰ April)

Watching our children grow is, as you might imagine, a pleasure that almost cannot be described. A fearless two-year-old who absorbs and regurgitates everything around him, Rather has now amassed the lexicon of a toddler, and it's amazing quite how far in life it seems you can go with a vocabulary consisting of No, More, Up, Choo-choo and Pub. He has also just learned how to say his own name, which is so endearing as to make me ask him to tell me several times a day.

Quite a different kettle of fish is Jolly, who regards her brother with what appears to be a blend of awe, tolerance and curiosity. What she presently lacks in speech, she more than makes up for in vocal ability, and has just perfected the technique of rolling onto her tummy. As the inability to do so is sometimes what prevents me from getting out of bed in the middle of the night for a pee, I am suitably impressed. Between the pair of them, it feels like we are watching two curling stones slide across the ice, and all Barbara and I can do is sweep.

The inside of Stone House is awash with sharp corners, hard surfaces and low ceilings which provide a steep learning curve for them to learn about life's physical knocks. Outside there are all manner of hazards that provide the same challenge, and although we constantly wrestle with the balance between protective care and experiential learning, there has been nothing that we felt represented an unreasonable or especially worrying danger. Not until I discovered that the cover to the well had given in to the relentless attention of the elements. Sat quietly in the far corner of the garden and often overlooked, we presume the well must date from the days before the house was connected to the water mains, and it appears to still be in full working order. We have yet to really explore it, but what we do know is that the water level is around thirty feet below the surface, and is both clear and clean. Due to its proximity to the septic tank, we plan on doing little with it ourselves, but we have a vague notion of one day using it to fill a duck pond.

At three feet in diameter, it must be safely covered and locked from inquisitive youngsters, and so Barbara quickly found a carpenter who promised to replace the entire cover with new tannelised wood based on the old lockable design. His work was completed whilst I was away and when I came back to inspect it, I look the opportunity to lower a video camera to the bottom to see what it looked like inside. Having only expected a muddy hole in the ground, I was quite impressed to see evidence of the effort put into its construction.

I have no idea what's beneath the water, nor how deep it is, but the sides seem to have been formed using a drystone walling technique to hold the earth back as it was excavated, giving it the appearance of the sort of tunnel in which Indiana Jones might find himself trapped. Both the well and its superstructure appear sturdy enough, so should we decide to build a pond it should be easy enough to feed it with a pump from the bottom. Until then, we will do little with it apart from making sure the cover and well handle stay safely locked, and possibly tossing the odd coin in it to support the hopes and dreams we have for our children. Happy Easter!

Home Eggonomics (5th May)

During my student days in the 1990's, I did my fair share of cheap living and pushing the boundaries of nutritional research by thriving on a balanced diet of Smirnoff, Pasta & Pesto and the occasional weekend treat from Tesco's of one whole roast chicken, which then cost the princely sum of four pounds fifteen and sometimes never made it home. Twenty-five years later, the same meal costs five pounds seventy-eight, which is still a great deal by any stretch of the imagination.

Now, I'm the first person to hold my hand up and acknowledge that the finish of my formal education is more vinyl matt than deep gloss, but it seems to me that if a chicken is sold in a large supermarket for such a price having been raised, fed, slaughtered, transported and then cooked, then there is some serious leverage at work to generate a profit. As I see it, it's a matter of exploiting the economies of scale. Or perhaps exploiting something else.

Following the wholesale slaughter of seven chickens before Christmas by Mr Fox, Barbara and I have been planning on adding to our clutch for some time. Costing anywhere from a couple of pounds from a local livestock market to just under twenty pounds for a twenty-week old hen at point of lay, it can be expensive to buy chickens and, as with most things, you get what you pay for.

About a month ago Stripper, one of our chickens, started exhibiting some strange behaviour. Preferring her own company to the exclusion of others, and remaining in the coop for most of the day I began to fear the worst and went to investigate. For removing the eggs beneath her, I received a sharp peck, which sent me scurrying off to Google, and it seemed clear that she was answering the call of nature and had become broody.

Having seen the sheer exhaustion some hens suffer from after they have been on the receiving end of a cockerel's affections, not to mention the fact that Walt Disney's assertion that a cockerel only crows once or twice at sunrise is a blatant lie, we have little intention of allowing one of the annoying buggers anywhere inside our boundary. However interfering we may be, nature's way will not be for our birds.

Barbara then found out that Busy Bantams, the nearby chicken farm, were offering fertilised eggs for sale at ten pounds for half a dozen. The idea of letting Stripper's biological urge take care of the problem whilst saving us about a hundred pounds was too tempting an opportunity to pass up, and so three weeks ago we gently pushed six Cream Legbar eggs under her and left her alone.

With her changed temperament and the other hens overly inquisitive presence not helping things, I fenced off a small area within the enclosure and recommissioned our old coop which had been stored in the Cider Barn. In privacy, she has sat all day and every day for the last three weeks staring at the wall, her only exercise being a short ten-minute leg stretch in the morning before settling back down on her eggs to keep them warm. Having checked on her most days, I am now convinced that it is possible for a chicken to look bored out of its mind. The incubation period for an egg is meant to be highly predictable at twenty-one days, with a two-day margin of error either way. As the bank holiday weekend approached, so our sense of expectation increased and we waited with baited breath to see what would happen. Friday passed without incident, as did Saturday. By Sunday I began to worry and gently lifted her to check all was well, and had to remove one crushed egg and its lifeless contents.

By today our hope was on the wane, and as we made our way home from a morning play date at a friend's house I wondered whether we might try with six more eggs, especially as it seems some of our other birds might have caught the broody mood. To my complete surprise and utter delight, when I opened the nesting box I found three chicks burrowed under their mother's breast and the other two eggs still intact.

In a rush of excitement, I dashed to our local Countrywide to buy some chick crumbs, and then Barbara and I fashioned some protection from aerial predators using garden netting, string and staples. We don't know how many will hatch in the end, but we'll do all we can to make sure those that do aren't despatched too quickly.

With Barbara's egg-selling cottage industry growing slowly but surely, having more birds makes sense and this seems by far the best method of expansion. I estimate that our birds should generate enough revenue during their egg-laying years to pay for themselves about twenty five times over at today's prices, and if we can exploit their broody periods, that increases to almost thirty times as well as being a lot of fun. It's not the biggest money-spinner there is, but every little helps.

Fair Trade (11th May)

Spring typically heralding an explosion of growth in all areas, the atmosphere around Stone House since March has been a delightful cacophony of bleating lambs, chirping chicks and squealing children. Trees have burst into blossom, grass has started growing vigorously and hedgerows are thickening out. I am amazed and not a little grateful at the enormous appetite that thirty odd sheep can have, the result being that I have not had to put a foot in the field this year for anything other than pleasure.

Several months ago, Lewis and I spoke about the possibility of letting the sheep into the orchard field as well, which we decided would be mutually beneficial as the sheep wanted the grass on the ground and I wanted their poo in its place. As the big field was now smooth and short like velvet, and would need chain harrowing before it could produce new growth in respectable quantities, it seemed a good idea and only required a new stock fence to be erected along the roadside border for safety.

The only other job that would need to be done would be to keep the sheep away from the compost heap in the corner, whilst continuing to allow chickens access to it. In exchange for his agreement to repair my earlier shoddy work, build the fence and cordon off the compost, the sheep would be granted access to both fields. To make it even more of a fair trade, I would supply the fence and he the posts.

Turning up one lunchtime with a colleague, Lewis set about doing exactly what I did last December; namely banging a number of wooden posts into the ground and then attaching the wire to them. To the untrained eye, it looked as though they were using the exact same technique as me, but with one subtle difference which he shared with me conspiratorially; "See, like, I'll be doin' it properly."

In open admiration, I watched the posts go into the ground with the greatest of ease. As they attached the stock net and tensioned it with a winch, a tiny part of me began to think that this job might be one that I could learn to do properly if only I were to not only buy the correct tools but also actually use them. As far as I can tell, there are three things that I need to get and two things that I already have but need to use.

Fence post diggers are rather clever devices which allow you to quickly excavate a hole into which a fence post can sit snugly, ready to be hammered home securely without the need for an extra pair of arms. Fence post drivers are an excellent tool that can do just that without shattering their tops at the same time. I plan to invest in one of each of these as well as a winch that I can attach to the back of my car, and provided that I use them all with patience and a spirit level, all should be well.

By late afternoon the compost area was enclosed with a fence and access gate, the finishing touch of a length of barbed wire was added to the posts and the job was done. The flock, who had been keeping an eye on progress all afternoon, now resembled an impatient queue waiting for the Boxing Day sales to start, and the scene was set for a smorgasbord.

Lewis opened the gate and an ovine torrent poured through, stopping immediately in the tall grass and the sound of ripping and chewing soon filled the air. Over the next few hours they slowly spread out across the field and before nightfall the efficiency of their digestive system had caught and passed the ferocity of their appetites. Within a matter of days the field sported closely cropped grass, the bordering hedge had taken on a neatly trimmed look and the ground already looked better as dose after dose of manure had landed on it, been trodden in and left to work its magic.

In exchange for letting Lewis use our land, we receive expert fence maintenance, free manure, trimmed hedgerows and the companionship of a large flock of child and chicken friendly sheep. What's not to like?

Gerrymandering (18th May)

In 1812, Governor Elbridge Gerry redrew part of the state of Massachusetts to favour his own political party, and with the resulting borders suggesting the shape of a Salamander to the political satirists of the day, a genteel term for an underhand practise was born. Although formerly eligible, I never once took part in the US Elections simply because I felt it would be inappropriate to influence, however slightly, a political process that I had no stake in.

With the 2014 European Elections taking place in a matter of days, and the certainty that they will be immediately followed by exhaustive campaigning for the general election next year, I thought it prudent for me to try out my new-found voter muscles in safety by messing about with my very own sandpit and swing-o-meter here.

Barbara and I formed our own junta on arrival here in 2011, and since then we have employed a scorched earth policy against any and all unwanted infrastructure. Our victories so far include a hawthorn hedgerow, four garden sheds in various states of disrepair, fifteen cider apple trees, forty metres of fencing and a few other sundry items. Now, after almost three years in control, only one obstacle remained that prevented us from gathering all territories together under our leadership.

The Leylandii hedge that connects the house to the garage has long been an eyesore, and in the past I had made a few attempts to despatch it. As I have the tools to inflict damage on it but not mortally wound it, I once again turned to the mercenary forces of Rupert, a local tree surgeon. In the past he had made short work of other hedges and trees, and so I felt he was the just the man to come along and remove all traces of the hedge.

Within the space of a few hours, he deployed an impressive array of power tools to fell the trees, convert them into an enormous pile of wood chip and cut the remaining stumps into the ground. All that remained of thirty trees was a strip of stumps awaiting the grinder before being ready for grass seeding in a few weeks. Once the greenhouses have been relocated to their new home on the south side of the garage and the last of the concrete has been broken up and removed, the garden will finally be open, safe and visible in its entirety from the house.

As underhand as gerrymandering can be in a democracy, it can deliver excellent results in a totalitarian state. When I cast my first ever vote, I shall do so in the full knowledge that I

am a tin-pot dictator aiming to empower those who I imagine
wish they were.

Blot on the Landscape (1ˢᵗ June)

Since we arrived here in July of 2011, Barbara and I have
spent a great deal of time getting rid of the clutter that Ted and
Jan had accumulated over their forty odd years in residence
before us. Much of it had to be cut down and chipped, and a
good deal had to be dismantled and taken to the recycling
centre, and the rest burnt. Over time I have become a deft
hand at fitting an extraordinary amount of rubbish inside and
on top of a Volkswagen Passat, and the car's condition reflects
this rather well.

Sat alongside the animal shelter in the field is an ageing
chicken shed which can't have been moved or used in the last
thirty years. Barbara had once voiced a romantic idea of
restoring it, and when we first inspected it she opened one of
the doors to discover a small fruit bat cowering inside. I had
visions of finding an entire colony up in the rafters, but sadly
this was a lone traveller resting on its way somewhere more
comfortable, and it has never been seen since. When the soak
away was installed two years ago, I asked one of the
contractors if he might accidentally reverse his tipper into it,
but he didn't think I was being serious and so it remains intact.
Uninhabited and unused, it is too big and heavy to be removed
in one piece, and I was undecided how it should meet its end.
Crowbar? Axe? Flamethrower? All were equally tempting, but

at nine feet long and a shade over six feet wide, it would be hard work whichever method I used to nudge it from this life into the next. Every time I noticed it, I found something else that required my attention very quickly.

On one of his visits, Lewis saw me eying it up warily and asked what I used it for. "Nothing", I said and then told him that I would soon be taking a sledgehammer to it. "Well you could do that, or you could sell it on eBay and save yourself the bother" he said. Then, with a grin, he watched the rusty cogs in my head begin to clunk and squeak as I took his idea on board.

I had spent so much time despatching ageing wooden structures through brute force and fire, that it had never occurred to me someone else might want them. Admittedly one of the sheds had been in reasonable condition when I took it down, and I have stored it in the Cider Barn, but this was a whole new approach that would cost me no money, time or effort. I immediately took a few photos of it and listed it for 99p with no reserve as a "traditional chicken coop in need of complete restoration; go on, you know you want to."

The bids didn't exactly come flooding in, but a trickle was all that I needed and at the end of ten days I had sold it for £12.50. Now all I had to do was make sure the buyer, a local contractor, came to collect it, which he did and promptly discovered that it was a little harder to shift than he had anticipated. He looked at it this way and then that way, and concluded that he to come back with the right tools for the job.

As it happened, these turned out to be a mini-digger and a flatbed lorry which he reversed up to the gate. When he fired up the digger and slowly manoeuvred it down the ramps, he caught the look of envy on my face. "I should put one of these on my Christmas List, if I were you" he observed, and then trundled off in the direction of the chicken shed. When it comes to machinery like this, my face is an open book it seems.

Using chains, hydraulic rams and a mixture of timing and subtle control, he dug the shed from its muddy clutches and inched it towards the back of the lorry where, after fifteen minutes, it was positioned at the foot of the ramps. From there it was a matter of nudging, shoving and pushing in equal measure until the shed sat squarely on the back of the lorry.

A series of canvas ties were then used to secure the shed down. Attached to the axles, they were easily tightened and fixed the base firmly. Sitting proudly on the lorry, it soon became apparent that the superstructure was gently swaying as the rotting wood flexed in its newfound freedom. More canvas ties were thrown over the roof, and as they were slowly tightened the top of the roof began to buckle and I had visions of the shed beginning to resemble the Sydney Opera House. Thankfully it held, and with a few audible creaks the new owner gently started to make his way across the field towards the road. I reflected on the fact that I had just been paid to let someone else clear away some old clutter, and the only muscles I had used were those that created the big smile on my face.

As I watched the lorry and shed cautiously disappear in a northerly direction, I said farewell to another piece of the past from Stone House. Walking back to the house, I chuckled knowing that whatever happened when they encountered the first of the many potholes that litter the B4220, it wouldn't be my problem.

Another Place (8th June)

I've never been able to tell the difference between some of the paintings by Mark Rothko and a colour swatch from Homebase, and for this reason the only opinion about art that I have ever been prepared to express is simply whether it inspires me or not. Rather than let a critic decide for me, I employ a yardstick that is both basic and literal; whether or not the work causes me to have a sharp intake of breath.

One of the longer term projects that currently occupies my time requires infrequent visits to the northeast of England, and the logistical planning for these has allowed me the chance to see first-hand a work of art which passed the test the moment I first heard of it; Anthony Gormley's Another Place, which is now a permanent installation at Crosby Beach in North Liverpool.

It is a collection of just under one hundred cast iron statues that stare out to sea, made from 17 moulds of the artist's body and arranged in a haphazard fashion across two miles of the beach. At low water all are completely exposed, and at high water most are submerged. What the work is about depends on who you ask, and over the years I have heard and read enough interpretations to suspect that no one really knows, and now that I have seen it I know that it doesn't really matter.

I had asked Barbara if she wanted to make a weekend trip out of the visit I had to make, and she said yes enthusiastically. With her on board, the planning process took on a whole new dimension, and while I researched the best route and times to drive she organised accommodation that would allow the children a quiet night's sleep and give us a cosy evening enjoying "du vin, du pain, et du boursin" overlooking the Mersey.

I also had arranged for us to meet at the beach a very dear friend of mine who lives nearby, and even the weather conspired to make the whole trip memorable; from clear roads to dry grass and from evening sunsets to warm breezes, we revelled in our outdoor enjoyment. When Saturday dawned sunny and bright, we capitalised on being woken early by the children to make our way to the beach before anyone else.

Once down by the water, Rather ran free and his fascination ebbed and flowed between the shells he found in the sand and the iron figures that rose from it. As he ran towards and explored the first of them, Barbara and I followed with Jolly in the pram. We were silently grateful for the success of her most recent steroid injection that allowed us to cover a mile or two, before we found a bench on which to rest and where my friend joined us.

In the warm sunshine we chatted, squinted out to sea as if trying to spot what the figures were staring at, soaked up the sunshine and took time to consider whether we wanted squirty cream or pouring cream in the coffees that we bought from the catering van in the car park. For some of the time we sat doing absolutely nothing, and I realised how hard it is to do just that at home; there is always something to fix, to break or to build.

As the sun rose higher and the figures began to disappear beneath the waves, we made our farewells and were on the road again towards home. We stopped to meet another friend at Chester Zoo who had kindly offered us some of her precious weekend to help us show Rather that Lions weren't exactly like Ra Ra, Penguins weren't much like Pingu but, mercifully, a tractor was a tractor wherever you see it. He absorbed as much as he could, but after 48 hours and many hundreds of miles of unfamiliar sights and sounds, he had reached the end of his considerable tether, and he treated those who had gathered by the Giraffe enclosure to a toddler meltdown.

It was time for a reasonably sharp exit, and thankfully once in the car both children slept on the last leg home. Several hours later we arrived exhausted and got the children washed, fed and into bed. As we relaxed with a well-earned glass of wine, we exhaled slowly and reflected that as wonderful as it had been to visit other places, it felt just right to be back in ours.

Caravan Morrison (15ᵗʰ June)

I have never liked caravans; they're just not my thing. When they are moving, it's the way they fishtail around the back of a vehicle like a salmon that can't quite make it upstream. When they are parked in rows connected to every utility under the sun, I see them as a cramped bed & breakfast on wheels. Camping is an activity that offers the romance of outdoor cooking and sleeping under the stars in a trade for creature comforts. Caravanning on the other hand seems to be about mobilising microwave ovens, satellite television and ruched blinds, the net result being simply to change the view from your front room while making it noticeably more damp.

As a family of four living in a three-bedroom house we enjoy the perfect blend of personal privacy and domestic efficiency, but being in Herefordshire it presents friends and family with the option of a long journey or a poor night's sleep. Barbara's mother has stayed with us enough times to decide that a mattress on the dining room floor is preferable to our sofa bed in the living room, but it's clearly the lesser of two evils. For quite a while we have known that something had to be done.

Barbara has always loved caravans; often taking great delight in threatening me with the idea of a holiday in one, but I have each time pointed out that it would constitute grounds for an instant divorce. In the absence of the lottery win that will allow us to build an extension to the house, not to mention the cost of putting a yurt up in the field, it was always the obvious solution and a compromise was reached whereby we could have a caravan as long as I didn't have to look at it.

Give her a mission and access to the Internet, and nothing takes long it seems. Fully equipped with advice and information from the four corners of the world of caravanning, she targeted Gumtree and eBay with laser-guided precision, and forty-eight hours later we were eagerly standing outside the gate to the orchard field watching a van approach from the south with our guest bedroom flapping around behind it.

Small caravans are cheap when compared to camper vans, and twenty-year-old ones are very cheap indeed. They are also quite hard to find, and I put this down to the fact that most of them will have either fallen apart or been destroyed by Top Gear presenters by now. However, ours seems well built and free from any damp.

Things got off to a good start when Adrian, the chap who brought it, misjudged the turn from the road through the gate, and managed to get his van stuck against the open gate on the inside whilst the caravan was wedged against the gate post on the outside, with most of it sticking out onto the road. I thought the best option was to reverse and try again with better aim, but he had other ideas. At this point no money had changed hands, so I was content to follow his lead.

While he considered his options, I stood on the road waving traffic past feeling only moderately foolish. One car approached and, rather than pass at my signal, chose to stop with its hazard lights flashing. The driver got out and wandered up to see if he could help, and I had visions of this becoming a local talking point. Meanwhile it had been decided that the best policy was to unhitch the caravan, free it from the gatepost and then reattach it from a different angle so it could make the corner. We did so with the help of the passing motorist, and I thanked him. As he returned to his car, I swear I heard him mutter "bloody caravaners" under his breath. I felt his pain.

Now we were all set to tow the caravan up into the big field and position it by the animal shelter, and Adrian's eyes passed from the long wet grass to his rear wheel drive van and back again. After what felt like an eternity, he advised, "You'd better push from the back, just in case." Dutifully I positioned myself at the rear and waited for something to happen. He floored it, the caravan shot forward and I clung on for dear life, my welly-boot shod feet getting tangled in the long grass as I attempted to simultaneously find traction and stay upright.

We shot though the next gate, past the puzzled faces of Barbara, Jolly and Rather, and ended up more or less where I had previously indicated. Adrian then set about unhitching the caravan while I caught my breath and managed to say "You'd never have made it without me pushing, y'know." Even though he had a large wrench in his hand, he generously interpreted my comment as humour.

The last step was to swing it around and push it up against the animal shelter where the old chicken shed used to stand, which we almost managed. As one of the wheels left the grass it buried itself in soft mud right up to the axle, and it was game over with the caravan now firmly beached and listing worryingly to one side. Adrian grinned, his body language clearly saying "It's your problem now, matey" before holding out his hand, accepting our money and leaving.

A few days after its arrival we managed to free the caravan from the mud with help, and move it to the hard standing between the Cider Barn and Animal Shelter. We then set to work emptying it of what we didn't want or need, cleaning it from top to bottom and figuring out how the water, electricity and toilet worked. From what we can tell, it is dry, clean and in good nick for a 1993 vintage Compass Reflection 360/2.

Once I have cleared out part of the Animal Shelter, it will live in there protected from the elements, out of view and easy to get to with a torch after a long late night. With a little wiring work in the Cider Barn, we'll be able to power it safely, and then we will have a guest bedroom that will boast heater, kettle, fridge, ensuite toilet and two beds.

Whether because ours may never see the open road again, or because we can now accommodate guests in comfort, I find that I may now like caravans just a little. After all, as Van Morrison says:

> *And the caravan is painted red and white*
> *That means ev'rybody's staying overnight*

Predictably Irrational (29th June)

During the 1940's, the economist Professor Theodore Levitt suggested that "differentiation is one of the most important strategic and tactical activities in which companies must constantly engage." His idea was then taken and developed by television advertising companies into one of today's foremost marketing tools; the Unique Selling Point. Like many people, I like to think that I am intelligent enough to see beyond slogans, gimmicks and hype, but I suspect a behavioural economist like Dan Ariely would say that I am just stupid enough to select the ones I want to justify.

When we moved to Stone House we were swapping a suburban garden for a rural smallholding, and one of the adjustments I had to make was that mowing the lawn was a very different proposition. I estimate that there is just over an acre of lawn to cut, and I have always been glad of the foresight Barbara and I had in requesting that Ted's old tractor be included in the sale of the house, even though a design flaw that prevents it from collecting grass hampers it.

In a fit of frustration this spring, it became clear that spending three hours to cut the grass every week was more than I or my back were happy to give, and the shortcomings of the Honda were never going to be overcome by my use of brute force, bodging or whining. Thanks to some advice from a local expert and a timely article in a newspaper, I ordered and had delivered what is probably the only vehicle I shall ever own from new.

Built by Cub Cadet, a company in the United States that only recently began exporting them to Europe, it is perfect for my needs. It's probably little different from any other lawn tractor in its class, so if I wanted to win a game of lawn tractor Top Trumps, I reckon I'd have to highlight the sporty faux-leather steering wheel, ergonomically contoured seat and infinitely adjustable driving position; all of which make no difference to its ability to cut and collect grass.

If I were to wait until the grass were dry before I cut it I might never be able to do it, and so the feature that actually made it the best choice for me was the fact that you can unclog the grass vent without having to stop or get off; you just pull and release a lever. It's something no other similarly priced model is equipped with, but the result is to reduce the time I spend mowing to just under one hour. I'm no expert, but when it comes to selling equipment for rugged and manly outdoor activities like larger scale mowing, it seems the USP of laziness doesn't sell.

Now with a surplus of lawn tractors it seemed sensible to sell the Honda, but having researched its resale value, it was unlikely to fetch as much value in currency as it can still provide in utility. Therefore it is now used for the edges of the fields where grass collection is not required and, when hitched to a trailer, it serves to pull, drag and carry all manner of stuff from one side of the plot to the other. The joy of having two tractors to play with is not lost on me either.

Having invested in the new one, I felt that my usual approach towards things mechanical of yank, shove and shove harder might not be the wisest choice. Instead I uncharacteristically chose to start on the path of maintaining it properly to safeguard its value and longevity, and hoped that the hidden USP would reveal itself further. Leafing through the virgin white pages of the manual the other day in search of how to unclip the grass catcher correctly, my eyes wandered over the sentence; "The CC1018HE has also been fitted with a drinks holder to enhance the mowing experience of a summer's day." Now we are talking my language.

Instantly forgetting about the grass catcher, I raced back to the machine to confirm that indeed this was true. Located with pinpoint accuracy in the place where your left hand naturally falls when driving with one hand in an affectation of nonchalance, it holds cans, beer bottles and wine bottles but draws the line at anything larger. I interpret this possible oversight as a deliberate design decision underlining the fact that it is meant for large gardens or small farms.

Out of interest, I checked the specifications of all the other mowers that I had considered and discovered that while many were more expensive, better equipped and perhaps more durable, none were fitted with the same accessory, and none even offered it as an option. If only Cub Cadet had branded their mower as "designed for the lazy gardener who likes to mow with a cold beer" I'd have ordered one without having to compare it to others, and I'd probably have been willing to pay more for it too. Predictable maybe, but irrational? Never.

Stilt House (6ᵗʰ July)

Having kept chickens at Stone House for over two years, we have learnt a good deal about their habits and needs. We have also discovered that many of the companies that supply equipment for smallholders and hobbyists such as ourselves have not. Obviously many aspects of chicken care are nuanced and it can take time to grasp them properly, but the fact that chickens produce a surprisingly large amount of poop is neither hard to notice nor difficult to plan for.

Chicken coops are built without plumbing, and so cleaning out their waste every few days is an obvious and essential chore that needs to be done. To aid this, coop designers have thoughtfully made the floor a tray that is both removable and moisture-resistant, and the theory is that you should be able to simply slide it out, tip it into the compost and that's it. Unfortunately they make them far too thin, and on removal most of the content gets squashed against the inside before dropping to the ground in one large mess. Nice.

To prevent all sorts of unpleasant things from growing and living in the fertile guano beneath a coop, it should be frequently moved and this, quite frankly, is too much like hard work for me. With the on-going plans to convert the existing chicken enclosure into the new vegetable garden, there was no time like the present to kill two birds with one stone, and I put into action my plan to relocate the coop, banish forever the need to move it or clear beneath it and give the flock permanent access to the orchard field from the relative safety of the garden.

It was one of those dream jobs that involved plenty of banging and absolutely no finesse; I was in heaven. All I had to do was butcher an old wooden palette to make a pair of sills, rummage around inside the cider barn for some spare posts and I was ready to start. It took fifteen minutes to dig two holes about a foot deep using a set of post diggers, and another ten minutes using a 12-kilo post driver to bang them two feet further into the ground. As fast as that may sound, it is nothing when compared to the brief second or two that it took me to forget to measure the position of holes before siting them in exactly the wrong place.

There is an old adage that says "measure twice, drill once" and it's fair to say that I have never seen the value in it, preferring instead the joy that comes from finding the right spot through a thorough investigation of numerous wrong ones. However, in this instance, my standard operating procedure would have resulted in something akin to a lunar landscape, and so the overall design was changed to accommodate my error. This made most of the reasons for elevating the coop in the first place redundant, but by this point the ship had already sailed.

After a good deal of sweat, swearing and assistance from Barbara the supporting framework was anchored in position and the coop precariously balanced on top. If it had been built as originally envisaged, it would have been totally safe, but it wasn't and so there followed an extended period of hammering and sawing in order to lash the two together with offcuts and odd brackets.

In a feat of civil engineering that would make any surveyor run for cover and weep, the chickens now enjoy a penthouse apartment view with a veranda boasting a southerly aspect and direct access to the field via an elegant walkway. Despite the errors made during construction, cleaning the house no longer requires bending over and anything that falls beneath can be easily hoovered up with the lawn mower.

As we head into the height of summer, the garden is now free from marauding hens and the children can play without fear of stepping or rolling in poop. The old enclosure is ready to be cleared before fences are moved, greenhouse bases are installed and raised vegetable beds are built.

This Be The Verse (20th July)

My innate optimism and lack of formal training in literature mean that I take the work of Philip Larkin at face value, and enjoy it for its simplicity and deadpan dourness. Actually, I don't take his work very often and my knowledge of his writing is exclusively limited to the poem from which this letter takes its title. As our children continue to grow, their objectives will change in line with nature's way, and I have little doubt that I will prove Larkin right to a certain extent in time.

Jolly remains wholly focussed on satisfying her physiological needs, and is not so much interested in movement as she is frustrated by her inability to move. That being said, she has recently discovered that she is capable of forward propulsion, but has yet to find any benefit associated with it and so remains largely immobile.

Having gained a high degree of physical control and confidence in his movement, Rather has now set his sights beyond his body and is all about interaction with people and objects. When not contentedly going about the business of playing, he naturally tests boundaries and ebbs and flows between sampling the satisfaction that comes from having control and experiencing the frustration that arises when he is thwarted.

He is also all about language, and is jumping headfirst into becoming bilingual which is something that Barbara and I consider very important. As his English and Swedish vocabularies start to form, mine improves and the hope is that in the end all four of us will be able to understand each other in both languages, although in my case perhaps never fully.

This effort may create potential hiccups, for example when learning the difference between saying "Ta" and "Tak" when thanking someone, but it does not explain from where he sourced the name for one of his favourite animals, the Giraffe, which he insists on calling a "Halfway".

In the way that parents can have when they find things their children do unbearably cute, but which are faintly annoying to other people, I have taken great delight over the last few months in pointing at pictures of giraffes in order to ask him what they are. I find it funny; I can't help it. A few weeks ago when picking him up from a day at nursery, another parent overheard our little ritual as I asked him what animal he was playing with, and as they rolled their eyes upwards I instantly remembered how I used to feel at school when I was forever told to stop being silly and grow up.

Regardless of the rights or wrongs of this, the fact remains that it is my job to ensure Rather knows that a giraffe is called a giraffe (or a giraff in Swedish) if for no other reason than the confusion he may cause when he asks someone to "Meet me halfway."

Last week when he and I were playing with plasticine and cut-out shapes on the living room floor, I asked him what the shape pictured above was. "Halfway!" he cried. "No, it's a giraffe. Can you say giraffe?" I asked. He looked at me quite seriously and searched my eyes. "Duff?" he asked after a pause, and I grinned. Right first time, my boy, right first time.

I have long believed that instinct and intelligence often exclude each other to a large extent, and having just chipped away at a little piece of his childhood, I had to wonder whether Philip Larkin was on to something, even if he was only halfway right.

Lab Report (3rd August)

Barbara and I have long wanted a dog, but there have always been reasons not to have one. When in London and both working away from the house full time, we felt it was never really an option for us. When we moved to Herefordshire, we felt that the presence of a dog would have complicated an already labyrinthine legal battle. With the conclusion of our court case and the construction of our roadside defences, not to mention the arrival of our children, we felt finally in a position to seriously consider getting one this spring.

Since meeting one in the flesh many years ago, we have always rather fancied a Flat-coated Retriever; there being in our estimation something calm, playful and loyal about them. Ever keen for research, Barbara soon found out that they also have a tendency to err on the loopy side of sane. Whilst this makes them an ideal candidate for us they also seem to have a penchant for eating their own poop, and with children around this put a rather unpleasant finish on an originally bright idea.

We had previously discounted the idea of a Labrador owing to their clear predisposition to gain weight and develop hip-dysplasia. I mentioned this in passing to a local friend of ours, and it turns out that he not only trains working Labs but has six of them. "I'll bring them over one day and you can see what they're like for yourself" he said. He was as good as his word, and on a recent beautifully sunny summer afternoon he and his wife arrived with five of their dogs, each one blacker than night.

Commands were issued after opening the tailgate of their car, and as I stood on the driveway with Jolly in my arms, we were enveloped by a synchronised swarm during which they quickly sampled the scents of four new people. They were inquisitive, calm, silent and always in control. They were then released to roam the garden as they wished and it took them about 0.157 seconds to find and swallow the remnants of Rather's al fresco lunch. Shortly after their blanket and water was spread out in the shade under an apple tree and they settled down.

We chatted over tea, coffee and cake and Barbara and I began to learn more about the differences between show dogs and working dogs, and we instinctively knew that we would want the latter. When the subject of weight came up, our friend reiterated the information freely available on the Internet indicating that "unless your lab has developed opposable thumbs, the only people with control over the food cupboard, are the people he lives with." Just then Lewis arrived for an evening inspection of his flock, and eyed the dogs appreciatively. "Nice to see a Lab that isn't fat!" he said. I mumbled in agreement whilst simultaneously reaching for more cake and loosening my belt.

Conscious that all we ever notice of dog ownership is the good, occasionally the bad but never the mundane, I asked what they felt was the most common mistake made by new dog owners. "Remember that they are dogs and not people", he said. "As long as you treat them according to their needs and not yours, you can't go far wrong." It seemed like sensible advice, and we reflected on it whilst gently fussing the dogs in the evening sunshine.

The children's bedtimes were approaching and as they had promised to put on a bit of a show for Rather, the dogs were called to order. Whilst his wife distracted their attention, our friend set a series of tasks for them in the big field. Dummies that ranged from a sausage shaped bean-bag to a plastic pheasant with all-to-real broken neck were hidden in various places around the two acres. Then, using line-of-sight indications, calls and whistles two of the dogs were despatched at high speed to hunt and retrieve, which they did with unerring precision.

It was an impressive display of skill and training, but the aspect with which Barbara and I were most enthused was their placid and calm behaviour at rest that was clearly contrasted by the iron discipline that allowed the dogs to work closely amongst the sheep and chickens without upsetting or being distracted by them.

Our friends and their dogs packed up and headed home, after which Barbara and I retired to the Breeze House for sundowners and to reflect on what we had learned. We felt that it was no longer a question of if, but when and just as had been the case before both our children were born, the name was agreed on in advance. With fair winds and a following sea, we hope to welcome a puppy here at Stone House by late next spring.

Black Hill (10th August)

With Barbara away in the United States at present, my current routine consists of getting the children up and out of the house as soon as breakfast is cleared away in order to visit playgrounds, take walks and pick up supplies. Ever one with a keen eye for the short-range weather forecast, yesterday dawned bright and held much promise of being the last warm and sunny day before the remnants of Hurricane Bertha arrived.

We piled into the car by nine and disappeared towards Malvern singing songs from The Little Mermaid as we went. There are a bewildering number of walks up, across and along the hills, and I had recently heard of an easy-access path that had been created in the late 1990's to give prams and wheelchairs access to the top of the ridge. Given that our explorations have been limited to the lower slopes of the British Camp so far, I had decided that it was a good day to try the climb at Black Hill.

With the car park already at 800 feet, it didn't take long for us to meander up a gentle incline. Preferring to err on the side of safety I kept both children in the buggy which meant that I was wheezing and sweating by the time we reached the tree line. It was still before ten, so there were few people about, but those we met offered encouraging words and, on one occasion, water.

Having enjoyed the dramatic shape of the hills from our field on many occasions I have often wondered whether I might be able to see the reverse view. I stood searching for any landmarks that might give me a fix, but short of flying an enormous pink balloon from the house I was never going to find the needle in the haystack that I was looking for.

By this point Rather had grown somewhat frustrated by not being able to wander on his own, so I released him and was glad of the pram's lighter weight. Without the shelter of the trees, the wind had picked up considerably, and whilst Jolly and I steadily climbed Rather stopped, started and reversed according to whatever it was that took his interest. Every time I called for him to either catch up or wait, he smiled at me and squealed "Schwindy!"

The perfect place to stop for a rest was found about twenty minutes later by the careful triangulation of the level of incline suddenly becoming much steeper, the last bushes affording shelter from the wind being reached and Jolly deciding that she had waited long enough for her mid-morning bottle. With legs feeling a little like jelly I flopped onto the grass and began setting out bottles, snacks and toys.

Sitting as we were on the spine of the hills, we had views for miles in every direction except due north. Although one day I plan on climbing the Worcestershire Beacon that loomed above us, I felt it was too steep for me to push the buggy up on my own. As the world passed lazily by, we sprawled on the grass at its foot, munched our snacks and chatted with passers-by.

Like a little red standby light on a television, the numbers of speed, distance and time had been quietly crunching away in the back of my mind throughout the morning. The calculations were designed to allow me to get back home with both children still awake; an absolute imperative if the daily respite of the children's afternoon nap was not to be sabotaged. When the warning buzzer sounded, we collected our belongings and set off again.

Heading back down towards the car park it became clear that we had been among the early birds on the hills, as group after family after lone walker passed us heading in the opposite direction. Stopping to chat with strangers is as acceptable in Herefordshire as it was odd in London, but walking in the Malvern Hills seems to be in a class of its own. Shallow and fleeting it may be, but the lady from San Francisco who wanted to fuss over the children, the walkers with Dizzy the eager puppy and the gentleman from Dumfries who needed change for a fiver to pay for parking were just some of those who helped to make my day.

Are We There Yet? (17th August)

During a conversation about Life, the Universe and Children with a colleague a few months ago, I was asked if I was going to send Barbara back to work at some point. Although I understood what was behind the question, I found the phrasing odd, struggled to find an answer and the best I could come up with at the time was "That's for her to decide." With the luxury of hindsight, I now think I've got a better one.

Not only do we live in a relatively remote part of the country, but also we live beyond the reach of family support. These and other factors were never far from our minds when Barbara and I first discussed an invitation we had all received to North Carolina for her best friend's wedding at the beginning of August, as we knew that it was not going to be possible for all of us to go. Previously I have looked after the children on my own for weekends and day trips, but she knew and I suspected that nine days on the trot was going to be quite a different kettle of fish.

With my work frequently taking me abroad for anything up to a week at a time, being in sole charge of the children was common for her, but in the days running up to her departure, she wisely and generously put a significant amount of effort in to planning ahead on my behalf. Meal plans were drawn up, nursery bags were prepared and some good advice was given. On the day she left I stood at the bottom of the cliff face that towered above me and looked up.

Some aspects were predictable and expected such as mealtimes. With two young children, it would not be inaccurate to say you are never far from preparing, serving or clearing away meals, and so it was a case of developing a routine which could generate a rhythm. The same cups and plates travelled from cupboard to counter to tray to dishwasher with metronomic regularity and the only variable was whether the food would be eaten, worn or used to decorate the walls and floor. Even so, routines like this are precisely the sort of thing that can make the days seem endless.

Aware of this, Barbara had urged me to take outings every day in order to break up the monotony. I had made a few plans to meet friends for walks and play dates, but most days we went out on our own. Errands were combined with visits to playgrounds, new exploratory walks were taken and as the days passed I realised that Bob the Builder and Postman Pat just weren't stimulating enough for me; I was starting to miss adult conversation. Being possessed of an extroverted nature that can border on the garrulous when the need arises, I took eye contact from any stranger as an invitation to a conversation and thrived on a sparse diet of banality.

The only times that my mind was not wholly occupied by the children or their needs was either when they were in bed or strapped into their car seats. This explains why on the day a delivery van broke down immediately outside the house, and the young man driving it knocked on the door to enquire whether I had any petrol he could buy, I chose to say I didn't when I did. I then leapt at the chance to throw the children in the back of the car and ferry him to and from our local town where he could buy some. What he may have mistaken as a good deed was in reality an exercise in maintaining my mental equilibrium, as we chatted about news and current events on the way. Whatever he may have thought, for me and for his van it was wonderfully refreshing.

It is often claimed that men cannot multitask. Be it a statement made in jest or not, I have learned that it is an indispensable skill for childcare. As the days passed, old habits long submerged that I developed through spending time on boats resurfaced. A place for everything, and everything in its place may sound trite, but as my brother once discovered all it takes is one object left on the chart table and a large wave to create chaos out of order, or in his case, a forehead. The same is true when juggling the hundred and one things that children need, and as a rule they aren't shy about complaining when chaos dictates that those needs are about to be left unmet.

I also found myself remembering my days working in technical theatre; an environment where a time and motion expert could learn a thing or two. I fondly remember being part of the stage crew having to structure the scene changes for a number of productions where any time spent moving from here to there without either setting or striking a prop or a piece of furniture was deemed fat that needed to be trimmed in some way. Similarly, it's a waste of time and energy to take a dirty nappy to the bin unless you put an empty cup in the dishwasher on the way and collect the laundry from the dryer on your return.

These are all logistical challenges to plan for, meet and overcome and all are perfectly possible however tiring and repetitive they may be. With practise and familiarity they become easier, and I was increasingly aware of having to operate in three dimensions by dealing with now, planning for next and making sure I was on schedule for later.

Such choreography has its price, and the part that I found the hardest was the complete absence of any space in which I could think. All the mental processing and daydreaming that I normally engage in whilst doing other things never saw the light of day, and it was this I felt most keenly every evening just before seven o'clock when I was putting the children to bed. Only afterwards could I at long last sit on the sofa with a glass of wine and relax. By the end of the week I had become too exhausted even to think, and in my semi-conscious stupor I understood all too clearly what life can sometimes be like for Barbara.

I love my children dearly, would happily lay down in traffic for them and am fiercely protective of them. I had a fantastic time with them and enjoyed intimacy, a sense of reward and a greater depth of bond. However this letter focuses on the less glamorous aspects of childcare in an effort to articulate the learning journey I have recently been on. It also gives me the opportunity to share my revised answer: "She's working now; just not getting paid for it."

And with that, it's now time for the four of us to forget about routines, pack our bags and head off to enjoy two weeks' relaxing holiday by a pool in the sun with family waiting for us there to help. Hasta la vista, baby.

Virtual Vice (7ᵗʰ September)

When I started these letters in July of 2011 it was to create a virtual connection between us and our friends and family, given that we had chosen to pack our bags and leave London. Over the last three years, it has attempted to chart the ups and downs of a couple of townies who swapped a suburban London home for a less frantic and more peaceful existence. Its purpose was clear in my mind at the outset, and as a result much of our lives and thoughts haven't featured in it.

In one of the more acerbic passages in his autobiography, Peter Ustinov described the Hollywood gossip columnist Hedda Hopper by saying, "Her virtue was that she said what she thought; her vice was that what she thought didn't amount to much." His antipathy may have been magnified by her decision to name suspected communists during the McCarthy era, but there was more than a grain of truth in what he said.

There is so much that Barbara and I have yet to learn, accomplish and make a pig's ear of as smallholders, but it's hard not to notice of late that these letters have been increasingly suffering from Mission Creep. I have discovered that the joy writing brings me often can't wait for the often slower speeds at which relevant material arises; a frustration that can't have been entirely unknown to Ms Hopper.

As so much of what Ustinov wrote about rings true for me, and I clearly enjoy writing about our trivialities from week to week, I find that his description of Hedda Hopper articulate in the most appropriate way the continued broadening of the remit for whatever letters appear here in the months ahead. However, you will be relieved to hear that Barbara retains full editorial control.

The Wall (14th September)

When Barbara and I were house hunting in 2010, the part of the country we would move to wasn't important so long as motorways and airports were within reach, but the situation was. We therefore spent almost a year hunting high and low from south of Bath across to Northamptonshire and back towards the Welsh border. Although many properties seemed promising, Stone House was the only affordable and viable candidate, being the best compromise with the most potential as we saw it. Oddly though, I remember well that it was the only property we viewed where we liked absolutely nothing of the inside. It was dated, damp and dark and not one room was as we would have wanted.

On moving-in day when the house was completely empty, we ripped out all the 1960's pub style carpets and replaced them with wood laminate flooring which made an immediate difference, but that was it for the time. We have made no other significant changes since then, as all things cosmetic have had to take their place behind those we consider more pressing like weather-proofing, utilities and security.

As two cottages spliced into one, the layout of the house was always too symmetrical to be practical, and so we decided that some internal remodelling was also needed. Given that we spend the vast majority of our time in the living room when indoors, and almost none in the dining room, it seemed logical to kill a small flock of birds with one stone.

By removing the wall between the two we would increase the size of our living room, add light to a dark space and make eating at the dining table a social rather than formal occasion. We would also begin to chip away at the damp problem by allowing air to circulate where it hadn't for so many years, and allow our wood burning stove to spread its warmth to the north face of the house in the colder months.

The first stage of this project was to get a structural survey done, which was completed in ten whole minutes after some chin rubbing and teeth sucking. The resulting document had all the hallmarks of the twins of turnover better known as copy and paste, but when it comes to removing a load-bearing wall Barbara and I wanted some professional indemnity insurance between us and any mishaps that might occur, and so we swallowed the fee with a smile.

Maintaining our practise of watertight legal conformity, we then placed a phone call to the local council to inform them of the work we were planning to do, and they surprisingly but no less predictably charged us handsomely for what turned out to be a five minute visit during the building works which amounted to a declined offer of tea and a quick chat about the weather. It also contained a bravura performance of the consultant's expression; the special one that combines a studiously furrowed brow with an utterly vacant stare that I've worn myself during many a client briefing.

The work itself was almost sublime in its simplicity. It was a case of cover the floor, prop up the ceiling above and hello sledgehammer! Once the rubble was cleared and the dust had settled, it was followed by the arrival of the roof-supporting joist which was precisely five inches too short due to the builder's worryingly inaccurate measurement. Being a man who knows more than a little about discrepancies of this magnitude, I was both understanding and sympathetic when he admitted his oversight.

Facing each other over a coffee, he proposed that one way to solve the problem and keep the job on schedule was to use the beam as it was and simply make the opening between the two rooms a little narrower. It took me all three years of drama school training to fix him with a stern look and say; "Well, if it were up to me I'd say that's fine, but I'm fairly certain my wife would notice the absence of five inches of rigid steel, so it's probably best you make the beam a little longer and work a little quicker to make up any lost time." He gave me no answer, but our eyes met and we smiled at the same time.

A replacement beam was sheepishly brought in due course, and once it was installed and the remedial plumbing and electrical work was complete it was a case of plaster and make good. Barbara and I then applied our hasty and slapdash decorating skills to what the builders had left, and we now have an open and bright living room that we can happily live with until such time as we can afford to lay a proper floor and redecorate to our taste.

To some the adage of "if it's worth doing, it's worth doing well" applies. To us, that can wait until the lottery win as it's the effect and the serviceability that we want. Having said that, as with all the projects that are undertaken here, we have learned a little bit more about promises, contingencies and the need to oversee.

However, my main regret is that I was on a conference call during the twenty minutes it took the builders to knock down the wall, and I never got the chance to take a swing with the sledgehammer myself. I feel utterly robbed.

Autumnal Manoeuvres (28th September)

As a wonderful summer sounds the retreat, the sun remains bright but weakened and wildlife all around has launched the offensive in search of warmth over winter. As usual, the harbingers of change are the spiders who divide their time equally between sending their air force to drape every possible outdoor surface with food-gathering webs and mobilising their infantry divisions to mount wave after wave of assault to secure the dark corners inside the house.

So far we are keeping them at bay, and it has to be said that Barbara has a low tolerance of them and employs a fair degree of artistic licence when describing their size and danger. One afternoon when moving some boxes around in the garage to make room for a new project, she came across a rather splendid specimen and radioed for special ops, in the form of me, to remove it. By way of forward intelligence she told me to expect something the size of a small family car that was about to eat her alive.

Taking the sizeable monster and the sheet on which it was clinging to for dear life to the garage door, I put it on the ground and was about to let it go when Barbara stopped me, explaining that it would only head straight for the house and join the rearguard there. The dice were cast and it received a mercifully quick end as she extinguished it with her boot on the spot. We then we returned to the job at hand.

Other invasions seem rather more disorganised as we discovered just five seconds later when clearing to one side an assortment of material that had been lying in the middle of the garage floor for some time. With forces totalling one, a hedgehog equipped with full body armour but no map had evidently blundered inside one day when we weren't looking and annexed the pile for her nest. She hadn't chosen her spot with any discernible care, but then I imagine anyone armed to the teeth like her would feel confident of a good night's sleep pretty much anywhere.

At first we saw no movement and were not sure if she was dead or already in deep hibernation. After a few moments it became apparent that she was still awake, though somewhat groggy. She slowly got her bearings before heading off towards a pile of boxes by the wall, and the race was on to find a pair of gloves so that we could pick her up in time. We made it, but only just.

Clearly tired, surprisingly smelly and very cute she regarded us with suspicious eyes as we determined where to release her. Our first thought was the Cider Barn, but as I plan on emptying it and re-organising it over the winter, we opted to release her inside the animal shelter and let her find a quiet and dark corner there.

Over the three years that we have lived here, my opinions about animals, their rights and their place in the world haven't altered. However, I am more aware of different points of view over touchy subjects like foxes and badgers, and I suspect they remain arguments at least if not more emotional than they are reasoned.

In addition to repelling an army of spiders from the house we are waging chemical warfare in the chicken coop which is infested with millions of red mites; two highly effective species that punch well above their weight are giving us a run for their money and we are showing no mercy. At the same time we happily downed tools to rehouse a dopey hedgehog that couldn't distinguish between its nest and a canvas bag. I am once again amused by and perhaps a little ashamed of the attitudes we have towards some of those around us in the food chain.

Regardless of this, I look forward to seeing Mrs Tiggywinkle sometime next spring. If we hear of her before then, it will presumably be because someone staying in the caravan blames her for snoring.

Las Ruedas del Autobús (5th October)

The perfect holiday for Barbara and me is one during which we accept our lack of cultural hunger and embrace a cocktail of sun, water, wine and sleep. Her favourite pastime of reading and mine of idly splashing about in either a pool or the sea both act as dawdling preludes to our shared affection for sundowners and catching up on rest. In the second half of August we travelled to the east coast of Spain for a fortnight of just that, and Barbara's mother and sister had agreed to join us there for the first week.

Arriving after a lengthy day's travel that included helpful flight attendants, a selection of highly non-nutritional bribes and an eye-watering queue at the airport car rental kiosk we arrived at our house in the hills to the west of Montroy; an unremarkable town about half an hour inland from the city of Valencia. An old whitewashed building with a pool, Villa Peñazo was the perfect place where we could splash about in peace and from which we could explore when the mood took us.

We spent a lazy week of sunbathing, sightseeing and wrestling with the indecipherable modern art that is the Spanish road marking system. At the same time it became apparent quite quickly that the notion of waking up and considering the day's possibilities over a leisurely breakfast coffee and morning swim was just not purposeful enough for the children. We had completely failed to realise that for them it was just like being at home, only hotter and with less toys.

We found ourselves leaving the house every morning after their morning bottles and then wandering the streets of our local town, which was kept tidy by the most glamorous municipal cleaner I have ever seen, while we waited for the cafes to open. Our patience was rewarded by heavenly coffees, and the mornings then filled with playground visits, walks and food shopping. Jolly in particular found it hard to remain entertained, and as singing The Wheels on the Bus was the only reliable way to keep her happy, we found ourselves singing it more and more each day. Not, it has to be said, always with the same key, tempo or even lyrics.

When we drove to the train station in Valencia after a week to send Granny and Auntie on their way, we were on our own and only then did we realise that we hadn't quite learned our lesson last year when we took Rather to a gîte in the South of France. One plus one do indeed equal five, and holiday isn't really the right word for it.

We left the house every morning and headed out towards the coast. Barbara administered breakfast over the back of her seat while I took potluck with the road markings, and we usually managed to get to our destination by nine o'clock. We visited the celebrated L'Oceanogràfic aquarium, the Bioparc nearby and also made a few visits to the beaches in the beautiful nature reserve of El Saler. In all cases our early bird approach resulted in prime parking places, deserted beaches and empty attractions; all of which helped to make it easier on all of us. We can't remember the last time a two week holiday felt like a long time, if indeed one ever has, but this time we were more than ready to pack up and go home at the end.

For the vast majority of the time we feel lucky to have two children who seem to travel with reasonable ease, but it seems that Rather has a fuse that is as long as it is powerful. The few moments that it took for his beloved comfort blanket to be scanned at airport security were enough for him to bring the airport to a standstill with an unprecedented public meltdown that echoed around the departure hall. Worried travellers all around us prayed that we weren't on their flight, and we could do nothing but sympathise. Thankfully the storm blew itself out as suddenly as it had arrived.

As it turned out, both children coped admirably with the flight itself, and for all the wriggling, shuffling and obvious signs of boredom there was not much more than a whisper to be heard. When we landed, we found out how well Birmingham Airport's passport control copes with three simultaneous international arrivals, and we were all relieved when we at last strapped ourselves into our car for the last leg of the journey home.

Assuming we will be in a position to take a similar amount of time away from home during next summer, we have already decided to do things a bit differently. However much we enjoy tranquillity, there is little chance that this kind of holiday will provide it for the time being. With our desire for at least some mental shutdown and the childrens' yearning for activity, distraction and diversion, it's time for us to embrace an all-inclusive child-friendly resort where there is a little help at hand to help grease the wheels on the bus as they go round and round.

Stormin' Norman (12th October)

She is thrifty and tenacious but admits to a difficulty in visualising things that are not in front of her. Perhaps these reasons explain a little of why Barbara's love affair with car boot sales has endured for longer than I have known her. It is no exaggeration to say that we would not be able to live the way we do were it not for her dedicated bargain hunting. I frequently join her on Sunday mornings, the joy for me being a bacon roll and the opportunity to wander by tables strewn with goods while muttering, "Tat... Crap... Utter shite... Oh Lordy will you look at that!" while she roots around in boxes and bins in order to clothe the children and, to a certain extent, furnish the house.

Some seven years ago, she bought a plant that caught her attention at a busy car boot sale near Bath, and has spent the years since cultivating a strong relationship with the species. The Aeonium Schwarzkopf, also known as the Black Rose, is an odd looking rubbery plant that is, even in my care, impossible to kill. She gives them as gifts, donates them to fundraisers and spends snatched hours of peace here and there propagating them. About a year ago she first mooted the idea of seeing if they would sell well at a car boot sale, but the idea faded from the forefront of her mind as Jolly's arrival and several household projects took all her time. Since that time the plants have thrived and multiplied, but with the approaching Autumn came the realisation that I had yet to rebuild the greenhouses in which they must be to survive the winter frost.

As the car boot season ends by October we checked our diaries for a free Sunday, but by curious coincidence I was booked to work over every weekend during September with the only exception being my birthday. As there was no way she would be able to look after the children and run a stall, I was more than happy to spend the day with them while she sat in a deckchair, read her book and sold her flowers to the good people of Ledbury.

That morning, I thought it would be fun to take the children there and see if they could spot Mummy from a distance through the crowd. With the car packed with children, buggy and snacks we set off and joined the queue of traffic waiting to get into the site. Thanks to other car boot sales in the area being reduced in size, Ledbury's had expanded to accommodate the surplus trade, and it took a few phone calls to find out where she had set out her stall.

We were about twenty feet away when I spotted her, but the children had absolutely no chance of seeing through the crowd that had gathered around her carefully staged display with comments of "Oh - something different!", "are they indoor or outdoor plants?" and "what on earth are they?" Arranged by height and price she had something in the region of sixty plants for sale, and I've never seen her look so proud or in control as people gushed and started to reach into their pockets.

If you frequent car boot sales, you will know that a great number of vendors set up their stalls in front of their cars using tables, rails, boxes and blankets. On them they spread out their wares and then retreat with a drink or a book and wait for buyers to arrive. Whilst this is a pleasant way to spend a Sunday morning, it's also an excellent way to avoid having to deal with customers which means that if you want to sell, it's fairly easy to stand out.

Ever one with a keen eye for presentation, Barbara kept her plants glistening in the bright sunshine with a spray bottle and happily engaged in conversation anyone who showed interest. With what rapidly became her sales patter, she explained how trouble-free they were to look after, how easy it was to propagate them and that they needed protection from frost in the winter. I noticed that people seemed to be attracted by her open and friendly demeanour as much as they were by the plants, and from the depths of their canvas chairs her neighbouring sellers noted the brisk speed of her trade.

By now the sales were coming thick and fast, and on more than one occasion it turned out to be a good thing that the children and I had shown up as reinforcements. I started to sell the plants when the crowd got too big for Barbara to serve alone, Rather disappeared with the spray bottle to amuse himself by cleaning the wheels of the car and Jolly sealed every deal by steadily munching her way though a bag or two of Pom Bears. Teamwork in action.

After what felt like about twenty minutes, but was in reality more than ninety, the pace started to slow as stock dwindled. I bundled the children into the pram and disappeared in search of a chuck wagon and my customary bacon roll. I arrived at the food area with a huge grin smeared across my face having passed a number of shoppers tightly clutching their new plants.

Then, with the majority of my bacon roll either inside Rather or on my shirt, I returned to find that Barbara had sold all but two of her stock. She decided to keep them for propagation, and so our work was done and the rest of the day was free for birthday celebrations.

Once back home with the children fed and put down for their naps, she opened her purse to count her earnings. Estimating her loot to be in the region of sixty or seventy pounds, we were amazed to find it to be three pounds short of two hundred. An early dinner at the Pink Pub was definitely on her, and as we walked up the road in the afternoon sunshine I was reminded of something that Norman Schwarzkopf once said: Leadership is a potent combination of strategy and character. But if you must be without one, be without the strategy. Amen to that.

Leaf Peeping (26th October)

In the parts of New England and Ontario where I have visited, as well as the many others I haven't, such is the beauty with which the foliage changes from green during autumn that an entire tourist trade exists to exploit this transition. Lasting only a few weeks from start to finish, reports in the local media predict when will be the best few days to see the landscape change colour through red, yellow, purple and brown before the leaves finally fall, and tourists arrive in their droves to feast on the sight.

Europe, Wikipedia tells me, has far less of the varieties of deciduous trees required for this spectacle, and so has no such tradition on a comparable scale. Perhaps this explains why most of us here regard the onset of autumn with either a shiver and a mutter about turning on the central heating or, as in my case, a search in the garage for a wheelbarrow and a rake.

Returning last Saturday from a week's work in Galicia, Barbara had planned to spend the following day unwinding with friends at a health spa in Malvern, and so the children and I had the day free to play on our own. At her suggestion, we headed off to Queenswood Park, a local arboretum that boasts an incredible variety of trees, free parking, a playground and good coffee.

Taking advantage of the sunshine, the children and I wandered slowly along the paths, stopped to chat with other young families and fussed over passing dogs. Less than a twenty-minute drive from the house, it is fast becoming a firm favourite of ours as a destination for a cheap and enjoyable morning out.

In the middle of the park is the Autumn Garden; an enclosure of about an acre in size in which whoever responsible has replicated the phenomenon of fall colours, albeit on a much smaller scale, by planting a wide variety of trees side by side. Unremarkable for most of the year, the garden comes to life for a few weeks each autumn, and to me the effect is absolutely breathtaking. I felt like a two-year-old as I walked slowly under the canopy, my "oohs" and "aahs" serving only to make my two-year-old eye me quizzically.

We stopped to read the inscription on a large rock that detailed the timeline of the garden and the species growing in it, and whilst we were there we were approached by a beaming toddler named Ollie with hair as red as the leaves on some of the trees. Under the watchful gaze of his mother, he offered my children each a handful of mud-caked leaves that he had collected on his travels. Without a prompt from me Rather solemnly thanked him and Jolly stuffed them in her mouth.

Twenty baby wipes later, we were ready to head for the playground and I spent the next twenty minutes shuttling between bribing Jolly with treats as she sat harnessed in the pram and encouraging Rather as he scaled every climbing frame, rope bridge and slide that was on offer.

Later, on our way home, I asked if the children had enjoyed themselves. They said they had and, further embracing the delights of middle age, I wondered whether we should all go back the following weekend to see how the colours had changed further.

Unfortunately, two days later the remains of Hurricane Gonzalo passed slowly across the UK and, if the state of the land around Stone House is any indication, laid completely bare all the trees of the Autumn Garden in a matter of hours. Ah well, there is always next year.

Waste in Haste (2nd November)

It's been over a year since Barbara and I first met Lewis and agreed with him a mutually beneficial exchange of favours. In that time our hedgerows have been maintained, new stock fencing has been erected and ton after ton of nutritious sheep poop has fertilised the fields. We have also had the benefit of a wandering flock of sheep to look at, and I have not had the problem of cutting an enormous amount of grass. As a bonus every now and then, I also get the chance to learn a little about animal husbandry.

One weekend during July I spotted some activity up by the Cider Barn, and wandered up to say hello and catch up on news. A pen had been erected against the southern wall and Bonnie, the young sheepdog who treats praise and criticism with equal disdain, was creatively interpreting Lewis' instructions to bring the flock in for worming. Once in the pen they pushed, shoved and clambered over each other before settling down and staring at absolutely nothing in the way that only sheep can.

With his DIY methods being very similar to mine, the only trifling difference being that his actually work, Lewis is a man after my own heart and teaches by example. Attaching an old piece of string that he found on the floor of his truck to the bottle of worming liquid, he upended it on his back before jumping into the pen. He then grabbed the nearest ewe who nodded to her neighbour, bleated "why me, what's wrong with her?" and wriggled to absolutely no effect.

The drenching gun was inserted into her mouth before a dose of what I presume to be horrible tasting medicine was delivered. Adding insult to injury he then smeared her head with blue wax to signify she was 'done' and moved on to the next one. He worked methodically, quickly and quietly and it took him less than ten minutes to worm all twenty-three sheep.

As I watched I tried to imagine how Rather and Jolly might react when the days of Calpol end and the time comes for them to have a dose of foul-tasting medicine for some reason. Noting how crude but effective this system was, I reminded myself that social services might take a dim view if I cornered my children in quite the same fashion even if I wouldn't need to use wax.

With the job finished, Lewis handed me the worming kit from inside the pen and made ready to release the flock. "So, is it fast-acting? Will they feel better right away?" I asked. "They will do once they've finished shitting themselves stupid on this stuff" he replied. With that he opened the pen, the flock bolted for the field and I wondered if Senakot's marketing department might learn a thing or two from his brand of simplicity and directness.

As we loaded the pen into the back of his truck, we chatted about the price of lamb being half what it was a year ago and made vague plans for chain-harrowing the fields sometime next spring. Then he left and I took a tour of the field to see how much thatch there was.

Half an hour later anyone within earshot could have been forgiven for mistaking the large field for a gents' toilet in an airport arrivals hall. Taking comfort from the knowledge that the field was being given the very best nutrition possible, I wandered back to the house through noticeably scented air whilst humming the theme tune from The Dambusters and proclaiming to the air "Goner!" every time I heard a fart.

LFA 4 (16th November)

I've long suspected that there is such a thing as pilots' voice training; a course during which airline pilots are taught to speak in a certain way so as to convince passengers through their tone, pace and vocabulary that all is well regardless of whether or not it actually is. I did once seek confirmation of this from a retired pilot I shared breakfast with at a B&B a few years ago, and he dismissed it with a casual wave before telling me to sit back, relax and enjoy the toast.

Nonetheless, I find there is something deliberate about the voice used by the vast majority of the pilots that I have heard inflight over the years. I say "used by" as it strikes me rather like a phone voice; a purposeful work persona that would raise either a laugh or an eyebrow if not quickly dropped when home for tea. But if I am wrong and it's just happenstance, it calls to mind this old joke that's been doing the rounds for years:

Q: How do you know when there's a pilot in the room?
A: Don't worry, they'll tell you.

Truth be told, there is more than a little envy in my words, as I know only too well the joy that being in control of machinery brings me. Despite my relatively mundane arsenal of internal combustion engines, it's not too big a leap for me to imagine how my personality might alter if given absolute mastery over 40,000 pounds of thrust and a speed of Mach 1.25 with a price tag of £125 million dollars, and this might explain what often happens in the skies above Stone House.

The UK is divided into twenty Low Flying Areas, which is pretty much the whole country outside of CAA air corridors and urban areas. The MOD rotates their use so as to minimise disturbance, which is wise given the upset that can be caused if a barely subsonic Eurofighter passes 250 feet above your head. Our scheduled day is Thursday, and the area we live in is LFA 4 which borders the central Wales area LFA 7(T), the letter 'T' denoting it as a tactical area.

In tactical areas, the minimum altitude is lowered from 250 to 100 feet and, one presumes, the thrill rises in inverse proportion. Having studied the surrounding area from the top of the Malvern Hills, I note that the rolling hills and valleys that lie between the Severn Valley and the Black Mountains look rather like the early computer flight simulators that I used to play. Insert coin and away we go balancing thrust, weight, drag and lift.

I imagine that if I were travelling at Mach 0.95 and wanted to suddenly turn left, I would have covered quite some considerable distance by the time my brain, motor neurones and muscles had collaborated sufficiently to effect such a manoeuvre. This might account for the fact that the boundary between LFA's 4 and 7 seems to be blurred somewhat as I've seen Jolly Green Giants pass by below eye level, Eurofighters doing barrel rolls overhead and Hercules dipping their wings as they hug the hills.

Combat readiness is of course a serious business, but if the look on the face of the pilots who fly around here differs that much from that of Jeremy Clarkson at the wheel of an Ariel Atom with the pedal to the metal, then I'm the pope. They'd be daft not to, and I have little doubt that the thrills on offer are quite extraordinary.

Whenever I am working in the office and hear the ear-splitting howl as they pass overhead, I run to the window hoping to catch a glimpse. If I'm outside, it's a case of first determining the direction in which the sound is travelling and then scanning ahead in order to make eye contact. Then, and often only for the briefest of moments, I can marvel at the machinery regardless of its purpose.

The only aircraft we have a chance to see properly are those flying in a far more sedate manner; transatlantic jets far up in the sky, light aircraft crabbing through crosswinds and the indomitable Midlands Air Ambulance. As for Thursday's boy-racers, it's a case of keeping our seatbelts fastened as unexpected turbulence is always a possibility.

Grass, Glass and Plaster (23rd November)

Another year of change is starting to draw to a close here at Stone House, and the end of landscaping is at last in sight. Whilst a few small jobs remain, the final large pieces of the jigsaw have been completed in fits and starts over the past eight months. First, the breaking up and removal of all the concrete behind the house, then the filling in of the old vegetable plot and the grassing over of the whole space to make it safe for the children. Finally, the creation of a new area on the south side of the garage where we plan to build a kitchen garden.

Due to their size, complexity and how much of a pig's ear I might make of them, jobs like these are still best left mostly if not entirely to the professionals. This is something that both Barbara and I agree on, but even she would tell you that the day is not far off when I will give in to temptation and hire myself a mini-digger for a weekend's play. I mean, work.

Having last year tipped some sixteen tons of wood chip into the old vegetable plot, I had managed to raise its level almost to that of the land around it, but it would need six more tons of topsoil mixed with it before it would be level and ready for grass seed.

Morton, a local contractor, brought his wealth of experience and local contacts to bear and after a few weeks' work he had transformed what used to be a muddy trapezium shaped vegetable plot into beautifully lush grass that blended seamlessly with the rest of the lawn. He had also broken up all the concrete areas and done the same with them, burying a new electricity cable for the Breeze House along the way.

That left the garden around the house complete at last, and by the end of the summer it had become a safe and beautiful space for the children to play in and for us to watch the setting sun with a glass of wine. From now on it will only require maintenance and the adding of whatever shrubs, plants and features we feel belong there.

In order to maximise how much material was reused, Morton had effected a clever swap at the start of the job by first excavating topsoil in preparation for laying the greenhouse foundations, and using it for the lawn. He later used most of the broken up concrete removed from the lawn as hardcore for the bases. Having learned in previous years that our exposed location often means greenhouse doors can be dislodged and sometimes removed in high winds, we wanted them to sit snugly in the lee of the garage with only a wheelbarrow's width of a walkway to separate them.

With bases made for Ted's old greenhouse and our well-travelled second hand effort from eBay, we decided to keep an eye on the future by having another one constructed for an eventual third and slightly larger greenhouse. Nestling against the southerly facing wall, they now offer winter protection to Barbara's clutch of Aloe and Schwarzkopf plants and stand ready for next years' crop of tomatoes and peppers.

Within the last few weeks I have been able to lay some armoured electrical cable from the garage to provide power in each greenhouse, and at some point during the winter I will be installing tanks capable of storing several thousands of litres of rainwater that will almost certainly flow from the garage roof this winter.

The design for the kitchen garden that Barbara has imagined calls for raised vegetable beds to be built in runs alongside the greenhouses, and so the last piece of the landscaping puzzle was to then create the space where they will soon be built. With chickens and sheep only too happy to devour anything we grow, we wanted to reposition the old orchard field fence, thereby creating a roughly rectangular area measuring some twenty metres by fifteen.

Calling on Stan, another local contractor who has forgotten more about fence building that most of us will ever learn, he set the upright posts and supplied the rails. This left me the job of removing the old fence and attaching the rails to the new one. The former was achieved with the greatest of ease by attaching chains between each fence post and the back of the lawn tractor, and then driving slowly forward. One by one the posts and rails fell and, once freed from old wire, were stored in the Cider Barn for future reuse.

The latter was slightly more tricky and definitely more painful. After using Barbara's car to tension thirty metres of stock fence, I nailed it to the uprights and was then ready to attach the rails. Cutting each one to length and securing it with four-inch screws and my well used Bosch power screwdriver, I made slow and careful progress.

Sadly not careful enough as I managed to create a perfect storm in the space where bodily weight, poor aim and utter stupidity meet. Holding a rail in position with my left hand, I started to drive a screw in with my right, and leaned on it to give it better purchase. This might sound pretty stupid to you and certainly does to me now, but for some reason it didn't at the time. Even when it slipped, hit my left hand and fell to the ground.

It happened so quickly that I thought I had simply put a gash in the top of my hand, and carried on for a short while until I noticed rather more blood than was usual for a day's work that involved relatively simple drilling, sawing and hammering. Such was the weight I had put on it that I had actually driven the screwdriver clean through my hand and out the other side.

When later getting a tetanus shot at the local surgery, I was told that I had been extremely lucky to miss everything vital and would have to contend with nothing more than a bruised hand and fractured ego for a short while. Feeling more than a little lucky, I felt it only fair that I absorb the feedback that I was offered by those around me. 'Idiot' was one of the most common terms used, 'foolhardy' was the gentlest and 'twat' was by far the most accurate.

Free ranging Children and animals in June 2015

The finished garden in April 2015

The new wood burner in December 2014

The Kitchen Garden in July 2015

The open plan living room in August 2014

Stone House in June 2015

Rainlater at six months in July 2015

Al fresco dinner in the field in August 2015

Bouquet Garni (7ᵗʰ December)

Originating in France sometime around 1850, a bouquet garni is a bundle of herbs tied together in a cheesecloth bag and used to flavour soups and stews. I have heard from foodie friends that they are an absolute must for certain dishes requiring authentic and strong flavours, but I wonder if the far less glamorous and more modern freeze-drying process mightn't be a good deal easier.

A few months ago during one of his visits to check the flock, Lewis stopped on his way out and asked if I wanted the dags. For those of you who may not be up to speed on things rural generally and things ovine specifically, he was asking me if I wanted the bits of poop-encrusted wool that he had recently cut from around his ewes' bottoms. Now, I know what you're thinking, and that's exactly what I asked him.

I remain ever-grateful to him for teaching me everything he knows whilst not judging me for being a bit thick, and it seems that sheep dags are the bouquet garni of plant fertilisers. Apparently all I need to do is put the dags into a hessian bag and leave them in a large vat of water for a couple of months, giving it an occasional stir in order to create a nourishing drink that can be diluted with water to make next year's tomato crop the absolute envy of everyone who listens to Gardeners' Question Time.

He warned me that I should keep it a reasonable distance away as the smell can be predictably rather pungent, and so I quickly concocted a plan and gathered up some spare concrete blocks that were lying around from the summer's building works. It took fifteen minutes to fashion a pedestal at the corner of the Cider Barn, fill a hessian bag with poop and throw it in.

Feeling a bit like Keith Floyd, I imagined a cameraman following my every move while I added two hundred and twenty litres of water, gave a cheeky smile and judged it to be a fine brew that would be ready by the end of winter. Whenever I pass by the Cider Barn, I lift the lid and give the string tied to the bag a quick tug to keep the contents stirred, but apart from that its job is to sit and steep.

With one eye always on saving money, my plan is to dig out another of our old water butts and let the roof of the Cider Barn fill it over the winter. Some time in February or March next year, I will swap the poop from the other one and hopefully be able to brew another batch by summer. With any luck, we will have almost five hundred litres of poo stew that will give our tomatoes a tremendous boost next year. Of course Tomorite tomato food from our local garden centre is probably just as good and doesn't require this much effort, but at £3.99 a litre I would need to spend well over £1,000 to get as much. Tidy job.

Agnes of Log (14th December)

Right from the very first day we arrived it was clear that life in Herefordshire would be very different and having only ever been city dwellers before, winter warmth was always going to be an issue. The obvious solution was the curiously designed wood-burning stove which has attracted a good deal of attention from contractors who have visited the house over the years since. None had seen anything like it before, and it certainly looked a bit eccentric with its complicated set of vents. I did my research into how it worked in my haste to appear knowledgeable about something, just anything to do with rural life. I discovered that it was exceptionally clever in theory and, truth be told, I became quite the bore in explaining the science behind it to anyone who would listen, but all the hot air I produced could not make up for the stove's mediocre performance in practise. This was then confirmed by a local specialist, who studied it with great care and pronounced it quite the most efficient way he could think of to place the heat extracted from a fire directly into the air above a house without actually heating much of the space in between. Given that we consumed an enormous amount of firewood last winter without ever being too warm, the decision to replace the stove was effectively made for us. We explored the many options available and carried out all the research we could. Cast iron seemed to win over welded steel in terms of efficiency and a larger stove running at lower output seemed preferable to a smaller one running flat out. In the end we decided upon a model made by the Norwegian company Jøtul which appears to be the model of choice throughout much of Scandinavia and North America.

With the removal of the old unit, some remedial structural work was needed, and for the better part of a week I worked in my office with jackhammers pounding behind me whilst Barbara ferried the children from one play group to another. As with previous structural projects, we both found that living amongst chaos took its toll on our humours, and we carefully counted the hours as they slowly passed.

After four days of upheaval the stove was finally installed and the engineers tested it to make sure all was as expected. They pronounced themselves satisfied that a good job had been done, and we were grateful that they had managed to accommodate during the build a few of the house's previously unseen architectural peculiarities. Just moments after they left, we settled down in the spreading warmth.

In the three days since, we have already discovered that it is a far more forgiving fire than any we have previously known. Lighting it seems remarkably easy, and even just a few glowing embers in the grate are enough to ignite freshly added wood. On a reasonably light but steady diet of logs it can keep the entire ground floor comfortably above 22°C.

Venturing out with the children yesterday afternoon to meet with a friend for a seasonally crisp walk around Westonbirt Arboretum to see the Enchanted Christmas display, we managed to squeeze a large log cut from the old apple orchard into it before we left. On our return over six hours later, we found the fire still alive and the house toasty and warm in its welcome. "We really need to give it a name" mused Barbara as we settled on the sofa with a glass of wine having ferried the children up to bed. "I don't know if stoves are male or female, but I think we should call this one Agnes. It's the name of someone warm, old fashioned and reliable." That's fine by me as long as she can spew out more hot air than I.

Santa Plod (24th December)

Santa Pod Raceway in Bedfordshire is the centre of European Drag Racing where speed freaks regularly hurtle themselves down a three quarter mile track in the pursuit of glory. Some make it and others spectacularly fail as I remember when once I visited it as a young boy with my family. Although a budding petrol head, it left me cold with only its odd name staying with me.

We approach Christmas this year with a two and a half year old son possessed of a decidedly firm grasp on the concept of presents and a one year old daughter who is determined to copy him in as many ways as she can. Given that they'll probably be fixing our computers in a year's time, we thought we'd try to make Santa Claus as real as possible this year as our window of opportunity may not be open for too long.

A few clicks on Amazon was all it took for a full Santa outfit to be ordered and dispatched, and so just like the Canadian Mounties, we had our man. What we didn't have was a way of getting him here, and as far as we know there are no EU grants available for the rearing and keeping of reindeer. The only animals near us that stand a chance of looking similar are a herd of Alpacas on a farm about half a mile down the road, but even if we managed to borrow six for a day, sleighs are not the best way to navigate the clay-rich mud that pretty much covers Herefordshire in December.

Facing the very real prospect of no snow, no sleigh and no reindeer, Santa was going to need a complete transport makeover if he was going to get to Stone House at all. Such urgency and a blank canvas were an open invitation for me, and I disappeared into the workshop to hatch a plan. Drawing inspiration from the clutter strewn all over the workbenches and the need to involve at least one piece of petrol-powered machinery, I set to work.

Using gaffer tape, a crowbar and my latest weapon of choice; a rather nifty pair of 36 inch bolt cutters, which if I didn't already own, would be the first thing on my Christmas wish list, I soon fashioned the basics. Before long STS-1 (Santa Transport System) was born with little more than some swearing, half a clue and a modicum of bloodshed. With construction complete, it became clear that my creation lacked a certain seasonal touch.

I bundled the children into the car and disappeared to Hereford in order to take advantage of B&Q's Christmas Clearance sale in which everything that no one had wanted was re-priced in pennies rather than pounds in an effort to clear space, and came away with what I felt was a serious bargain. Back in the workshop I set to work with battery powered baubles, tinsel and two of the most interesting mini Christmas trees you will ever see.

Having already agreed a theatrical plan with Barbara, I will disappear to the garage tomorrow afternoon before proclaiming, "Tonight Matthew, I'm going to be..." I'll then chug out of the back of the garage in first gear through a cloud of smoke dressed as Santa sitting astride STS-1and towing a pile of presents. I probably won't be singing, though.

Taking the scenic route of about a quarter of a mile through the fields to the front of the house will hopefully allow maximum visibility for Rather and Jolly who will no doubt be prodded by Barbara, Granny and Auntie if they fail to notice. Once dismounted, I shall try to channel three years of drama school into whatever accent I can manage to put on, and with a large sack of presents create a little scene before heading back to the North Pole.

The current record at Santa Pod is 3.58 seconds, and it's safe to say that I will not threaten it in the slightest. Historically most meetings between Santa and young children do not always go smoothly, and so it is entirely possible that the wheels may metaphorically and literally come off my highly decorated wagon. Happily there is no law against driving a lawn tractor while three sheets to the wind, so any embarrassment will be brief and quickly forgotten. Merry Christmas!

New Year's Solutions (1st January 2015)

As Barbara and I have done nothing to the upstairs of the house yet, Ted's 1970's Porn Bathroom is largely as he left it. Probably installed around forty years ago, the taps on the sink and bathtub have long been difficult to operate, requiring more effort than is usual to turn them on or off. In the off position they drip, and when on they sometimes don't provide much in the way of water. Fixing them has been on my list of things to do since day one, but somehow has never seemed urgent and so we have learned to live with it.

Until one evening a week or so before Christmas that is, when I went upstairs to run a bath for the children. The hot water tap turned stiffly, strange gurgles emanated from beneath the floorboards and there was no sign of anything coming out. With both children too big to fit in the kitchen sink, the job of fixing the bath taps was a new chart entry at No 1 up from No 713 on the list of things to do, and they went to bed unwashed that night.

With my DIY skills probably best characterised as amateurish and eager, it is just this sort of job that I will consider a challenge and have a crack at before calling in the professionals. The next day in less than fifteen minutes I had shut the water off in the house, emptied the pipes and started to dismantle the taps. It was a safe bet that new seals would be required, but the internal mechanism was still sticking after removal. Pausing to discover via Google that what I had always known as the tap-twisty-turny-thing was actually called an Insert by those in the know, I then set off to town in search of replacements.

On entering our local plumbers' merchants, I was greeted with a cheery smile by the shop assistant and we exchanged pleasantries before I outlined the reason for my visit. "I need to replace these as they have a fault." He gave my inserts a quick glance before saying "Oh dear, they haven't made them in that size for years." Feeling a bit like J.R. Hartley I immediately began imagining the price of new taps, whether or not they would fit an old bathtub and the cost of a plumber to rectify the mess that I would make. "I guess it looks like I'll have to replace the whole mixer tap unit then." Taking pity on me he picked up one of them for a closer look and said, "Here, just give me a minute."

Over the next five minutes, using nothing but his fingers and a screwdriver, he took the insert apart piece by piece inspecting each one until he found the fault; a piece of broken seal that had managed to wedge itself up inside the thread of the valve. Using his shirt he cleaned it and then applied some silicone lubricant. Noticing the expression on my face, he beckoned me closer. "If you watch me put it back together, then you can service the other one just the same and then they'll both be good as new." It was an impressive performance, and I said as much as I left.

Back at home and half an hour later the bath taps were reinstalled and working perfectly for a cost of 20 pence and less than an hour's labour in total. I can't remember the last time a shop assistant went out of their way to be courteous, polite and helpful whilst doing themselves out of a sale, repairing my broken goods for free and teaching me a new skill. He won't win The Apprentice with behaviour like that, but he's won my business from now on.

With an infinite list of things to do both in and outside of the house and a finite amount of resources with which to achieve them, this episode fills me with a certain amount of confidence for 2015. Happy New Year!

Mind the Gap (11th January)

The hedge that separates Stone House from the B4220, on which cars and bikes sometimes whizz past in excess of the motorway speed limit, is mostly a mixture of holly, ivy and honeysuckle. Almost totally evergreen, it blocks the view from and of the road, but there is a small section of it that is hawthorn. Apart from being my sworn enemy from the world of flora, hawthorn is particularly useless as a visual barrier as it sheds its leaves in November becoming a threadbare and nasty tangle of twigs and thorns for the next five months.

During our first winter here, I identified it as something I wanted to take care of but, being a matter of aesthetics, it was never going to be high on my list. With the driveway gates installed last year giving us a sense of privacy and security, it began to irritate me as soon as it lost its leaves, and so I decided the time was right. A little bit of research revealed that whatever I replaced it with would need to be planted before the spring, so I went online just before Christmas to order some English Holly to fill the gap.

A pallet with six bushes wrapped in cling film and some detailed planting instructions arrived in early January, and with the ground soft from rain and the temperature unseasonably warm, I set aside a whole day for the job. Working from the roadside, it was fairly straightforward to remove the hawthorn and dig a small trench. Having piled the earth to one side I considered all the preparation done, and it was a simple matter of dropping each plant in before covering the root balls with soil.

Holly is not nearly as deadly as hawthorn but it still has prickly leaves, and you would think that anyone with half a brain planning to plant a number of six-foot tall bushes would protect themselves from flailing branches. For some reason that even I cannot quite understand, I had decided that a t-shirt, body warmer and gloves would be sufficient protection, and by the time Barbara appeared on her way to town for some supplies, I was reasonably well lacerated.

I'm still not sure whether I can blame my stubbornness or my laziness for the fact that I didn't stop to put something on with sleeves, but by lunchtime all the plants were in and my arms were sore in more ways than one. The instructions called for the root balls to be "thoroughly soaked", so I dragged out the hose, attached a sprinkler and left it on for an hour. Standing back to survey my work, I noted that all the bushes had been planted and were in a straight line. Job done.

Or so I thought as shortly afterwards the heavily publicised westerly gales arrived. Before long the chimney pot was whistling a tune, the roof tiles were clapping like a bored audience and the bushes were all leaning over at a 45 degree angle as though ready for bed. Re-reading the instructions, I discovered that the plants should be protected from excessive wind for their first year in the ground. After raising my fist towards the skies in a futile gesture, I set about creating a windbreak for them.

Normally my shoddy DIY work is hidden from view but on this occasion it was going to be on full show, and the increasing wind and failing light encouraged me to cut every corner imaginable. I buried three half-rounds on the verge in a vaguely upright fashion and then strapped two old fence panels to them with wire, nails and screws. Given that this structure needs to withstand both gales and vortices from HGV's passing just two feet away, I then dug out an old rail from the Cider Barn and lashed it over the panels for extra safety.

Pretty it isn't but it is solid and does give the bushes some much needed shelter before they're firmly bedded in and start to thicken. Another benefit is that we don't see it from the house, and I'm also keen to hear the words Lewis uses to describe it when he next visits.

Red Mite (25th January)

I'm one of those people who presses the lift call button even when I know it has already been pushed. Once inside the lift, I then repeatedly press the button of the floor I wish to go to in the belief that the doors will somehow close quicker, and I'll be on my way sooner. It could be because I have been conditioned by the adage 'if at first you don't succeed, try, try, try again.' but it equally might be because I can sometimes be a bit dense. It's a close call as stupidity often masquerades as persistence, but as the end justifies the means in this particular case, I'm happy either way.

When we brought our first three chickens home in 2011, we had consulted Google about the best way to look after them, and bought a typical wooden coop with pitched roof and nesting boxes. The manufacturers assured us it would be more than up to the task of housing Jodie, Jade & Jordan and as our flock began to expand, it comfortably accommodated several new birds. We quickly established a weekly routine of cleaning it out, refilling the feeders and making sure the birds had all they needed for a healthy and happy life.

Sadly its construction was far from robust, and before it was a year old the signs of rot were increasingly evident thanks to rain and the staggering volume of waste produced by its occupants. When it was close to collapse, we chose to replace it with a slightly larger one of exactly the same rather poor design, and blamed our stupidity on the limited choice in the market place. We made it feel like an improvement by adding an automatic door and raising it off the ground to save our backs, but as acid has a knack of dissolving thin plywood, we had merely erected a new deck chair on the Titanic.

Late last summer, in addition to the second coop starting to rot, we discovered that it had become infested from top to bottom with red mites. They had infiltrated the coop by turning the local Magpies, who on occasion help themselves to eggs, into unsuspecting Trojan Horses. Once ferried inside they had immediately made themselves at home and promptly claimed squatters' rights. Barbara, ably helped by Rather, emptied the coop and soaked it with soap and water in an effort to counteract the insurgency.

Like all parasites, these tiny blood-sucking mites are highly developed and through evolution have turned survival into a fine art. Able to grow from egg to adult in under a week given the right circumstances, their life cycle is so quick that populations not so much grow as exponentially explode. It's rather like an Englishman in the queue for passport control at Rome's Fiumicino airport; for every minute he waits, thirty more people appear in front of him.

In addition to this they are hard to find as they hide by day only coming out to feast at night, giving them the upper hand against diurnal organisms like, chickens and humans. We were facing an infestation of biblical proportions, and under Barbara's instructions, the coop was quarantined before being subjected to chemical warfare of the kind banned by the Geneva Convention. With their ability to survive for almost a year without a host, such aggression was needed to drive them out of every crevice and kill them.

It took months of treatment before we were happy to let the birds use the coop again, but now with an eye for how the mites operate we knew how hopelessly inadequate our coop was. The design's heavy reliance on tongue and groove woodwork was its Achilles' Heel, which was compromised yet further by build quality and an almost non-existent ability to resist moisture, whether water or acid.

We scoured the Internet for a solution. The answer seemed to be a plastic coop, but finding one that would be large enough for our flock of twelve and compatible with our automatic door mechanism was not going to be easy. It seems that in the world of chickens people either have broods of three or three thousand, and this is evidenced by the scarcity of mid-sized coops on the market. After exhaustive research we found only one viable option, and ordered it.

Arriving in five rather heavy flat packed sections, it took me the better part of six hours to interpret the instructions and assemble in such a way as to mostly resemble the picture on the website. I choose to elevate it in the same way as the previous house, and after a brief period of acclimatisation the birds rewarded us for their new condominium with a noticeably increased level of egg production that has shown little sign of abating even in the depths of winter.

Designed with the minimum of corners and crevices, the inside is as smooth as a mirror and affords the mites very few footholds or hiding places. When the warmer weather returns, with it will come the red mites and the war will resume. They may remember me as a hapless fool who is no match for them, but this time I know just what I am up against. Sporting a grubby undershirt like John McClane in Die Hard, I'll be packing heat in the form of a pressure washer and when the coop door opens the last thing they will ever hear is me screaming "Welcome to the party, pal!"

Man Cave (8th February)

Paula Aymer, an Associate Professor of Sociology at Tufts University, rather dramatically describes a Man Cave as the last bastion of masculinity. Here, according to the psychiatrist Scott Haltzman, "rules are relaxed; it is a place where other people's sensibilities about standards of cleanliness are not necessarily observed." Now call this definition a sweeping generalisation if you will, but almost all people blessed with the good fortune of an indoor flushing toilet are able to operate them, even if a surprising number can't fathom the public ones. I therefore find the idea of a link between lack of cleanliness and gender, as opposed to anonymity, unpleasant and stereotypical.

Be that as it may, Stone House is littered with a number of such spaces; some are where Barbara turns her fingers increasingly green and others where I drive nails through

419

mine. Regardless of their cleanliness, most are less useful than they could be, and so it was with great excitement and not a little effort that last autumn I was able to install power into the two greenhouses so that Barbara's plants can withstand winter frost, and fit lighting inside the Cider Barn so that I can actually see what's inside it.

For the last three and a half years, along with the Animal Shelter, the Cider Barn has been something of a junkyard. Apart from the collection of traditional pub signs that Ted had liberated over many years, it contains the remains of several sheds, some old fence panels, an assortment of roof tiles and, more recently, Jolly and Rather's outdoor toys. Truth be told, I was no longer exactly sure what was in there as I had taken to throwing things inside when I couldn't think of anywhere else to put them.

Wishing to do things correctly for once, I contacted two local electrical contractors and asked them to quote for installing two fluorescent lights inside it and one electrical point in each of the greenhouses. Both responded eagerly and spent in excess of two hours to travel here, inspect the area and make copious notes before leaving. What then became clear was that for some reason neither actually wanted to do the job. The first produced an eye-watering quote in excess of £1,500, which he then steadfastly refused to itemise despite requests, and we never received a quote from the other.

Nonplussed by their logic, Barbara and I shrugged and gave them no more thought. Given that the job involved about fifteen feet of armoured cabling that I already had, two outdoor plug sockets that had been disconnected when we moved the greenhouses and two fluorescent lights that were available from B&Q for £10 each, I quickly resorted to Plan B which came with the added bonus that I could play with drill, hammer and saw.

Drawing on my somewhat rusty experience from studying theatre electrics in the late 1980's, I soon rigged up a couple of cheap fluorescent tubes and connected the electrical sockets. The lights worked first time, but true to form I had forgotten to mirror the wiring on the back of the plugs, and so when I turned the power on, the whole system suffered a short circuit. Rather was not best pleased as it happened halfway through an episode of Bob the Builder, and as I traced along the wiring for my error, the consumer unit continued to trip. Happily I found the problem quite quickly, and before you can say "Can we fix it? Can we buggery!" all was well.

Given that most things I built at Drama School were designed to last for no more than a couple of weeks, and not all of them actually did, I will be more than pleased if my work withstands a whole winter. Thus far, Barbara's crop of Schwarzkopf plants have been busily growing since October in their frost-free home, and if all is still well by the time the Spring comes, I shall pick my nose, let rip with a mighty hurricane of flatulence in every direction and consider all man caves tested and fully operational.

After that Herculean effort, I'll probably need to retire for a long soak in a hot tub laced with something sparkling and fragrant from Molton Brown.

Kitchen Garden (22nd February)

Although total self-sufficiency is not a realistic objective, growing as much of our own food as we can has long been a dream of ours. During our final years in London we had enjoyed the modest output from our greenhouse and vegetable plot and, even before we knew our city days were over, felt sure that one day our food production would make the transition from hobby to more serious endeavour. One of the reasons that we could afford Stone House in the first place was the fact that it was completely un-modernized inside and somewhat unplanned and overgrown outside. I imagine a farmer with the right equipment would have cleared the entire space in a weekend and had a huge bonfire, but for a pair of amateurs it has taken considerably longer. The mistakes have been educational and occasionally quite painful, but having created a blank canvas it is with a certain delight we have now started to build our kitchen garden.

Work began on a chilly January weekend when we planted nine new fruit trees up in the orchard. Ably assisted by the chickens who can smell a worm at twenty paces, Barbara and I first dug and then positioned two apple, two pear, two plum, a peach, an apricot and a fig tree. Once set with earth and bark chipping, they were braced against the prevailing wind with wooden posts and their slender trunks protected from hungry wildlife with plastic shields. It will be a season or two before they start to bear fruit, and we have allocated enough space to at least double our production in years ahead. With this investment in trees, it seemed only sensible to construct a post & rail fence around the new saplings so they could be protected during their early years from inquisitive sheep. Having used a local contractor in the past to set posts, this time I felt it only right to have a go at the entire job on my own. Adopting the "how hard can it be?" approach, I ordered the wood that I needed and one sunny morning set about burying around twenty-five uprights by hand. I now know that it is very hard indeed to set posts if you want them vertical. Although my technique is clearly poor it is surprisingly consistent, and this has resulted in a perfectly straight run of posts that all stand about 10 degrees off the vertical. It then took about half a day to attach the stock fence before nailing it all together with rails. Somewhat squint it may be, but I think my effort frames the new orchard perfectly and fills me with a sense of achievement and pride.

Next it was time to move closer to the garage in order to plant berries. In a long line open to the sun we installed a forty foot run of raspberries, and constructed a wood and wire trellis inspired from my times at sea for them to cling to. Just behind them in another row we planted blueberries, gooseberries, rhubarb, blackcurrant, redcurrant and whitecurrant. In time we will build two small bordered areas nearby; one for strawberries and the other for asparagus. We positioned everything in rows with just enough room between them to make mowing easy during the summer months, and the ground around each bush will be covered with weed fabric and, in time, some form of decorative fill. Like the trees in the orchard, little will grow while the roots settle in and stretch out, but we look forward to all manner of jams, jellies and flavoured alcohol.

The last stage was the most complicated and labour-intensive. Due to Barbara's injured foot and my inherent laziness, we wanted our vegetable beds to be tall enough to allow for relaxed gardening from a sitting position with a glass of Pimm's, so we decided to build them sixty centimetres high. At over ten metres in length, a large quantity of strong timber would be needed to construct something that could hold back around ten tons of earth, a fact I found rather sobering. Barbara's design calls for two such beds, but with my track record of DIY disasters I thought it best to start by building just one to begin with. The entire plot around Stone House sits just under the crest of a small hill, and there is no flat land anywhere. Beds this long were going to have to be level, and that meant a bit of excavating would be needed to fashion some sort of foundation. The only way I was going to achieve this was to dig a little bit each day, and so that is exactly what I did. From the very start it was a case of sweat, swear and shout as with every spadeful of earth I uncovered rubble, broken glass and twisted metal just below the surface. Eventually the footprint emerged, and I was further motivated when seventy metres of pressure treated wood arrived on the back of a lorry. Having tested a number of options with Rather's *Duplo* bricks for quite a while, I was fairly certain of the sturdiest design to use. With the help of a new and rather powerful circular saw that I had been itching to add to my collection of tools for some time, it took only a few hours to build and all that remains is to add some structural support to the outside so it can withstand the weight of the soil.

With the days now noticeably getting longer and the start of the growing season heralded by Barbara preparing her tomato seedlings, we look forward to our first proper year of growing food in greenhouses, on trees, in raised beds and in the ground. It remains to be seen how well we can protect our crops from all the local wildlife, but with plans for nets, shrouds and other such devices, it has to be said that we fancy our chances. Pausing to catch our breath, we now see clearly that the views around the garden, orchard and field are so very different from when we first came to see the house in February 2011. After three and a half years of hard work there is little left to remind us of Ted, and our footsteps are increasingly being left on fresh ground.

Empty Plinth (8th March)

From the peaceful backwater of Stanford Bishop we like to punch our weight with the very best and so we, just like London's Trafalgar Square, have an unoccupied plinth in need of filling. We had felt somewhat avant-garde by using it to artistically display all manner of gardening paraphernalia, but as skeletons are the latest thing we felt the need to keep up with the Joneses, or rather the Nelsons. Having worked like a trooper to design and create a kitchen garden that includes orchard, fruit bushes and vegetable beds, Barbara very recently turned her attention to this matter. The plinths were put in last year as part of the landscaping effort, and our intention always was to put a third greenhouse on it.

Small greenhouses are two a penny, but larger ones are harder to come by simply through their relative rarity. Ever the queen of bargain hunting, she scoured the Internet as there was no way she was going to pay brand new or even healthy second hand prices. In the end she found one quite locally that was being sold for next to nothing as part of a hurried garden clearance. Having arranged for a man with van to help us with the job, we showed up last Thursday when the children have their day in nursery. We were greeted by spring warmth and an absence of rain, and with an assortment of tools we set to work and carefully removed its ninety-two panes of glass; a laborious process that we eventually completed with only one casualty. Encouraged by this we then started to dismantle the structure and, thanks to the size of the man's van, were able to load each of the sides in their entirety thereby reducing the difficulty of the rebuild.

Once safely back at Stone House, it was fairly easy to get the basic structure in place before too long. It was immediately evident that the plinth was too short and too narrow by a matter of centimetres, so extra foundations to bear the weight will be needed before the glass can be refitted. Not having taken it apart on my own I lacked a complete visual memory of how it all fitted together, and so needed to use a little more common sense on the job than is my habit. About halfway through I had a very worrying moment when it became clear that I had not actually brought one of the most important pieces home; a section of the base. We therefore made a quick dash back yesterday with fingers crossed, and were lucky enough to find that the former owners had kept it to one side for us. By this morning it resembled a greenhouse once more, and unglazed it will sit until I have done a little research into mixing concrete and laying bricks. Surprisingly, there were no leftover parts at the end of the rebuild.

This afternoon, when I went to collect eggs from the nesting boxes in the coop, I found that our parallels with Central London were even greater than I had first thought*. Trisha, one of our oldest and dearest hens who had the faintest hint of powdery blue in her feathers, had evidently been prompted by the arrival of a skeleton on the plinth to leave hers for good. Another example of life imitating art as it so often does.

*At the time of writing 'Hahn', Katharina Fritsch's statue of a 5 metre tall blue cockerel, was the temporary installation on Trafalgar Square's famous empty plinth.

Shipping Forecast (14th March)

Introduced in February 1861 by Vice-Admiral Robert Fitzroy after 450 people lost their lives when a steam clipper foundered in a storm off Anglesey, the Shipping Forecast has been a stalwart of the British airwaves for over a century. In truth it has long been obsolete thanks to modern technology, but it resolutely persists in a world where change is the only constant, once prompting parliamentary debate when a twelve minute shift to its dependable 00:48 broadcast slot was mooted. For sailors, insomniacs and curious listeners alike, its poetic structure, sombre delivery and use of archaic names can bring an extraordinary sense of calm to the end of a tumultuous day. Dispensing with all but essential vocabulary, it is a metronomic recitation of the predicted wind direction, wind strength, precipitation levels and visibility for thirty-one sea areas. It also provides readings from twenty-two coastal weather stations, and after more than thirty years of listening to it, *Scilly Automatic* never fails to raise a snigger from the depths of my pillow.

If ever our lives were predictable, that time has long gone. Barbara and I live amongst piles of laundry and boxes of toys. We lurch from soft cuddles to occasional tantrums. As we fix one part of the house another calls for our attention. Part funny farm and part madhouse, we work hard to keep as much order as we can and so it is with considerable excitement that we welcome to Stone House our latest, and last, family member. Barbara had done a little research into which breed would be gentle towards both children and livestock, and last summer we were persuaded by a local contractor, who breeds and trains working Black Labradors, that they would fit the bill perfectly. One of his pack is regularly put out to stud, and so we made some enquiries, put our name down and then waited. Just after Christmas we received an email telling us that we were fourth on the list for a litter of seven. We had only eight weeks to get things shipshape, and all the paraphernalia that comes with dogs like bed, crate, bowls and leads were sourced from eBay and online car boot sales. As travelling by foot on the B4220 with two toddlers and a puppy is not even worth considering, we have trimmed the hawthorn hedge to open up an old access gate in the big field which leads directly out to the small lane at the back. In the years ahead it will also serve for the children to come and go with their bicycles. When the puppy was a month old, we went to see him with his brothers and sisters. I say this like we knew which one he was, but as the breeder couldn't tell them apart we were happy to chat and coo at seven cuddly lumps of fur. We visited again at six weeks' old and the seven lumps of fur were bigger but no easier to distinguish. Both Jolly and Rather seemed quite taken with them, and we left knowing that we had to pick a name from our shortlist of three.

This morning we went to collect him and found that buying a puppy is remarkably similar to buying a car. First we had to fill out a transfer of ownership form and were then given his service history in the form of a record of his pedigree. Then there was a care leaflet suggesting oil change and service intervals. Finally there was a brief demonstration of the basics like ignition, alarm and exhaust. He even came with a free tank of fuel and four weeks' free insurance. We were all smitten from the word go, and our journey home was faintly reminiscent of both drives home from hospital with newborn babies. Once back he seemed to settle in quite quickly and the children have smiles from ear to ear as they pet and cuddle him. Now, as I write this in the afternoon, he is sleeping at my feet and his gentle snoring is the perfect background noise for my office.

His place in our family will be utterly central; the constant shadow who keeps an eye on things and the one to watch us go and welcome us back. Personally I particularly look forward to his company during bouts of insomnia and when work demands unsociable hours of travel, and I have little doubt he will soon become as much a comfort to me as the

Shipping Forecast. We had even toyed briefly with the idea of naming him after one of the sea areas, but none were suitable. Not even the area of the North Sea that lies between the coasts of Denmark and Lincolnshire called 'Dogger'. For these letters however, his nom du plume will be the contradictory yet strangely comforting phrase that is probably mentioned more often than any other during the broadcasts. I am therefore delighted to announce that the forecast for the immediate area is Labrador puppy, eight weeks and growing, *Rainlater Good.*

Off the Grid (29th March)

Although not particularly cold, this last winter has felt long with Barbara and I often so tired by the time the children go to bed that we can manage little more than a light supper on the sofa in front of the television. We usually search for anything that appeals to our escapist dreams, and almost always first choice are programmes about people who choose to live in remote places where they must work with nature to make ends meet. You know the kind of thing; views to die for, fishing for food and generating your own electricity. We know we'd be there if only we had the stamina and the guts. Leaving a lighter footprint on the planet was always part of our plan when we moved here, and we have taken many small steps in this direction. This week we took a giant leap forward by covering the roof of Stone House in solar photovoltaic panels and joining the growing ranks of small scale electricity generators. As environmentally kind as this may be, the opportunity to make a significant dent to the high cost of a tumble drier and washing machine that never seem to stop was not lost on us either.

With almost four acres of land we had explored the magic of ground source heat pumps, but found a legal clause in our property deeds that prevents the excavation such a system would need. Being in an exposed location we are ideally placed to exploit a fairly constant source of wind from the west, and were it not for an influential local lobby that seems dead-set against turbines we might have investigated this further. Existing legislation means a solar PV system requires no planning permission, and with a roof that faces two degrees off due south, it was the obvious and only realistic choice. Early last Wednesday morning a yellow van containing two men and enough electronics and gadgetry for the next *James Bond* film arrived, and immediately set to work. Scaffold towers were erected, and before long a series of mounting rails were fixed to the slates. Onto these wiring was attached and then the fourteen panels that almost cover the entire roof. The array was then connected via something called an inverter that was installed in our loft, and from there to our mains electricity distribution board, and with a ceremonial nod the system was commissioned.

The power was instant, and for the next twenty years we will be paid for all that we generate during daylight hours as well as any we export to the national grid. Rather than measuring how much that is, the powers that be simply assume it will be half the amount produced, so our current calculations indicate that we will earn enough money from the system to cover the cost of the firewood that we burn each winter. Carbon neutral energy may still be some way off, but we're inching closer. Not only do we earn money by being a mini power station, but anything we generate is ours to use for free, so with an electricity bill traditionally four times that for gas, we look forward to savings too. With the ability to monitor the system in real time we hope to learn the right balance as we can't store any for overnight use and if we consume more than the amount produced at any one time between dawn and dusk the grid automatically kicks in to make up the difference. It's very early days of course, but we are hopeful as on overcast days it seems that we have enough capacity to power all but our peak use.

With winter finally over and the clocks put forward, it is with a sense of achievement and pride that to our growing list of homemade produce, we now add just under four thousand *Kilowatt Hours* of energy per year. Here comes the sun, and I say it's all right.

Back to the Future (5th April)

As child of the late sixties, my formative years were during the 1980's and my taste in music, film and clothing probably reflects this. Okay, perhaps it's just my taste in music and film. Putting that to one side, I note that this year is the one to which Marty McFly and Doc Brown travelled in a *De Lorean* from 1989 and discovered that, amongst other exciting novelties, lawyers had been abolished. Regardless of whether or not this might be possible, desirable or even beneficial, the idea is one for which we have some time. It has been a year since the farcical conclusion of Barbara's court case on April Fools Day 2014, and the last twelve months have given us some relief in that we are no longer required to give every spare moment to it. The topic is now almost never raised between us but, as we cautiously admitted to each other a month or so ago, both our private internal dialogues have continued more or less unabated.

Now remarkably thin-skinned when it comes to our privacy being invaded, our hands being forced or our words being twisted, we also remain highly sensitive to cars stopping on the road outside the house. Sometimes we pull over to let those visible for a bit too long in our rear view mirror pass us, or drive around the block once or twice before parking. Paranoid these behaviours may be, but through repetition over the years they have become second nature. I find it difficult to articulate the difference and the distance that lies for me between forgive and forget. Perhaps it's nothing more than a matter of *once bitten twice shy*, but we have come to realise that some things may have changed for good, although arguably not for the good.

Coincidentally, the current climate of austerity has dictated the closure of the police station in our nearest town, and whilst we neither live in fear nor expect any form of trouble, experience suggests that our safety and security rests primarily, and almost exclusively, in our hands. In view of these changes and the fact that I spend a great deal of time away from home, we took the decision last year to equip the house with surveillance cameras. Installed as "fit and forget" equipment, the cameras record what they see around the clock and in high definition. The novelty now having passed, we ignore them and on the few occasions that I have checked to see that they are working from my hotel rooms around the country, I have seen nothing more than cobwebs swaying in the wind and inquisitive nightlife. When I once verified that they keep a rolling record of the previous two weeks, I found only proof that I should eat less, exercise more and not only be grateful that we have an indoor loo, but actually use it too. We realise that the cameras won't prevent anything that can't be stopped by a warning sign. However, should something untoward happen, we will subscribe to the philosophy of *publish and be damned* given that both are acts over which we have some control, whereas the definition and interpretation of *due process* will always belong to the highest bidder.

"Time heals" was an adage I often heard when I was growing up, and I have come to the conclusion that it doesn't because, being only a measure, it can't. However, it is an interval during which wounds that are aired, cleaned and dressed have the opportunity to heal, whilst those that are ignored, denied or suppressed are almost certain to become infected. It's probably got something to do with powering the flux capacitor and not interfering with the space-time continuum.

Harrow on the Hill (19th April)

To be smallholders like us is, if I'm being totally honest, simply to garden on a slightly larger scale with bigger machinery. Mowing, digging, raking and pruning are the same whether on three acres or thirty square feet. Sure we have chickens, but millions of suburbanites feed birds every morning in the same way. True, there are often sheep in the field, but we have nothing to do with them apart from the enjoyable duties of admiration and fussing. It has been a creeping worry of mine that under oath I'd have to say that we remain phoneys; plastic pretend farmers who still smell of Hanwell.

Last autumn when Lewis collected the sheep to be put to the tup, we chatted about things in general and he opined that the field could do with "a good chain harrowing." I squinted at the land, sucked my teeth and solemnly nodded in firm agreement without having the slightest clue what he was on about, and then we said our farewells. Later that day I discovered through Google that there is indeed such a thing as chain harrowing, and people seem divided on its effectiveness. Some describe it as the perfect way to remove thatch and rejuvenate grass so as to produce a thick and lush meadow, whilst others disparagingly refer to it as *recreational tractor driving*. Both descriptions, particularly the latter, sound ideal to me, so obviously I'm now all for it. Delving into further research with uncharacteristic eagerness, I then found photographic evidence not only that a chain harrow is simply a set of metal hooks attached to a chain mesh, but it can be dragged on the ground behind a lawn tractor. As I'm pretty sure that no one does this in Hanwell, I immediately felt a clear and urgent need, supported by carefully selected evidence, to engage in some springtime chain harrowing of the entire field.

I mentioned my plan to Lewis when he popped around to check for any winter damage to the perimeter, and he looked me straight in the face. "You're going to chain harrow?" he asked. Adopting an air of tired experience, I gestured dismissively towards the field and nodded. "The whole field?" Again I nodded. "With your lawn tractor?" At this point, a little voice in my head suggested that a vague mumble coupled with a mild shrug was, of all the available options, probably the best course of action to take. He then cast his eyes over the nearly three acres of uneven, molehill-infested and somewhat damp grass and then muttered, "You're brave, I'll give you that." I studied him carefully for a moment and then gently asked, "When you say brave, do you actually mean stupid?" There followed the most enormous pause whilst he seemingly searched through his pockets and scratched the back of his neck thoughtfully. Finally he let a barely audible "Yup" escape his lips. I'll admit that I felt somewhat deflated, and for the following few weeks I contented myself with nothing more than eBay searches and daydreams. Driving around towing a set of chains, no matter how desirable, is quite far down my list of things to do but Lewis clearly is of the opinion that it's more than just recreational.

When he turned up a few weeks later with his orange and rather ancient *Fiat* tractor, I was thrilled to get a chance to see some chain harrowing in action. Attached to the back of it was a slightly mangled iron frame from which a mass of hooks and chains dangled rather ominously. To me the whole contraption looked like something leftover from the Spanish Inquisition, but he assured me that it would do the job. He even offered me a go, and had I not been halfway through the first grass cut of the year at the time, I would have jumped at the chance. It took him about half an hour to criss-cross the field, leaving it looking a bit like it had been to the hairdressers for a blow dry. On closer inspection it was clear to see that the dead thatch had indeed been ripped clean out of the ground and left on top of the grass for the wind to disperse. In its place the spring warmth and April showers would quickly start to produce fresh growth.

A few weeks later, in a scene rarely witnessed in suburban West London, a flock of ewes and their newborn lambs were unceremoniously tipped into the field from the back of a battered livestock trailer. They were duly greeted by a delighted *Rather* and *Jolly*, a playful *Rainlater* and twelve inquisitive chickens. With introductions over, they dispersed and immediately began the tasks of feasting, frolicking and fertilising in equal measure. With everyone now on board at the funny farm, we are ready for a long hot summer whatever the weather.

Nanna and Ambrosius (26th April)

We have now been here for nearly four years and, barring upsets, plan to remain until the day *Rather* and *Jolly* have either flown the nest or been gently pushed out of it. It is undeniable that an increasing number of our decisions have been influenced by both our history and the fact that we now live much closer to nature than before, but it's equally true to say that we have very little to learn from ducks. For a start they like rain, and that's just wrong. In the early spring of 2012 we noticed a distinct quacking noise from various parts of the garden which, at the time, had more than a few hiding places in the form of hedges and sheds. After some half-hearted sleuthing we found that a pair of ducks had arrived and spent most of their time lazily wandering from one sheltered part of the garden to another. They showed little sign of moving on, appeared unfazed by our attention and were promptly granted full asylum with Barbara naming them *Nanna* and *Ambrosius* after a pair of ducks that used to visit her grandmother.

Over the following week or two we noticed them noisily wandering around in the rain searching for food and building materials. Soon there was a pile of twigs, moss and assorted detritus piled on the hedgerow outside the kitchen window, which was clearly meant to pass for a nest. They duly moved in and shortly afterwards we found a number of broken eggs on the ground below. With their parental plans foiled by wind and gravity, all activity ceased and we thought no more about it until we realised that we hadn't seen them for a while. Laying the blame for their disappearance at the feet of Mr. Fox, our interest in ducks then returned to the menu of our local Chinese takeaway, from which it has rarely strayed since.

In the spring of 2013 they came back. At least we think they did, as one duck looks pretty much like every other duck to us, and they went through the same waddling charade as the previous year. It seems that ducks can live up to twenty years and clearly, if these two are anything to go by, are predisposed to build nests and lay eggs in completely unsuitable places. They have been back every year at the same time since and always with the same result. We hardly remember them from one year to the next, and their pattern seems set to continue. For whatever reason, our garden is where they choose to nest once a year for a week or two and, ever hopeful of seeing a flush of ducklings stumbling around the garden, we look forward to their next visit.

It's anyone's guess for how long *Nanna* and *Ambrosius* will continue to make their annual pilgrimage here, but for the present they, along with *Gerald* and the rest of the transient wildlife, bring occasional colour and entertainment for which we are grateful. Nevertheless, in the distant future Barbara and I will probably leave them behind and build a new, perhaps smaller nest for ourselves somewhere a little warmer and a little drier. Who am I kidding? A lot warmer and a lot drier.

A Penny Ode (1st May)

I'm not a particularly big Van Morrison fan; it's just that he's always managed to worm his way into my music collection. And it's not just my iPod, as it's a safe bet that I'll hear him before too long on those rare occasions when I tune in to a radio station that broadcasts popular music.

It's as if his job is to remind, or rather insist and nag me, to live in the present tense. *"These are the days, the time is now. There's only here, there's only now."*

Being in my later forties, there are certain inevitabilities that I face. My arms are now far too short when I hold up a menu to read in a restaurant, my bladder has long been too weak to afford me a whole night's sleep and a variety of aches and pains cover my body like confetti. However, my memory is mostly intact and I note with neither joy nor sadness that it was exactly twenty years ago today that I woke up and had a rather eventful *Mayday* that changed my life. Living with Multiple Sclerosis is a topic I seldom bring up, as I found out almost immediately that it's a conversation piece most often wedged somewhere between a faux-pas and a hot potato. Although its arrival had a tremendous impact on me at the time, the ramifications have since softened into the landscape. The combination of two decades passing, an extraordinary wife, two wonderful children and the strongest vision of the future that I have yet known have perhaps conspired to make it all feel slightly irrelevant by comparison. However once in a while someone offers me a penny for my thoughts on the matter, and so here they are.

I grew up with films like *Love Story* and *Terms of Endearment*, and used to imagine that there was something deeply moving about having a chronic medical condition when surrounded by loving friends and family. I then learned very quickly that this is not the case. At least, not for me and not by a long shot. What these and similar films never want to portray is how utterly tedious much of it can be; after all, how moving is a character who sits on the loo in the middle of the night for over an hour desperate, but unable, to pee? Or how frustrating is it to have confirmed that a cocktail of overt symptoms like fatigue, slurred speech and poor balance accompanied by a smattering of needle marks are more likely to provoke prejudice rather than consideration?

Alfred Hitchcock once said, "theatre is life with the boring bits taken out" and so good drama is. I consider it rather ironic to have been diagnosed with a chronic illness just days after playing a character who was dying from one, but to learn that art is artifice through such a contrast can be a hard lesson to learn for one as young and naive as I was at the time. With hindsight I now know it was this realisation, more than my lack of talent, that brought my love affair with acting to an amicable end during my final days at drama school. John, one of my teachers who is himself no stranger to the problems of autoimmunity, acknowledged my diagnosis thoughtfully one evening by wishing me a great deal of luck as we queued for a pint in the local pub; a tender moment I will never forget. Many years before then, I remember my mother referring to me as a "bum in the butter" child and so far she has largely been proved right, given that I have been luckier than most with my illness. Of course I experience a wide range of symptoms from the mildly irritating to the frustrating and restrictive, and it is likely there is worse ahead, but nothing has yet come anywhere close to the one that doesn't make good television; the gnawing sense of futility, impotence and perhaps a twisted sense of guilt that comes from being the one with the disease that has to watch those around you without it accept that they cannot take it away.

Since they were born, Barbara and I have shared looking after our children as much as my itinerant working life will allow, and when home I like to make up for my absences by doing as much as possible. With parenting tasks ranging from the unpleasant chore of changing nappies through to the abandon of play, I see each one as a chance to give health in the form of cleanliness, comfort or some other small and perhaps inconsequential way. However, none is more precious to me than the one that follows a piercing cry in the middle of the night denoting nightmare, toothache or fever. The chance to restore safety and calm by creeping through the dark, searching for them amongst their sheets and folding them into my arms is a joy that I treasure like few others.

Van Morrison may have provided the obvious soundtrack to our lives here, but firmly lodged in my memory is a ballad by another Irish songwriter called Percy French. It's about a coach driver named Paddy Reilly who emigrates from Ireland to Scotland, and it appears in the script for Harold Pinter's play *The Birthday Party*, a production of which I was involved with over thirty years ago. Often I hum it to myself, and when I sing it out loud it always appears with a cod Irish accent much to Barbara's amusement. Now, when I cuddle my son or daughter in the small hours and gently rock them to and fro, this slightly altered version is what I half-sing half-murmur into their hair as they press their head into my chest and we wait for the demons to leave and *The Good Life* to resume. That's it for these letters; I'll have that penny now. So long, and thanks for reading.

Oh, the Garden of Eden has vanished they say,
But I know the lie of it still.
Just turn to the left at the foot of Ben Clay,
And stop when halfway to Cootehill.
'Tis there you will find it I know sure enough,
And it's whispering over to me;
Come back Red and Railay to Ballyjamesduff,
Come home Red and Railay to me.

End

13734235R00259

Printed in Great Britain
by Amazon